When Divorce Is Not an Option

Gregory K. Popcak

When Divorce Is Not an Option

How to Heal Your Marriage and Nurture Lasting Love

SOPHIA INSTITUTE PRESS
Manchester, New Hampshire

Sophia Institute Press
Box 5284, Manchester, NH 03108
1-800-888-9344

www.SophiaInstitute.com

Sophia Institute Press® is a registered trademark of Sophia Institute.

Library of Congress Cataloging-in-Publication Data

Popcak, Gregory K.
    When divorce is not an option : how to heal your marriage and nurture lasting love / Dr. Gregory K. Popcak.
        pages cm.
    Includes bibliographical references.
    ISBN 978-1-62282-188-4 (pbk. : alk. paper) 1. Marital conflict—Religious aspects—Christianity. 2. Marriage—Religious aspects—Christianity. 3. Married people—Psychology. 4. Married people—Religious life. I. Title.
    BV4596.M3P67 2014
    248.8'44—dc23
                                                                    2014017750

First printing

To all those who faithfully strive
to live the cross in their marriage.
May they live to see the resurrection as well.

Contents

1. The Secret of Saving Your Marriage. 3

2. What "I've Tried Everything" Really Means 23

3. Eight Marriage-Friendly Habits 53

4. Rituals of Connection. 85

5. Emotional Rapport and Benevolence 119

6. Self-Regulation. 131

7. A Positive Intention Frame. 155

8. Caretaking in Conflict 171

9. Mutual Respect, Accountability,
   and Boundaries. 197

10. Reviewing and Learning from Mistakes. 211

11. Getting Good Support 231

12. Is It Worth It? 251

Epilogue: Marriage and the Cross:
"It Is Consummated!" 263

A Note from Dr. Gregory Popcak 269

Exercises

Taking Charge of Your Marriage Exercise 273

Mindset Exercise 276

Love List Exercise 279

Clarification Exercise 287

Reframing Exercise 291

Increasing Accountability Exercise 298

Boundary Clarification Exercise 309

References 313

About the Author 319

When Divorce Is Not an Option

Chapter 1

The Secret of Saving Your Marriage

And I will betroth you to me for ever;
I will betroth you to me in righteousness and
in justice, in steadfast love, and in mercy.
I will betroth you to me in faithful-
ness; and you shall know the Lord.
—Hosea 2:19-20

"*I'm just completely worn out. I feel like I've tried everything, but no matter what I do, he just pushes me away. I don't want a divorce, but I can't make him love me. Sometimes I wonder if I should just go.*" (Emily, married twelve years to Jake)

"*I can't do anything right. She's constantly on me about everything I do. We fight about everything. I know that marriage is hard work, but there's no way it's supposed to be this hard. I'm distracted at work. I can't sleep. My marriage is killing me. I just don't know what to do.*" (Michael, married seventeen years to Elise)

"*I've tried everything. Nothing makes any difference. We've been to counseling. We've talked to our pastor. I've tried ignoring things, fighting with him, letting it go. I'm at a complete loss. My friends keep telling me that some things aren't meant to be. Maybe we're just bad for each other. I hate the idea of divorcing him. Upending the kids' lives . . . starting over . . . Ugh! But I can't keep living like this."* (Amy, married eight years to Stephen)

Does any of this sound familiar? If so, I have good news for you. There is hope. Your marriage can be saved—even if your spouse isn't interested in working on it. In fact, more than just saving your marriage, this book will show you what you can do to transform your marriage. Over the next several chapters, it is my goal to show you simple steps you can take to heal the hurts and create marriage-friendly habits that will enable you to resolve your conflicts efficiently, increase your caring for one another, create the love you have been longing for, and rediscover the passion you have always wanted.

I will draw from both empirically validated methods as well as insights from our Christian tradition. My hope is both to heal your marriage and to inspire you to use every aspect of your journey to draw closer both to your spouse and to the God who brought you together.

What Makes a Marriage Happy?

I don't want to lie to you. Transforming your marriage will take some work. This isn't magic. But, as a friend of mine jokes, "It isn't rocket surgery either." Anyone can do this. Even you. Especially you.

Over the last twenty years, marriage researchers have discovered that what separates happy marriages from unhappy ones isn't destiny, personality conflicts, differing values, life experience, how many problems you have, or how much you fight. In fact, regarding the last two points, research consistently shows that happy couples argue about as often as unhappy ones and have about the same rate of success in resolving their issues (Gottman,

2011). So what makes the difference between "marriage masters" and "marriage disasters"?

Researchers have discovered that happy couples — as opposed to unhappy ones — have certain habits they use to manage their conflict, repair damage, build rapport, maintain intimacy, and create shared meaning. These habits can be learned by anyone who is willing, and the more consistently these habits are practiced, the more they can transform even the most conflictual, unhappy marriage into a joyful, loving, relationship.

At the Pastoral Solutions Institute, the group tele-counseling practice I direct, we have a marriage-counseling success rate of over 90 percent. This rate is not unusual for marital therapists who know what I will be sharing with you. My associates and I teach both couples *and* individual spouses (about 30 percent of our marital-counseling work involves solo-spouse marital therapy) these habits every day, and they are powerful. You don't even have to learn to do these habits perfectly to have them work for you. You should start to see at least some changes within a few weeks of instituting even a few of these habits. The more you use these habits, however, generally speaking, the more satisfied you will be in your relationship. Almost every couple uses at least some of the practices I will discuss in this book some of the time, but the difference between consistently happy couples and others is that the consistently happy couples make a habit out of these practices, while others use them in fits and starts — or not at all. The fact is, how you practice these habits in your marriage is every bit as important as the habits themselves.

What About Your Issues?

This book does not address particular issues such as money, sex, parenting, differences in values, in-law problems, and other common topics couples argue about. This is not an oversight. Although you may feel that these topics have a special power to bring out the worst in you, there is really nothing magical about these issues. Rather, the way you and your spouse talk about these issues and the way you relate to each other provide the context for healthy (or unhealthy) conversations about these issues.

I don't wish to micromanage your fights. Instead, I want to teach you the skills you need in order to learn how to relate and discuss any topic—the one you are fighting over now and any ones you may experience conflict over in the future. You will learn that *what* you talk about is much less important than both how you talk about it and the overall health of the relationship in which that conversation is handled.

Let's look at one of the first skills that every happily married couple has to master: riding the marital wave.

Riding the Wave

Every husband and wife knows that marriage has its ups and downs, but for most couples, why the ups are up and the downs are down remains a mystery. That's especially true when a couple gets stuck in the trough of a down phase, and, rather than going up and down, the relationship flatlines. What drives this wave? And what causes some couples to get stuck at the bottom of the wave, sometimes for years?

Although it can feel like it, there is no god of marital mayhem that taketh and giveth joy at his whim. The thing that drives the marital satisfaction wave are the habits we'll discuss in this book. Figure 1.1 shows Mr. and Mrs. Happy. They have the kind of marriage that makes the angels smile and the neighbors sick with jealousy.

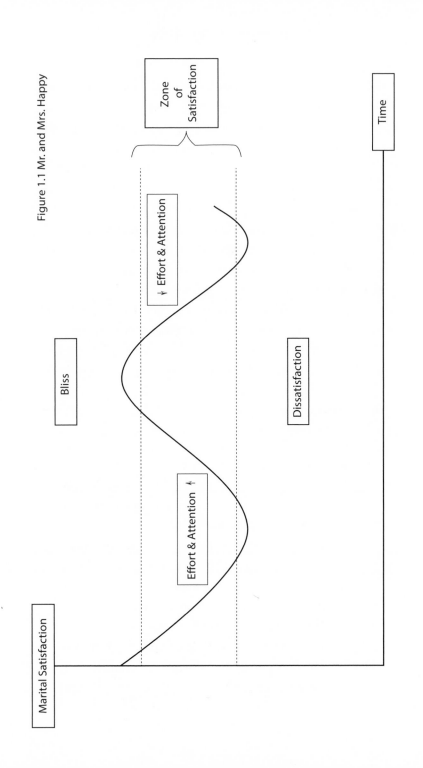

Figure 1.1 Mr. and Mrs. Happy

The Happys are consciously aware of the happiness habits that keep their relationship stable. At their peak, they are putting maximum effort into maintaining those happiness habits. If Mr. and Mrs. Happy start to crest and go down the other side, that's because they have been focusing their efforts on attending to other areas of concern in their life, which causes them to put a little less energy and attention into maintaining their happiness habits. That's okay. Those other areas need attention too. But the Happys also know that they can't take attention away from their marriage for too long, or they'll go into a marital dive and stay down in the dip. So they keep a mental list of the habits that keep their marriage working well, and they check themselves—and each other—regularly to maintain these habits. Their ability to make small corrections early, and on an ongoing basis, allows them to avoid dramatic peaks and valleys and keep their relationship in the healthy range.

Now let's look at two other couples: the Dramatics and the Flatliners. We'll start with Mr. and Mrs. Dramatic.

Virginia and Mark are both very busy—Mark with his electrical contracting business and Virginia with the kids, church, and community activities. They both admit they don't get a lot of time for each other.

Virginia says, "We go out on dates and stuff, and that's great. And we have a good physical relationship. But it just seems like it never 'sticks.' We'll decide to do something different, and it will last for a week or two, but then things go right back to the way they were."

"I love her so much," says Mark. "It's just depressing to put so much effort into getting things back on track only to have to do it all over again in a month or so. No change

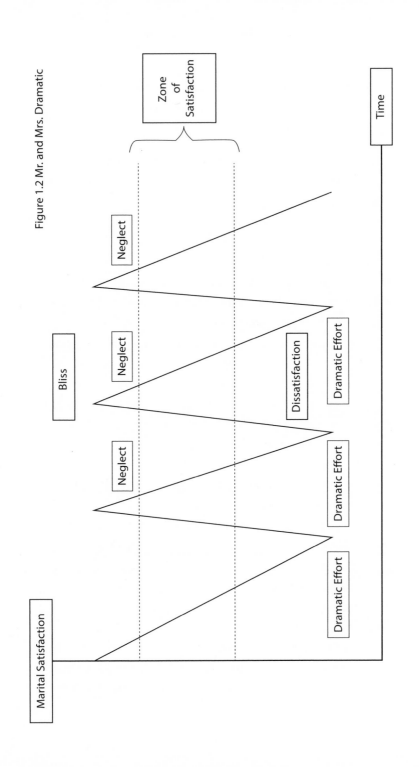

Figure 1.2 Mr. and Mrs. Dramatic

we ever make lasts more than a couple of weeks. I just feel like we're doomed to repeat the same cycle over and over."

Mr. and Mrs. Dramatic have an exhausting relationship. They swing wildly from marital bliss to marital dips. In part, the swings make them feel alive and excited to be together. That was especially true in the early years, when Mr. and Mrs. Dramatic didn't have too much to distract them from their marriage. But as time passes and life gets busier, the rollercoaster ride becomes less charming. In fact, as the Dramatics' lives get busier and fuller, they start experiencing even steeper peaks and valleys that transform their ups and downs from charming to downright alarming. But why is this happening to them?

The Dramatics tend not to be consciously aware of the habits that keep their marriage stable. They know that there are certain "things we do to set things right" (like dates, or sex, or a weekend away, or other such intensive effort). They do those things to prop the marriage back up, but then they immediately go back to ignoring the marriage, thinking that it should just take care of itself now. Despite the highs that this couple can generate, the fluctuating nature of the relationship can become a relationship problem in and of itself (Arriaga, 2001).

A frequent complaint of this couple is: "Things go well for a while, but then it all goes right back to the way it was!" When Mr. and Mrs. Dramatic make that dramatic effort to get their marriage back on track, they start to bliss out. After the weekend away, or that special date, or that especially intimate night, the Dramatics' relationship seems wonderful. They feel as if they are back on their honeymoon. Everything is terrific, and they rediscover why they fell in love with each other in the first place. But then they come back from the weekend (or step out of the bedroom), and life takes over. They immediately lose track of their marriage and focus on work and kids and all the other demands of life. As they do this, their marriage begins to plummet. At first they're too busy to notice, and for a while, they continue to experience marital satisfaction rooted in the memory of their special time together (illustrated by the duration they spend in the satisfaction zone in figure 1.2). But as that memory becomes more distant, they begin to fall out of love. They start bickering, and bickering turns to fighting, and fighting turns to misery until one or the other, or both, suddenly decides, "Enough!" And they schedule another weekend away or dinner out or sexual extravaganza, which rockets their marriage back into the stratosphere—at least for a while.

Mr. and Mrs. Dramatic tend to blame this cycle on the busyness of their lives and their hectic schedules, but in truth, their lives are no busier than the Happys'. The difference between the Happys and the Dramatics is the on-again, off-again nature of Mr. and Mrs. Dramatic's efforts to take care of their relationship. The Dramatics tend to think that having a good day or week means that "things are good" and having a really bad day or week means "things are bad." They don't understand that what actually determines the "goodness" or "badness" of their relationship isn't what's happening to them or how they're feeling from moment to moment, but rather the consistent practice of certain habits that enable them to manage effectively the feelings they're having and the things they're going through as a couple.

The good news is that if Mr. and Mrs. Dramatic learn to be conscious of the daily and weekly marital habits they must establish to maintain consistent marital satisfaction *in addition* to keeping up the periodic special efforts that allow them to experience marital bliss, the Dramatics can learn to have every bit as terrific a relationships as Mr. and Mrs. Happy ever had.

Now let's look at the Flatliners.

Ashley and Josh have been married sixteen years. Despite the fact that they love their kids and enjoy their family life, they feel very lonely in their marriage.

Josh says, "It gets so discouraging sometimes. She's always on me to come home from work early. Last Tuesday I did, but it barely seemed to register. I thought she'd be happy, but she just seemed as distracted as ever. We barely talked. After dinner, she went to do the dishes. I just ended up surfing on the computer all night. I don't know why she makes such a big deal out of it."

For her part, Ashley says, "I just don't feel like he really wants to be here, y'know? Like, the other day, I thought I'd try to do something nice. I make his favorite dinner, steak. He thanked me, but that was it. After dinner, he went to watch TV, and I hung out with the kids for a while. I can't make him want to be married, right? I don't know what to do."

Mr. and Mrs. Flatliner tend to have a fairly consistently depressive marriage punctuated by little efforts they make in an attempt to "shock" the marriage back to life — with varying degrees of success. Where the Dramatics tend to do bigger things that push their marriage up to bliss, Mr. and Mrs. Flatliner tend to do smaller things to take care of their marriage (give compliments, have dinner together at home a few nights in a row, work on a project, try to hug each other a bit more, and so forth), but their efforts are often tentative. This causes them to be able to

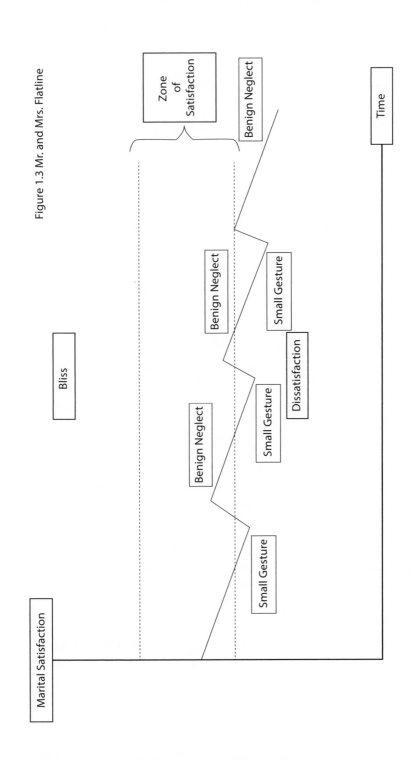

Figure 1.3 Mr. and Mrs. Flatline

get basic satisfaction out of their marriage but usually not make it all the way to bliss.

The absence of bliss, though, isn't necessarily the problem. While bliss is nice, some people crave bliss less than others. The real problem is that the Flatliners don't bounce. Because they don't pour the same energy into their marriage that the Dramatics do to get their highs, they have a lower distance to fall. Imagine dropping a rubber ball from an inch off the ground versus five feet off the ground. That's the difference between the Dramatics and the Flatliners. Because their highs aren't very high, they don't bounce much when they hit bottom. They just stay there. Flat.

Eventually, one spouse or the other will feel compelled to do *something* to try to make it work. Perhaps she initiates a conversation that evening, or perhaps he brings home some flowers, or perhaps they make a marriage retreat at their church. Usually, at least at first, these "nice" things shock the Flatliners' hearts enough to get a beat, but not enough to get a regular sinus rhythm. Eventually, the Flatliners may feel as if the effort they made never really paid off all that much anyway, and so they just stop altogether, causing the relationship to flatline completely.

Some couples are Flatliners from the start. Other Flatliners begin as Dramatics who, over time, have become exhausted from all the drama and invest less and less energy in the relationship.

In light of these marriage dynamics, take a moment to do the Taking Charge of Your Marriage Exercise on page 273.

What Role Does Conflict Play?

Having begun to address the ups and downs of marital dynamics, you might wonder where conflict fits into this picture. It varies. For the most part, the Dramatics' relationships tend to be punctuated by huge fights followed by passionate honeymoon periods. But there are variations on that theme. For their part, Flatliners tend to be more conflict-avoidant, but when they bottom out, they can have some fairly intense arguments too. And of course, their slow burn causes them to get stuck in tension longer.

Interestingly, research shows that despite what most people think, arguing and marital conflict aren't the cause of marital problems (Gottman, 2011). Rather, they are symptoms. Arguing and marital conflict are really just the *fever* that attends the *infection* represented by the poor establishment of good marriage-maintenance habits. Many couples, Dramatics in particular, think that when they aren't arguing, things are going "great" or at least things are "fine." But that is like saying that you don't have the flu anymore just because your fever broke. Couples have been taught to think that the fever (marital arguments) is the disease, and if they can just avoid or resolve the arguments, then the marriage will heal itself. Taking down the emotional fever in a marriage can bring welcome relief, but unless the underlying disease — the absence or inconsistent practice of healthy-marriage habits — is treated, the fever will always come back. Always.

How Will You Know If You're Making Real Progress?

Often, early on in marriage counseling (or sometimes even starting a new self-help book), a couple will go through a week or two of not fighting, or not fighting as much, or just feeling better about their marriage in general. Research shows that this early, post-interventional bounce is caused by the new hope the couple experiences just from doing something they think is potentially helpful (Weiner-Davis, 1993). Although it might encourage couples to double their efforts or to think it's time to wind down or stop therapy altogether, this bounce represents a break in the fever, not a curing of the underlying disease. So I always encourage couples to enjoy the break, but I also take the opportunity to assess what specifically is different: "That's terrific. It must feel awfully good to get a break from all that tension. But tell me: *what did you do differently to make things work better this week?*"

In asking that question, I look for them to describe the new skills, habits, or practices they have been employing to manage stress, care for each other, and protect the integrity of their marriage. If the couple describes at least a few specific, intentional, and conscious actions they have taken to care better for each other and their marriage, I know the change is real and reliable. I will then work with the couple to enumerate those "differences that made the difference" and discuss ways to turn these practices into Marriage-Friendly Habits.

More often, however, I will get one of two other responses. The first is, "I don't know. Things just went better." This could mean that the couple spent *less* time together or that they just happened to wake up on the right side of the bed or anything in between. If this is the response, I know that the break they are enjoying, while welcome, can't be counted on to last more than a few weeks on the long end.

The second possible response is, "Oh, the kids didn't have any games this weekend" (or "we had off from work," or "we went on a trip," or some variation on that theme), "and we just had the best time together!" Again, the break in the "fever" this couple is experiencing is certainly welcome, but unless they plan on spending the next fifty years of their life together on vacation, chances are it isn't going to last.

I share this with you because as you use this book to heal your marriage, you will need to know what real progress looks like;

otherwise, you will become demoralized as you think, "Everything's great," only to have your hopes dashed two weeks later when you have that huge fight "out of nowhere." Despite how it seems, the tension didn't come from nowhere. Again, arguments are not the disease; they are the fever that accompanies the disease. And what is the disease? The absence or inconsistent application of one or more of the Marriage-Friendly Habits. You'll know you're making real progress that you can count on over time when you have a good week and can list the specific, intentional things you have done differently than in the weeks when things didn't go so well. Until then, enjoy the breaks in tension, but don't fool yourself. There is still work to do.

Can You Use This Book Alone, or Should You Get Help?

This book offers many practical ideas to help you heal your marriage. In fact, I would go so far as to guarantee that if you consistently apply the ideas in this book, you will have an enviably happy marriage. That said, you may find yourself becoming frustrated at one point or another. Perhaps you will struggle to get yourself to use some of the suggestions at all. Or you may find that you start to take advantage of some of the ideas, but you can't make them stick for some reason. If this is the case, I would recommend that you seek professional assistance either through the Pastoral Solutions Institute or a local, marriage-friendly therapist you trust.

Marriage therapy isn't a class. Knowing the information well enough to pass a test isn't any guarantee of success. Healing your marriage is like trying to develop an exercise habit. The fact that I know how to do crunches doesn't mean that I'll do them or do them consistently enough to make a difference, or for that matter, that I'll do them properly so that I don't do more damage to my health by exercising than I would sitting on the couch with a bag of chips. That's why I might need a personal trainer either to keep me accountable or to teach me how to do my exercises properly or more efficiently (or even do different exercises that would work better for me).

Studies show that from the time they are first unhappy in their marriage, most couples wait four to six years to seek professional help (Gottman, 2011). This is foolish. Getting competent help early is key to your success. If you find yourself struggling with the material in this book at any time, for any reason, skip ahead to chapter 11, "Getting Good Support," for guidance on seeking the right kind of professional with the right kind of skills to help you heal your marriage. Remember, the success rate for competent, marriage-friendly therapists is over 90 percent. The guidelines in chapter 11 will enable you to choose well.

Inviting God In

Fr. Patrick Peyton used to tell couples that "the family that prays together stays together." It wasn't just a cute slogan. Research shows that couples who pray, and especially those who pray together, enjoy both greater marital satisfaction and marital stability than couples who don't (Rushnel and DuArt, 2011).

I understand that if you have not prayed with your spouse before, it is hardly the best time to begin when your marriage is in a tailspin, but I encourage you to propose it anyway. If your mate says no for now, you haven't lost any ground, and you can always start praying on your own, but if your spouse says yes, then you're already making progress!

God wants to be part of healing your marriage. In fact, he wants to be part of everything you do in your marriage. As

Christians, we believe that God brought you and your spouse together for good reasons, not because he has a warped sense of humor. Presumably, God has chosen both you and your spouse to play a role in helping each other become everything he created you to be and helping each other get to heaven. You and your mate play an essential role in God's plan for each other's sanctification and perfection that is second only to the saving work of Jesus Christ! That's one of the reasons Scripture says that God hates divorce (Mal. 2:16).

Of course, God can get you to heaven with or without your spouse—in him, all things are possible (Matt. 19:26)—but he has chosen your spouse to be a help, to challenge you in just the ways that you need to be challenged to become the person he is calling you to be, and vice versa. Sometimes we grow because of our spouse, and sometimes we grow in spite of our spouse, but we must always realize that God wants to use the circumstances we are in, regardless of how challenging they may be, to facilitate our growth in grace, strength, and emotional and spiritual maturity.

Sometimes the challenges we face on the road to these good things are harder than others, but they are almost always necessary. Regardless, it only makes sense to go to God, especially in the midst of your marital struggles, and ask him to teach you exactly what he was thinking when he made this crazy match! Scripture tells us that if we seek his wisdom, we will find it (Matt. 7:7-12). Praying about your marriage, especially if you can manage to do it with your spouse, will help you see your marriage from God's point of view and enable you to see his blessings in your challenges, as well as the path he wants you to walk through those challenges.

Many people ask how they can begin praying for their marriage—whether together or on their own. There are as many

ways to pray as there are people on the planet, and ultimately
you have to choose what you feel most comfortable with. That
said, I recommend the following suggestions.

- *Pick a time.* Try to choose a time that can be consistent
from day to day. It's okay if you have to move the time
around (the truly important thing is not *when* it happens
but that it *does* happen), but the more variation in your
time, the more difficult it is to be consistent with your
prayer.

- *Keep it simple.* Especially if you are new to prayer — or
to praying as a couple — keep it simple. Prayer doesn't
have to be frilly or longwinded to be effective. It just
has to put you in a place where you are genuinely open
to receiving the wisdom and grace God wants to give
you. A short, simple, heartfelt prayer for help is worth
a million more complicated, time-consuming, "dutiful"
approaches to prayer.

- *Be humble.* When we have marital problems, it is easy to
believe our spouse is to blame. Sometimes, it's even true!
But even if your spouse is 100 percent of the problem, be
humble in your prayer. Even when you feel as if you didn't
cause the problems and aren't responsible for them, God
can teach you ways to respond to those problems that can
begin to heal them. It's fine to ask God to change your
spouse, but it's a much better prayer to ask God to change
you so that you might respond in a more graceful and
faithful way to the things that irritate, upset, or infuriate
you about your spouse. I encourage my clients to say, in
their own words, some version of the following prayer.

Lord God, we're hurting so much in our marriage. We don't know what to do. Teach us your way through the problems we're facing. Help us discover the most graceful and faithful way to respond to each other and help us to live out the love that comes from your own heart when our own love has run dry.

Notice the request to respond in a more "graceful and faithful way." I chose those words carefully. Too many spouses think that the only godly response to a spouse's offensive behavior is to try to be "loving," which usually translates into "nice, tolerant, and long-suffering." Often this is true, but just as often, the godly thing to do is to learn to set limits charitably, to say no, or charitably to challenge one's mate to behave more appropriately. Asking God to show you the "graceful and faithful way" to respond to one another allows you to reflect more specifically on the nature of your response and choose the path that might work best—or perhaps hasn't yet been tried.

As with the other ideas in this book, prayer isn't magic. God can certainly grant you a miracle and spontaneously heal your marriage, but more often, God would like us to experience the healing of our hearts that comes from doing the work our marriage requires. Either way, turning to the Lord to ask his guidance to discover the path back to love allows us to open our hearts to the wisdom and grace he wants to give us and challenges us to take our hands off the wheel so that he can drive the bus.

So, What Are These Marriage-Friendly Habits?

Soon I'll introduce the specific habits that help couples stay happy with each other through life's ups and downs. As you might have guessed, prayer is certainly one of those habits, and

I'll discuss it in more depth later, as well as many other habits that can help heal your marriage. But before we dive into which habits you need and how to cultivate them, let me address one other potential problem that could undermine your progress.

Chapter 2

What "I've Tried Everything" Really Means

Spouses are therefore the permanent reminder . . . of what
happened on the cross; they are for one another . . . witnesses
to the salvation in which the sacrament makes them sharers.
—Pope St. John Paul the Great, *Familiaris Consortio* 13

One of the biggest challenges in trying to save a marriage is overcoming the exhaustion and frustration that most couples feel.

"I feel like I've tried everything," Mary Beth says of her eighteen-year marriage to Ralph. "I've tried talking to him about things. We've argued until the cows came home. Eventually, I get sick of fighting, and I just try letting things go, but that never lasts. We've talked to our pastor, we went on a marriage retreat, we've been to counseling a couple of times, but nothing seems to make a difference—at least, not a difference that lasts. I'm worn out. I never thought I'd say that I was past caring whether my marriage worked or not, but some days ... Of course, I don't want divorce, but I just don't know how much longer I can keep doing this."

Everybody says marriage is hard work, and there is no way around the fact that it is often much harder than we expect. The thing is, while every couple experiences marriage as hard work, happy couples know how to work smart. Unhappy couples also tend to work hard at their marriages, but they do so in a way that wears them down and drains them and produces little effort. Often I find that, through no fault of their own, spouses and even therapists make the work of healing a marriage much harder than it needs to be, and that's something we can start to fix today.

That Powerless Feeling

Many marriage-counseling clients often complain of a sense of powerlessness that comes from either trying and failing so many times or being unable to find effective solutions to the marital challenges they face. Understandably, they attribute this sense of powerlessness to their marriage. Feeling powerless—a sense that "I've tried everything" or "Nothing I do will ever change anything"—about one's marriage is terrifically demoralizing. When we experience that place of powerlessness in marriage, we often feel that there is nothing we can do to improve things, that nothing will work, and that our marriage is hopelessly broken. After all, you can't change anyone but yourself, right? (Actually you can, but we'll get to that.)

The Press of Troubles vs. Oppression

Even though it's natural to blame the relationship, the sense of powerlessness one feels in the face of a difficult marriage isn't actually a result of the marriage at all, but rather a sign that your brain is stressed, overloaded, and in a state of lockdown.

St. Augustine once distinguished between the "press of troubles" and "oppression" (Thigpen, 2001). The press of troubles is simply the fact that life is hard and bad stuff happens. Oppression is something more than this. Oppression is what happens when the normal press of troubles starts to wear us down, separate us from God, make us feel powerless, and cause us to behave in ways that don't reflect the kind of person we would like to be. Understanding how the press of troubles in marriage becomes oppression can help you feel more powerful and begin to discover new opportunities for change that you were previously blinded to. It has to do with how stress—and in particular, relational stress—affects your brain's ability to solve problems.

Stress does a number on the brain. Whether we are feeling stressed in the moment or stressed over a period of time, the stressed brain is less capable of either identifying solutions or following through on solutions that have been created. Sometimes, after living in a stressed-out state for a long time, it becomes the norm and we don't recognize it anymore. At that point, even when we *think* we're calm and put-together, we are *actually* almost constantly flooded with stress chemicals that essentially paralyze our brain and cause us to react rather than respond in an effective, creative way to the challenges in front of us. Chances are, if you feel powerless in your marriage, you may be living in an almost perpetual state of brain lockdown. This is the psychological manifestation of the more spiritual oppression Augustine referred to. When our minds go to this place of lockdown, we are less receptive to help, less flexible, less creative, and less motivated to try anything.

The behavioral reactions that the stressed-out brain produces are intended to be short-term fixes intended to get us out of immediate discomfort, but they tend to make long-term solutions harder to find. The result is that we burn up a lot of energy doing things that could never work in the first place. It is a bit like the exhaustion that comes from obsessively and repetitively pushing on a door that can be opened only by pulling it. (Admit it. I'm not the only person who has done this, right?)

The good news is that you can learn to recognize, control, and even escape the state of brain lockdown that causes your powerless feelings. Although escaping this powerless feeling will not make your marriage problems magically disappear, you will be surprised to discover that you are able to resist the temptation to be caught up in marital drama, and you might even be amazed to see the creative ideas you are able to come up with that open new avenues of healing for your marriage. It's okay if you don't believe me just yet. Most of my clients don't believe me either—at first. And then most of these same clients go on to experience exactly what I just described to you; a sense of calm that allows them to step outside the marital drama and identify creative new solutions to problems they have struggled with for years.

The Solution-Focused Brain
vs. the Misery-Making Mindset

If you are trying to solve serious marital problems, especially if you are trying to do it alone, you need to have all your wits about you. You will need to begin with two basic skills. First, you must be able to recognize when you are operating out of your Solution-Focused Brain and when you are operating out of your Misery-Making Mindset. Second, once you get good at catching yourself falling into your Misery-Making Mindset, you'll need to know how to switch your Solution-Focused Brain back on so that you can respond to problems with effective solutions instead of reacting to problems in ways that make them worse. By the end of this chapter, you'll know how to recognize the difference between these two brain states and how to switch back into the more productive, Solution-Focused Brain when you experience your less productive, Misery-Making Mindset coming online.

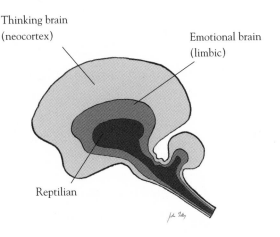

Thinking brain
(neocortex)

Emotional brain
(limbic)

Reptilian

The Three Sections of the Triune Brain

Troubles on Your Mind

To begin, you need to understand that the Solution-Focused Brain and the Misery-Making Mindset are not just metaphors. If you had a functional MRI machine in your house and you took pictures of your Solution-Focused Brain and your Misery-Making Mindset (say, when you were problem-solving with your spouse versus fighting with your spouse or feeling thwarted), you would see profound differences between the two brain states. What I am referring to as the Solution-Focused Brain is the state of mind that exists when your cortex (the part of the brain where learning and life experiences are stored and the part responsible for problem solving and regulating your emotions) is online and operating in cooperation with your limbic system (the part of the brain responsible for emotions and reactions). When these two regions of your brain are working together, you are able to discover emotionally satisfying solutions to your marital problems, or at least see how it might be possible to do so if you could just access the right resources. This is what makes this brain state solution friendly.

But as stress increases in your marriage—and especially if it becomes the norm—your brain tries to conserve energy to get through the day without burning out. It actually allows the cortex more or less to shut down (Cozolino, 2014; Seigel, 2013). At that point—since the cortex is the repository of life experience and knowledge—all the self-help books you've ever read, the life experiences you've had, the counseling you've received, and the advice you've been given becomes largely inaccessible to you. You can look at it all through the window, but you can't enter the room. The library doors are locked. The Internet is down. This is a tremendously frustrating place to find yourself, which is why I call it the Misery-Making Mindset. This is, incidentally, the precise mindset St. Paul was complaining about when he said, "I do not understand my own actions. For I do not do what I want, but I do the very thing I hate" (Rom. 7:15).

Now, with your cortex offline, you are left with only your limbic system and brain stem (the two regions comprising the Misery-Making Mindset) to solve your marital problems (and whatever other problems you have as well). Unfortunately, even taken together, they offer about as much brainpower as your average white-tailed deer or lizard can generate. From what I've heard, neither animal is a particularly reliable source of marriage-counseling advice. At any rate, these brain regions (limbic system and brain stem) are completely incapable of finding complex solutions. They are merely the seat of your "fight-flight-freeze response." When your brain is working as it should, this response should take over only when you are in imminent danger. The limbic system and brain stem should overpower the cortex only as long as it takes to get you out of immediate trouble, and then they should return control of your brain to the cortex so it can do the heavy lifting of finding long-lasting solutions.

Unfortunately, for many reasons, this God-given, life-preserving strategy can become hijacked by the stressors of everyday life. When that happens, you end up living in a state of reaction. If you stay in that stressed-out place long enough, your reactive, Misery-Making Mindset becomes the norm. Although all of this is happening in your brain, you can recognize the shift by becoming aware of your behavior. Certain ways of thinking and acting are more consistent with the Misery-Making Mindset. If you learn to catch yourself, you can learn to push yourself back into the Solution-Focused Brain state and begin feeling more hopeful about your marriage and, more importantly, begin being more open to finding ways to change your marriage.

Recognizing the Difference

Here is a side-by-side comparison of the Solution-Focused Brain and the Misery-Making Mindset.

Solution-Focused Brain	Misery-Making Mindset
1. Aware of emotions but focused on solutions	1. Emotionally focused on futility
2. Intellect engaged	2. Ruminating
3. Collaborative mindset (even if mate uninterested)	3. Blaming mindset (If only he or she would do X, then ...)
4. Intentional about identity	4. Feelings justify actions

Let's look at each point to see how it plays out in marriage.

Aware of emotions and focused on solutions
vs. emotionally focused on futility

It is never healthy to deny our feelings, but the Solution-Focused Brain handles emotions very differently from the Misery-Making Mindset.

Let's first look at the Misery-Making Mindset:

> Jenna was tired of the constant arguments with her husband. She and Trey had never been in such a low place in their relationship. They had tried counseling before, but Trey quit when the therapist suggested that Jenna was not the actual source of his angry outbursts. Trey insisted that there was nothing wrong with him except that Jenna was unwilling to be sensitive to how stressed out at work he was. Her constant demands on his time were selfish and just added to his misery. Jenna was tired of Trey's excuses and frustrated with endless "conversations" that went nowhere and left them both feeling exhausted. She tried to pray about her marriage, but her feelings kept getting in the way, and she would just end up crying or daydreaming about how she wished things were. Sometimes a friend would suggest a counselor or a book that might help, but Jenna just knew that it was all pointless. Instead, she just tried to go from day to day as best she could, hoping that somehow, something would cause Trey to snap out of it and allow her to find some measure of happiness in her life.

Jenna, understandably, is allowing the stress of her marriage to cause her Solution-Focused brain to shut down. But just because a reaction is understandable doesn't make it healthy or useful. Let's look at how someone who knows how to turn on her Solution-Focused Brain responds to exactly the same marital dynamic.

Mary Elizabeth was tired of the constant arguments with her husband. She and Dave had never been in such a low place in their relationship. They had tried counseling before, but Dave quit when the therapist suggested that Mary Elizabeth was not the actual source of his angry outbursts. Dave insisted that there was nothing wrong with him except that Mary Elizabeth was unwilling to be sensitive to how stressed out at work he was. Her constant demands on his time were selfish and just added to his misery.

Mary Elizabeth was tired of Dave's excuses and frustrated with endless "conversations" that went nowhere and left them both feeling exhausted. As frustrated as she was, she continued praying about the relationship and looking for resources that might help. She realized that there are lots of approaches to counseling and maybe she needed to get a few more opinions on her situation. She interviewed several counselors about her situation and finally found one who she thought could help her even if Dave wasn't willing to participate at first. This counselor seemed supportive of the marriage and openly discussed the marriage-therapy training he had—that was something her previous therapist hadn't discussed. Mary Elizabeth made an appointment with this new counselor. Later, she told Dave that she planned to go either way, but that she thought it would be good if he would join her.

Mary Elizabeth's story is a good example of the Solution-Focused Brain at work. In the example, she didn't deny her feelings of frustration, irritation, and exhaustion, but even though she was *aware* of those feelings, she *focused* on possible solutions to her problem; solutions that included prayer, consultation, and making an appointment with a different counselor. There were probably lots of days she didn't feel like looking for resources and solutions, but in her Solution-Focused Brain state, she concentrated her energies on looking for answers to her questions.

Readers will note that the language describing the marriage problems faced by Mary Elizabeth and Jenna is exactly the same up to the point where I describe their responses to those problems. Both Mary Elizabeth and Jenna feel they are in an impossible situation, but while Jenna has fallen into the Misery-Making Mindset, which causes her to feel hopeless, powerless, and withdrawn, Mary Elizabeth has found ways to stay in her Solution-Focused Brain state, which enables her to continue the search for healthful solutions.

You might say, "But what if there really isn't anything she can do?" There is always the possibility that this will be the case, but the Misery-Making Mindset and the Solution-Focused Brain respond to this differently. The Misery-Making Mindset just gives up out of a sense of futility and frustration combined with a lot of doubt and self-recrimination. Spouses in this mindset know there are other things they could have tried, but they lacked the will, energy, and strength to try them. By contrast, spouses using their Solution-Focused Brain might hit a wall, but even here they feel a sense of peace and confidence, knowing that they have done everything that could be reasonably expected of them and more, and because they have been intentional about the process, they feel a greater degree of certainty about their next steps.

Intellect engaged vs. ruminating

Spouses in both the Solution-Focused Brain state and the Misery-Making Mindset feel as if they are thinking and working hard on their marriage. But only the efforts of the spouses in the Solution-Focused Brain state will bear any fruit. Let's start with the Misery-Making Mindset's tendency to ruminate and how this differs from the problem-solving approach of the Solution-Focused Brain.

> Phil and Michelle are at a low point in their relationship. After eighteen years of marriage, Michelle told Phil, "I love you. I'm just not in love with you." Phil was crushed. He had no idea that Michelle felt that way.
>
> For her part, Michelle feels that there is nothing that can be done to save the marriage. They've spoken with their pastor, but Michelle just went through the motions of the meeting. It is clear to Phil that she has one foot out the door. He's not sure, but there are signs that there might be somebody else Michelle is in love with, although he doesn't think she has acted on anything yet.
>
> All of this has caused Phil to feel paralyzed. All he can do is think about the end of the relationship and what that might do to him and the kids. He's not able to eat. He's just going through the motions at work. He has a hard time sleeping at night. He mopes and surfs the Internet when he's home. He tries to think about the marriage and what he could do to make things better, but he can't seem to generate any ideas that give him any sense of hope. His pastor has suggested some programs and counselors he thinks could help, but Phil just thinks, "What's the point?" If Michelle doesn't love him anymore,

he can't force her to change her mind. Besides, why would he want to be with someone who doesn't want him? Still, he desperately wishes things could be different. He thinks about it all the time. He just doesn't know what to do.

Phil is locked in his Misery-Making Mindset. He is not thinking about problem-solving as much as he is ruminating about his problems. Ruminating is the emotional equivalent of picking at a scab. You just turn the hurtful events over and over again in your mind, hoping that a solution will present itself, but of course it won't because you don't discover answers by focusing on the problem. You discover answers by seeking help and searching out resources. Phil is too paralyzed by his feelings to do anything useful. He is convinced that the marital problems are Michelle's fault, and of course, her actions are very seriously wounding to the marriage. But if Michelle's behavior is making the marriage sick, Phil's response to her behavior is poisoning what's left. His powerlessness and his sense that divorce is a foregone conclusion aren't caused by Michelle's actions. They are caused by his inability to recognize and come out of his Misery-Making Mindset.

Now let's look at how someone who knows how to turn on his Solution-Focused Brain might respond to a similar marital dynamic.

James and Rebecca are at a low point in their relationship. After eighteen years of marriage, Rebecca told James, "I love you. I'm just not in love with you." James was crushed. He had no idea that Rebecca felt that way.

For her part, Rebecca feels that there is nothing that can be done to save the marriage. They've spoken with their pastor, but Rebecca just went through the motions of the meeting. It is clear to James that she has one foot out the door. He's not sure, but there are signs that there might be somebody else Rebecca is in love with, although he doesn't think she has acted on anything yet.

James has been praying hard about what he could do to reach out to Rebecca—for both his sake and the sake of their three children, who will be devastated if they divorce. Working with his pastor, James has gathered a list of resources about local marriage retreats and marriage-friendly counselors and has a plan for approaching Rebecca. He knows that she'd refuse him if he asked her himself, so he has invited the pastor to dinner at their home for a follow-up meeting. James hopes that if he and the pastor—whom Rebecca respects—can encourage Rebecca to get help for their relationship, she will agree, even if only to save face. James knows it won't be easy to turn things around, but he has focused his energy on thinking of whatever ideas he can to move things forward toward healing. He knows that things are bad right now. But until Rebecca's gone, he's committed to coming up with whatever ideas he can to fight for the relationship and their happiness.

James's response to his marital difficulties is an example of how the intellect remains engaged when a spouse remains in his or her Solution-Focused Brain state.

Again, we see that the details of James's and Phil's marriages are the same; only their response is different. James is in the Solution-Focused Brain state. He is actively engaged in a process of problem solving. He isn't just desperately flinging out ideas and hoping that something will stick. He is giving serious prayer and consideration to Rebecca's feelings and trying to identify solutions and resources and an approach that will work, considering her specific attitude toward the marriage. It's true that he can't be sure any of these ideas will work, but that isn't the point. The point is that he is focused on claiming his power in a difficult situation by focusing on developing the most effective, grace-filled response he can to this situation. The sense of power that accompanies turning on one's Solution-Focused Brain does not come from being certain of a particular outcome, but from formulating the most godly and effective response one can to the situation and taking pride in responding admirably to a tough situation.

Collaborative mindset (even if mate uninterested) vs. blaming

It's hard to work on your marriage, especially if your mate doesn't want to work with you, but the Solution-Focused Brain and the Misery-Making Mindset respond to this challenge very differently. Let's start with how the Misery-Making Mindset chooses blaming over collaboration.

Sara and Frank are at a terrible place in their marriage of seven years. Frank loves his work, and he's very good at it. Unfortunately, Sara feels as if that's all that Frank loves. She has tried to be understanding of his long hours, but when she realized that it wasn't that he was being forced to stay longer than everyone else, but consistently chose to go in earlier and work later for his own reasons, she was deeply hurt.

Sara says, "Frank is a workaholic. I've told him a million times that there are more things in life than work, that our marriage needs attention. I try to tell him that he can't keep expecting me to sit around waiting for the crumbs of attention that manage to fall off the table when he is done with work and e-mails and meetings and everything he wants to do instead of be present to me. He just looks at me and says, 'I don't know what to do!' I just want to shake him. I've given him a million ideas, but he never uses any of them, or he tries for a week and then ... nothing. We've argued and fought. God help me, I even tried to get his attention by leaving for the weekend without telling him where I was going. He got furious, but nothing changed. I just don't know what the point is anymore. His mom put up with the same kind of treatment from his dad for years. He used to complain about it all the time. I thought that meant that he'd actually make different choices, but he's exactly the same person his dad was. He hates when I tell him that, but it's true. I'm not sure whether it even makes sense to keep working on the relationship. I honestly don't think he's even capable of meeting my needs. Maybe it's not even fair for me to ask him to. He's just not cut out for marriage."

Sara is obviously dealing with some very serious marital problems. Frank's behavior is causing her to feel completely unloved, and his inability to address his work habits would be frustrating to anyone. He needs to change. And yet Sara's approach to Frank's workaholism is rooted in her Misery-Making Mindset, which has only made her situation worse. She blames him for the problems and assumes that he wants to treat her poorly. Frank is the problem, and she must fix him. Obviously, she can't tolerate Frank's behavior, but her entire effort is focused on making Frank into a project. Although Frank's failure to take responsibility for himself makes Sara's response understandable, turning a person into a project never works. The person will simply become defensive in the face of blame and shut down even more, repeating the same unhealthy patterns, sometimes out of spite and sometimes out of genuine confusion about how to get his emotions to allow him to do what he knows is right.

Let's look at how the Solution-Focused Brain approaches the same marital dynamic, not in a spirit of blame but with a more collaborative mindset.

Jacinta and Louis are at a terrible place in their marriage of seven years. Louis loves his work, and he's very good at it. Unfortunately, Jacinta feels as if that's all that Louis loves. She has tried to be understanding of his long hours, but when she realized that it wasn't that he was being forced to stay longer than everyone else, but consistently chose to go in earlier and work later for his own reasons, she was deeply hurt.

Jacinta says, "Louis is a workaholic. His dad was too, but Louis always said he hated that his dad was that way. Still, he has a hard time breaking out of it. We've gone around and around about it, but even though we've come up with a million ideas together, he has a hard time following through. It's so frustrating; I think it probably is for both of us. Even though he loves his work, he likes to think of himself as a good husband, and I know he recognizes that he's letting me down. I finally sat him down and told him that I knew that neither of us was happy with the way things were and that we just couldn't keep going like this. I asked him what he thought needed to happen to help him be the husband I knew he wanted to be. He told me he didn't know, and I said that I didn't know either.

Then I asked if he had any ideas for where we could go to figure it out. He said he didn't. So I explained that if it was up to me, I'd have us set times when he would absolutely agree to be home to be with me and the kids, no matter what, but more importantly, we would talk to both our pastor for accountability and to a counselor to get the skills we needed to get past this—namely, for him to learn how to set boundaries at work and me to hold him accountable without nagging him. I explained that I didn't think we could do it entirely on our own.

"He didn't like that idea very much, and he got kind of upset with me. I explained that I wasn't telling him what to do; I was just proposing an idea. If he had an idea that would work better, I would happily defer to it. He didn't. I told him that I understood that he might need some time to think, but that things couldn't stay the way they are. So I just said that if he couldn't bring any other ideas to the table or we couldn't come up with some even better way to solve our problems, then I would call the rectory to talk with our pastor about meeting, and I'd set up an appointment with a marriage counselor.

"I knew he probably wouldn't have any ideas on how to fix this. He's stuck. I get that. But I would still rather try to invite him to collaborate with me than tell him what to do. By Sunday, he hadn't come up with another plan. So I just went ahead and called the rectory and also made an appointment for marriage counseling. Louis was surprised at first, but I just kept telling him that since things had to change, he could either come up with a better idea or go along with mine, but it was his choice. He was surprised at how assertive I was. I think he just thought it would blow over. Even though he was a little put out, he couldn't say I didn't ask for his input, and he came with me to the meeting with our pastor and made the commitment to counseling. It was hard to go through the motions of asking his input, but I honestly did hope he would come up with something, and when he didn't, it was easier to push my solution without being pushy.

Jacinta played this smart. Instead of blaming Louis and treating him like a broken toy she had to fix, she clearly stated the problem and her need and invited his collaboration to seek solutions. Every step of the way, he was invited to be part of the process. It's true that he opted out of the process, but by the end, he couldn't blame her for railroading him, so it was harder to justify his initial resistance to her ideas.

The collaborative mindset exhibited when our Solution-Focused Brain is turned on eliminates blaming, invites the other person to be our partner in solving the problem, and even if he or she doesn't partner with us, it gives us the credibility to assert our own plan without coming across as pushy.

Intentional about identity vs. feelings justify action

When you're dealing with a serious marital problem, it's hard not to want to put more and more fuel on the emotional fire, but that almost always backfires. Let's look at how both the Misery-Making Mindset and the Solution-Focused Brain deal with this pressure. First, the Misery-Making Mindset.

Jack and Chelsea have been married for ten years, and they're at a real low. It seems as if there is nothing they can say to each other that doesn't provoke some kind of reaction. The other day, Chelsea was furious that Jack forgot to stop and get paper towels on his way home from work. She'd had a rough day. The kids were crazy, and the kitchen was a wreck. All she wanted to do was get some order back in her life, and now Jack took that from her. She laid into him for his irresponsibility and told him that she was sick of never being able to count on him for anything.

Jack lost it. He told Chelsea that she should stop nagging him all the time. He told her that she was acting just like her mom — a sensitive point for Chelsea, who was estranged from her abusive mother. The argument continued like that for a while until they both burned out and spent the rest of the night ignoring each other.

Later, when they talked about it, neither Chelsea nor Jack would offer an unqualified apology. They both attempted to justify their own reaction by pointing to the other's offense and saying that "the only reason" they did or said X or Y was because the other did or said Z. Both believed that the other's behavior justified their own hurtful choices. Neither liked acting as they did, but what else could they do if the other one insisted on being such an idiot?

In the Misery-Making Mindset, we are never responsible for what we do. The things we do are always a response to someone else's earlier and more serious action — or at least it feels that way. It's a very seductive line of thought, but giving in to the belief that we are powerless over our responses to another's actions is not only objectively untrue; it is corrosive to the marital bond.

Let's look at how turning on the Solution-Focused Brain can make a difference.

Erik and Gabby have been married for ten years, and they're at a real low. It seems as if there is nothing they can say to each other that doesn't provoke some kind of reaction. The other day, Gabby was furious that Erik forgot to stop and get paper towels on his way home from work. She'd had a rough day. The kids were crazy, and the kitchen was a wreck. All she wanted to do was get some order back in her life, and now Erik took that from her. She laid into him for his irresponsibility and told him that she was sick of never being able to count on him for anything.

Erik was hurt, and he wanted to lash out, but something held him back. He was tired of letting the tensions between them make him so reactive. He didn't want to be "that guy" anymore. He just told Gabby that he was sorry he let her down and that she was right to be disappointed. But he also told her how much her words hurt him. At first, she tried to justify her reaction, asking how else she was supposed to feel when she couldn't even count on him to do a simple thing for her. He replied that he knew she was upset, and she had a right to be, but that when she calmed down, he hoped she'd see that lashing out at him just put more fuel on the fire, and they had already been through so many fires together. Maybe it was time they both just stopped blaming each other for their own bad habits. He told her again that he was sorry that she'd had such a rough day and that he wished he could have done a better job of being there for her. Then he left the room.

Later, Gabby apologized too. It was hard to admit it, but she knew he was right. She didn't want to be like her mom, who lost it over every little thing. It was a bad habit she had allowed herself to get away with for too long. They decided to find out when their diocese was hosting the next Retrouvaille retreat so that maybe they could learn some better ways to talk to each other when emotions heated things up.

When the Solution-Focused Brain is turned on, we can be more mindful of who we are and who we want to be. We stop justifying our hurtful actions by pointing to our spouse's offensive behavior. We realize that whatever our spouse's offense is, we are responsible for our own response. We don't have to let offenses go and take all the blame. Instead, we can take responsibility for our own behavior. Period. Then, without judging or blaming, we can invite our spouse to be better too by reminding him of who he wants to be or how you both are at your best.

Again, the power of this approach is not in any guarantee that our spouse's behavior will change. We can't directly control that. The power of this mindset comes from knowing that you have the strength not to let your mate's offensive behavior bring out the ugliest parts of yourself. As a bonus, sometimes that's also enough to challenge your spouse to change as well.

Living "in reaction"

Right about now, you might be rolling your eyes, thinking that you could never be like the people who illustrated the responses of those who have turned on their Solution-Focused Brain. But that isn't true. Chances are your Solution-Focused Brain works just fine with your coworkers or your boss, your neighbors, your extended family, the cop who pulls you over to give you a speeding ticket, or anyone you meet whom you might want to impress. A woman I know tells the story of how, when she was a little girl, her mom could be yelling at her viciously, but when the phone rang, her mother would pick up the phone, the portrait of charm and grace, and say, "Hello, darling!" The truth is, we control our reactions where it matters to us. We just forget that we have the power to do so in our marriage, where it counts the most. We get sloppy, and then we confuse our sloppiness with reality—the way it "has to be" because it always is.

Maybe you're not giving yourself enough credit. If you started thinking of your spouse the way you think of that customer who irritates you (but you still have to handle politely), or your boss, who drives you crazy (but you still have to respect), or your mom, who knows just how to push your buttons (but you still manage to be nice to), you would be on the road to learning how to turn your Solution-Focused Brain back on with your spouse. I'll offer additional suggestions in chapter 6 on how to turn on your Solution-Focused Brain and how to inspire your spouse to do the same, but for now, I wanted to get you thinking about how you could reclaim your sense of confidence, power, and effectiveness in your marriage if you stopped looking at how awful your mate is—even if he or she is—and started asking how you could leave your Solution-Focused Brain turned on, no matter what your spouse did. If you could learn to do that, not only would you stop feeling powerless; you might actually have enough presence of mind to be a positive force for change in your marriage.

Ask yourself:

1. When you are stressed but still manage to stay in your Solution-Focused Brain (e.g., at work or with friends or when you are handling problems "at your best"), how do you do it?

2. What situations tend to trigger your Misery-Making Mindset?

3. When you are in your Misery-Making Mindset, how do you think? What do you tend to say? How do you act?

4. Now that you understand the difference between these two mindsets, think back. Have you ever caught yourself falling into your Misery-Making Mindset and managed to spontaneously turn your Solution-Focused Brain back on? How did you do it?

5. Do you know anyone who is good at staying in his or her Solution-Focused Brain? How does he or she do it?

The Three Personas

Earlier, in our discussion about how different parts of the brain respond to stress, I referred to the "fight, flight, or freeze" response generated by the Misery-Making Mindset. In marriage, these reactions tend to manifest themselves as three powerless personas. The Pouting/Withdrawing Persona, the Tantrumming Persona, and/or the Contemptuous Expert Persona. Although, strictly speaking, it's enough to know if you are using your Solution-Focused Brain or your Misery-Making Mindset, sometimes it can be hard to tell. The presence of one or more of these personas can help clarify where your head is (literally) and warn you that have crossed the border of problem solving and are well into misery making. All of these personas share a sense of powerlessness, but superficially, they manifest this powerlessness in different and surprising ways.

* *Pouting/Withdrawing Persona.* This is the relational manifestation of the lower (limbic) brain's *flight* response. When you

fall into the Pouting/Withdrawing Persona, you organize your powerlessness along a continuum of emotional and/or physical withdrawal.

For instance, if you tend toward the pouting variation on this theme, you remain physically present but emotionally withdrawn. This persona is characterized by the idea that "there's nothing I can do, and the people who could do something about it don't seem to care, so I guess I just have to let it go/offer it up (*sigh*)." The person in this position is genuinely trying to be noble, but everything about his or her body language screams, "Please notice how miserable I am and fix things for me already!" Again, although this is never the conscious intent of individuals occupying this persona, if they ever had to watch a video of themselves, even they would be forced to agree that's what's going on.

The withdrawing variation on this theme is characterized by both emotional and physical withdrawal. This person believes that since there's "nothing I can do, I might as well not be here," hoping that the problem will either solve itself in his or her absence or, at the very least, he or she won't have to put up with it. Such individuals use their problems as an excuse to hide out at work, or in community involvements, or—if they have to be home—in various activities (TV, the Internet, car repair, scrapbooking, etc.) that make them unavailable.

Individuals who fall into either form of the Pouting/Withdrawing Persona tend to complain about feeling "controlled" by their spouses. What is usually truer is that the individuals occupying this persona are not really sure of themselves and tend to be less than assertive. It is simply easier to blame one's spouse for being controlling than it is to make and assert one's own plan. To escape this powerless mindset, individuals who tend to flee to the safety of the Pouting/Withdrawing Persona will need to begin to be much more intentional about life; thinking through problems, identifying solutions, and finding the strength to assert these ideas. If they can do this, they will reclaim their feelings of effectiveness and be able to create healthy change in their marriage. If not, they can easily sink into depression or even substance abuse.

A good prayer for the Pouting/Withdrawing Persona is, "Lord, you have the words of everlasting life. When I want to retreat, grant me courage to face the conflict, wisdom to advance godly solutions, and the words that come from your own heart."

• *Tantrumming Persona.* This is the relational manifestation of the lower (limbic) brain's *fight* response. It is both the scariest and the most powerless of the three personas. This persona is scary, because tantrummers are willing to go to ridiculous emotional lengths to intimidate their mates into submission. It is the most powerless of all the personas, however, because people who occupy this persona not only believe that they are powerless to do anything about the offense but also that they are powerless against the intense feelings of anger and injustice that sweep over them in the presence of the offense. These individuals often complain of feeling as if someone else has a remote that controls their emotional responses. This feeling of powerlessness is usually expressed when someone else complains about the tantrummer's behavior and receives the response, "What? You don't like how *I'm* behaving?! Well, maybe *you* shouldn't have done X in the first place."

Likewise, tantrummers often complain, "Everyone always tries to blame me for everything." They struggle to understand why, when they try to address a problem, the conversation almost immediately turns to their abusive behavior. Tantrummers rarely admit more than grudging, superficial responsibility for anything —which is actually the secret of their powerlessness. To return to a Solution-Focused Brain state, people displaying the Tantrumming Persona need to learn that other people's offensive behavior *never* justifies their yelling, name-calling, intimidating, or other angry, destructive outbursts. By learning to control their reactions by leading conversations with solutions instead of emotions, tantrummers can learn to reclaim their sense of personal power and channel their passion into becoming a positive force for change in the relationship.

Here is a good prayer for when the tantrummer feels the anger and angst coming on: "Lord, you are the source of the peace beyond all understanding. Give me your peace. Grant me a gentle spirit, ears to listen, and a well-trained tongue to speak only words that convey your grace."

• *Contemptuous Expert Persona.* This is the relational manifestation of the lower (limbic) brain's *freeze* response. This persona is tricky, because the person who exhibits it appears calm and fairly put together. Where the Pouting/Withdrawing Persona shuts down and becomes less vocal and the Tantrumming Persona blows up, the Contemptuous Expert becomes cold and irritatingly aloof and superior. People who are exhibiting the Contemptuous Expert Persona have a hard time admitting that they are in their Misery-Making Mindset because when their lower brain takes over, they become convinced that they can do no wrong. Like a peacock that spreads its feathers to convince an adversary that it is not to be trifled with, the Contemptuous Expert Persona becomes a puffed up, self-righteous know-it-all who is only too happy to explain in great, analytical, and intimate detail why everything that is wrong in the relationship is the other person's fault. Those who exhibit this persona don't usually come right out and say it, but you can tell by their tone that they mean to add "you idiot" at the end of every sentence, almost like a period.

Despite the superior facade (as well as, potentially, some reasonable ideas for solving the problems that get lost in all the lecturing and blaming), Contemptuous Experts continue to feel powerless inside exactly because nothing is their fault; they do not believe they are responsible for the problem, so they cannot take responsibility for finding a solution. They can only use the force of their words, lectures, and arguments to try to convince others to agree with them and do what they say. If the object of their lectures refuses to give in, they are rendered powerless as they feel that they have the right or ability only to talk, not to act. For all their bluster and superiority, they are like a hurricane blowing against a mountain. The mountain need only sit there to win. In fact, this is exactly the dynamic that occurs when a spouse who tends, when stressed, toward a Pouting/Withdrawing Persona marries a spouse who tends, when stressed, toward the Contemptuous Expert Persona.

To regain their sense of personal power and an ability to affect positive change in their marriage, those who fall into the Contemptuous Expert Persona need to remind themselves that they must build consensus by listening and asking questions to draw out the other person and be able to collaborate with him rather than attempting to force agreement by drowning him in a tidal wave of words. They also must remind themselves that if genuine and persistent attempts to work with their spouse to meet their needs fail, they are certainly allowed to act on their own without their spouse's agreement, if necessary.

Here is a good prayer for people who tend to fall into the Contemptuous Expert Persona: "Lord, you said, 'Blessed are the meek for they will inherit the earth.' Give me the kindness that will encourage others to work with me, the patience to wait for others to catch up with me, and the knowledge that actions speak louder than words."

Ask yourself:

1. When you fall into your Misery-Making Mindset, which persona (Pouting/Withdrawing, Tantrumming, Contemptuous Expert) do you tend to exhibit the most?

2. Which of the three misery-making personas do you tend to exhibit the second most (if any)?

3. Which of the three misery-making personas does your spouse tend to exhibit when he or she is upset?

What Does All This Mean?

Throughout this chapter, I have attempted to show you that while marriage can be full of many troubles and challenges, and some marriages more than others, the sense of futility, depression, and *oppression* you may feel about your marriage is due less to the presence of those problems and more to the tendency to let those problems turn on your Misery-Making Mindset. Often, when couples come to me, one or both spouses will say in exasperation, "I've tried *everything* and *nothing* works." When I ask what they have done to address their problems, they will say something like, "Well, first I just tried letting it go and not saying anything [i.e., withdrawing]; then I couldn't take it anymore. I blew up, and we fought about it all the time [i.e., tantrumming]. And there were lots of times I tried to be direct, and I just told him I couldn't believe how thoughtless he was being and how he just needed to X, Y, and Z [i.e., lecturing as Contemptuous Expert], but no matter what I did, nothing ever changed."

Of course nothing changed because the person saying this tried all the things that were doomed to fail from the start! The variations on these three themes (pouting/withdrawing, tantrumming, lecturing as a Contemptuous Expert) are merely the stressed-out brain's way to get someone out of an uncomfortable situation as quickly as possible. In this state, your mind is incapable of solving anything—ever.

The good news? Those who feel as if they have exhausted themselves trying *everything* to no avail have probably done a good job of ruling out all of the things that can't, won't, and wouldn't ever work. Now they can get down to the business of finally trying some things that actually will bring about the changes they are looking for! And that's what this book is about.

We will revisit these three personas in chapter 6 and talk in detail about how to leave them behind once and for all. But for now, it is important *simply to begin to become aware of how and when* you may be allowing the stress of your life or marriage to force you out of the Solution-Focused Brain and into the Misery-Making Mindset, in which you fall back on doomed-to-fail strategies such as pouting/withdrawing, tantrumming, and lecturing your mate like some Contemptuous Expert. The Mindset Exercise on page 276 will help you to gain this awareness.

Chapter 3

Eight Marriage-Friendly Habits

All happy families are alike; each unhappy
family is unhappy in its own way.
—Leo Tolstoy, *Anna Karenina*

Love . . . is a deep unity, maintained by the will
and deliberately strengthened by habit.
—C. S. Lewis, *Mere Christianity*

The previous chapters addressed some general information and attitudes you'll need as you begin the process of reclaiming and renewing your marriage. Now we're ready to get to work. In this chapter, I will outline the eight Marriage-Friendly Habits that couples in healthy relationships exhibit. This list is drawn both from the best marriage research available and my own clinical experience. Although these habits are present in happy marriages, any couple can learn and practice them. While each couple is different and should feel free to apply these Marriage-Friendly Habits in their own way, the research is quite clear that almost every happy couple, regardless of their background, their beliefs, or the circumstances of their life, practices habits very similar to the ones I will describe in this chapter.

Here are the eight Marriage-Friendly Habits almost all happy couples exhibit.

1. Rituals of Connection
2. Emotional Rapport and Benevolence
3. Self-regulation
4. A Positive Intention Frame
5. Caretaking in Conflict
6. Mutual Respect, Accountability, and Boundaries
7. Reviewing and learning from mistakes
8. Getting good support

The following pages will serve as an outline of these habits and include a self-reflective quiz that will help you decide which habits you need the most work on. This way, you'll know which areas of your marriage might require the most attention. After this overview, I will dedicate one chapter to each of the eight habits to give you more in-depth help in establishing those particular practices in your relationship.

Before beginning the overview, there are four thoughts I would ask you to keep in mind as you read this chapter:

1. *Resist the temptation to become demoralized* if you find that your marriage is missing most or even all of the habits I outline. The fact is, not every couple—not even every happy couple—practices all eight of these habits to the same degree and with the same degree of skill. Even if you find that your marriage is lacking in all eight habits, it does not mean that your marriage is not worth saving or couldn't become emotionally satisfying. Adding even one or two of these habits to your relationship will most likely make a huge difference in the level of satisfaction you can experience in your relationship. Enjoy these changes, and

allow the encouragement you may feel to inspire you to begin practicing even more of these habits over time.

2. *Feel free to start anywhere.* Even if the quiz indicates that you are lacking in one habit to a much greater degree than another, that doesn't mean you have to begin with that habit. Success builds on success, so start with the habits you think would be easier to master, and work from there. This will be critical to encourage you through the process of healing your marriage.

Although you should feel free to start with whichever habit would be easiest for you to master, try to resist the temptation to hop around from habit to habit. I recommend picking one or two habits at the most and sticking with them *only* for at least two weeks. At the end of those two weeks, ask yourself if you think you're ready to add another habit to the mix or if you still need a little time to feel confident about the one or two habits you've been working on. If you need more time, take another two weeks to practice and reevaluate.

Perhaps the best way to approach this is to read the whole book one time through to get an idea of how all the different ideas hang together and then go back and work on the chapters that relate most to the areas you would like to improve in your marriage.

3. *Take your time.* I know you want to change everything immediately, but please take your time. Chefs tell you that when cooking a custard, you have to pour the hot milk into the egg mixture a few drops at a time to *temper* the eggs (i.e., bring them up to temperature slowly); otherwise you'll end up with scrambled eggs instead of custard. The same thing can happen here. Taking on too much at once, rushing through the habits,

or bouncing from habit to habit will guarantee failure. Practicing one habit at a time and adding subsequent habits slowly is the key to working this program successfully. I know it's hard to be patient when you are hurting, but healing is a process. Trust the process, and you will enjoy the benefits of your patience.

4. *Be open to getting help.* As I have mentioned throughout the book so far and will mention several more times before you finish reading, if at any time you feel frustrated with the process, before tossing this book into the garbage and calling a divorce lawyer, please seek professional help. It is possible that you will be able to make significant improvements or even heal your marriage on your own with this book. But it is even more likely that at some point, you may get stuck and require the support, additional training, and accountability a good, marriage-friendly therapist can provide. If you find yourself becoming frustrated with your efforts at any point, please contact us at the Pastoral Solutions Institute (www.CatholicCounselors.com; 740-266-6461) or seek the support of a local, marriage-friendly counselor you trust.

Now, let's look at each of the eight Marriage-Friendly Habits that most happy couples practice. If both you and your spouse are working through this book together, you should proceed with the rest of this chapter separately. Don't compare scores until after you've completed the chapter. If you find that you and your mate have identified completely different issues, don't worry. It would not be unusual for you and your mate to be focused on separate concerns in your relationship. In fact, you can even begin working on whichever issues you each feel is most vital. It is not as important that you agree on where to start than it is that you are both doing whatever you feel you are capable of doing to bring about the change you desire.

Alternatively, if you are working through the book on your own, you will discover the issues in your marriage that will allow you to begin creating change even through your own effort. You will find that, because of the graces given to husbands and wives in marriage, you have tremendous untapped power to be a catalyst for change even if your spouse isn't participating. I'll show you where to start and walk with you through the journey.

Healthy-Marriage Habit #1:
Rituals of Connection for Work, Play, Talk, and Prayer
Rituals of Connection Quiz

Answer true (T) or false (F) for each statement.

T F 1. My spouse and I get at least a little time to work *together* almost every day (at least five days out of seven).

T F 2. My spouse and I get at least a little time to have some fun time *together* almost every day (at least five days out of seven).

T F 3. My spouse and I get at least a little time to talk with each other about feelings about life and our relationship (i.e., not just stuff that needs to be done) almost every day (at least five days out of seven).

T F 4. My spouse and I get at least a little time to pray *together* about our life and relationship (beyond Grace at meals) almost every day (at least five days out of seven).

T F 5. Once a week, my spouse and I usually spend at least an hour or two (over and above the daily time indicated in question 1) *working together* on some larger household project (e.g., cleaning or fixing things at home).

T F   6. Once a week, my spouse and I get at least an hour
       or two (over and above the daily time indicated in
       question 2) to do something fun (in or out of the
       house) *just as a couple*.
T F   7. Once a week, my spouse and I get at least an hour
       or two (over and above the daily time indicated in
       question 3) to talk together in greater depth about
       our life and relationship.
T F   8. At least once a week, my spouse and I attend
       church together.
T F   9. My spouse and I enjoy each other's company.
T F   10. Even when we are not getting along, our relation-
       ship feels comfortable and familiar.

Give yourself 1 point for each T.

You scored _____ out of a possible 10 points.

A score of 8 or higher means that your rituals and routines are a real source of strength in your relationship.

A score of 4 through 7 means that you could significantly improve your marriage by giving greater
attention to increasing the presence of rituals and
routines in your relationship.

A score of 3 or lower indicates that this is a critical
area for improvement in your relationship.

Why This Habit Is Important

One study examining fifty years of research on the effect of rituals such as eating together, praying together, and working and
worshipping together found that these simple activities had an
almost magical degree of power over marriage and family health

(Fiese, Tomcho, Douglas, et al., 2002). Couples who regularly worked, played, discussed more than just the tasks of life, and prayed together were significantly happier and more stable than other couples and exhibited far fewer problems that negatively impact marital well-being, such as anxiety, depression, and substance abuse (Fiese, 2006).

Research by the Baylor University Institute for the Study of Religion found that couples who prayed together were about 30 percent happier across every aspect of their relationship (e.g., sex, parenting, financial management, division of labor, and so forth) than couples who did not; and couples who prayed "a lot" were happier than couples who prayed "sometimes" (Rushnell and DuArt, 2011). Similarly, couples who enjoy "shared meaning" (i.e., similar beliefs and purpose in life) are also much happier in their marriages than couples who feel that they are unequally yoked regarding their beliefs and attitudes (Gottman, 2011).

It is easy to understand why this is so. Couples who make time to work, play, talk, and pray together at least a little bit each day and to a greater degree each week know that they need to prioritize their marriage; that marriage is an activity, not an accessory. It can be hard to have a stable, satisfying marriage if a couple tries to squeeze in time to work, play, talk, and pray together when all the work and chores are done.

Of course, as Catholics, we believe that the family is the domestic church. We know that the Catholic Faith is filled with rituals—Sunday and daily Mass, holy days, confession and other sacraments, adoration, Stations, paraliturgies, and prayers—that bind the family of God together, call us back to each other, and bring order to our lives. Taking seriously our role as domestic church means, at least in part, celebrating the power of marriage and family rituals and routines to bind us together similarly, call us back to each other, and bring order to our lives.

We'll discuss how to develop the habits of working, playing, talking, and praying together in chapter 4. But for now, consider the importance of this habit, and reflect on simple things you and your spouse could begin to do to shore up this aspect of your relationship.

Healthy-Marriage Habit #2:
Emotional Rapport and Benevolence
Emotional Rapport and Benevolence Quiz

Answer true (T) or false (F) for each statement.

T F   1. My spouse and I look for little ways to make each other's life easier or more pleasant each day.

T F   2. My spouse and I know and understand each other well.

T F   3. My spouse and I know and understand each other's needs.

T F   4. My spouse and I are thoughtful and sensitive to each other's likes and dislikes.

T F   5. My spouse and I share frequent, meaningful, non-sexual, physical affection.

T F   6. My spouse and I look for little ways to support and encourage each other each day.

T F   7. My spouse and I know how to encourage each other when we feel down.

T F   8. My spouse and I find comfort in each other's arms when we're stressed.

T F   9. My spouse and I turn to each other for comfort when we are upset or frustrated.

T F   10. My spouse and I try to be gentle and caring toward each other even when we are frustrated or stressed.

Give yourself 1 point for each T.

You scored _____ out of a possible 10 points.

A score of 8 or higher means that maintaining Emotional Rapport and Benevolence is a real strength in your relationship.

A score of 4 through 7 means that you could significantly improve your marriage by giving greater attention to increasing your experience of Emotional Rapport and Benevolence.

A score of 3 or lower indicates that this is a critical area for improvement in your relationship.

Why This Habit Is Important

Galatians 6:2 says "Bear one another's burdens, and so fulfil the law of Christ." Happy couples do exactly this in good times and bad times. They look for ways to take care of each other and make each other's lives a little easier or more pleasant, especially in times of stress and disagreement between them.

In the healthiest relationships, couples exhibit a 20:1 ratio of positive to negative interactions in the course of their everyday interactions and conversations (Gottman, 2011). That can seem overwhelming on the face of it—as if the only thing happy couples do is dance around in a state of blissful merrymaking, showering each other with presents and loving words. Relax. That's not the case at all. "Positive interactions" include simple acts like smiling at your partner when you walk into the room, acknowledging each other's presence and looking into each other's eyes when you talk, and brief touches as you walk past each other, as well as giving meaningful compliments, thoughtful tokens of affection, and being intentionally affectionate with one another.

Sometimes, it can be hard to convince couples of the incredible power these simple actions have on the overall well-being of a marriage. On more than one occasion, I have had couples challenge me by saying, "I feel like we're paying you a lot of money just for you to tell us to be nice to each other!" It may feel that way, but there is a great deal more going on than meets the eye. Studies such as the Gottman article I referenced earlier show that, when it comes to marital health, the devil (and for that matter, the angel) is in the details. Saving your marriage, for the most part, is not about big, dramatic gestures. It is about becoming more aware and sensitive and intentionally making more positive the ten thousand times you interact with your spouse each day and currently don't give a second thought to.

Simple actions such as the ones I just listed do two things. First, they help your mate feel cared for and valued in the moment, which draws you closer to each other and makes you actually want to be together instead of feeling like you want to flee the room every time your spouse makes an appearance. Second, these simple practices make you more likely to give each other the benefit of the doubt when you accidentally step on each other's toes. It's hard to take offense and react defensively to each other when you see that you are looking out for each other, happy to see each other, and trying to take care of each other thirty-eight times out of forty. If you're working to make all those little interactions just a little more positive, it's easier to let those other two out of forty times slide when you step on each other's toes. We'll discuss ways to develop this habit in chapter 5, but you can begin today just by doing the kinds of things I just identified. (And it's okay to fake it if you don't feel it just yet. As long as your intention is to feel it someday, that's good enough.) Don't expect your spouse to respond right away. It might even take a few weeks before your mate notices that there's something different in the way you're approaching him or her. I promise, though, if you stick with it, it will begin to make a difference.

Healthy Marriage Habit #3: Self-Regulation
Self-Regulation Quiz

Answer true (T) or false (F) for each statement.

T F   1. We are respectful in our disagreements.

T F   2. Our arguments result in solutions and concrete plans for improving things.

T F   3. Even when we disagree with each other, we are careful to avoid saying certain particularly hurtful things.

T F   4. If we offend each other in an argument, we are quick to apologize and forgive.

T F   5. If we offend each other in an argument, we bounce back and get the conversation back on track quickly.

T F   6. We look for ways to encourage and support each other when we're having tense discussions.

T F   7. Generally speaking, I wouldn't agree with my spouse just to get him or her to shut up.

T F   8. Generally, when I get angry, I do not lash out or say things that I think may hurt my partner even when I feel he or she might deserve it.

T F   9. Generally, when I get angry, I do not shut down, refuse to speak, or walk away from the argument.

T F　10. When conversations heat up, I am able to facilitate respectful breaks that give us time to cool down and start the conversation in a better place at a later time.

Give yourself 1 point for each T.

You scored _____ out of a possible 10 points.

A score of 8 or higher means that maintaining good self-regulation is a real strength in your relationship.

A score of 4 through 7 means that you could significantly improve your marriage by giving greater attention to increasing your ability to exhibit good self-regulation in the presence of disagreements and offenses.

A score of 3 or lower indicates that this is a critical area for improvement in your relationship.

Why This Habit Is Important

Self-regulation refers to our capacity to stay calm, to recognize that we are losing our cool before it's too late, and to regain our composure even under pressure. Your ability to negotiate conflict and tension in a marriage is directly dependent on your ability to stay in the Solution-Focused Brain state and avoid the Misery-Making Mindset.

As you saw earlier, when stress causes our emotional temperature to rise, we're unable to solve problems and we tend to react rather than respond. Psychologists refer to this process as *flooding,* and it causes a person to be rigid and reactive under pressure (Seigel, 2013; Manes, 2013). But, if you can learn to keep your Solution-Focused Brain turned on, even in conflict, you can stay in control of the discussion even if your partner loses control.

When I was engaged to my wife, an elderly couple gave us a bit of advice that was as true then as it remains today: "Don't ever go crazy at the same time!" If you have the ability to self-regulate, then you can keep discussions on track even if your spouse loses his or her cool. Developing this skill takes work, but it is well worth it because it is what enables you not to have to feel afraid or overwhelmed, no matter what problem you are facing or how emotional your spouse becomes.

Of course, beyond the psychological benefits we receive from practicing those habits that lead to self-regulation, Galatians 5:22-24 identifies self-control as one of the fruits that gives evidence that the Holy Spirit is dwelling in your heart. Proverbs 25:28 reminds us that the person who lacks the ability to regulate his emotions is like a city that is left defenseless and powerless in the presence of an invader.

Chapter 6 will discuss how to develop the skill of self-regulation in greater detail, but you can start working on this skill even now by reminding yourself that the most important thing to pay attention to in any conflict or disagreement is not what the other person says or does but how you respond to it.

Healthy-Marriage Habit #4:
A Positive Intention Frame

Positive Intention Frame Quiz

Answer true (T) or false (F) for each statement.

T F 1. My spouse and I are good at giving each other the benefit of the doubt when we hurt each other.

T F   2. My spouse and I tend to assume that offenses are due to momentary lapses in judgment rather than an intentional desire to be hurtful or offensive.

T F   3. When my spouse does something I find offensive or irritating, I tend to assume that I misunderstood his or her true intentions.

T F   4. My spouse and I rarely, if ever, react to each other as if we were *intending* to be offensive or hurtful.

T F   5. I feel as if it's safe to make mistakes around my spouse.

T F   6. I feel as if my spouse and I go out of our way to assume the best about each other.

T F   7. I am confident that my spouse is looking out for my best interests.

T F   8. Sometimes my spouse offends me, but I doubt he or she would ever do so on purpose.

T F   9. My spouse and I tend to be generous about extending forgiveness when we disappoint each other.

T F   10. When something goes wrong at home, my spouse and I are *not* quick to blame each other.

Give yourself 1 point for each T.

You scored _____ out of a possible 10 points.

A score of 8 or higher means that maintaining a Positive Intention Frame is a real strength in your relationship.

A score of 4 through 7 means that you could significantly improve your marriage by giving greater attention to increasing your ability to exhibit a Positive Intention Frame in your marriage.

A score of 3 or lower indicates that this is a critical area for improvement in your relationship.

Why This Habit Is Important

A Positive Intention Frame is what psychologists and marriage therapists call the ability to assume the best about your spouse even at his or her worst. This is not the same thing as making excuses for your spouse's bad behavior. Rather, having a Positive Intention Frame gives you the ability to refrain from reacting angrily to every slight and enables you to address bigger offenses in a sensitive and understanding manner. Having a Positive Intention Frame is the psychological basis for the corporal work of mercy "to bear wrongs patiently." Again, there is nothing wrong with addressing offenses directly and promptly, but doing so charitably as well allows the offender to save face. This increases the likelihood that the offender will work with you to find solutions to the problem instead of reacting defensively to what otherwise might feel like an attack or a criticism from you.

Having a Positive Intention Frame allows you and your spouse to feel comfortable making mistakes in front of each other because you know that you are both trying your best and that you will both tolerate each other's lapses and offenses and refuse to see missteps as intentional slights. Research by Hawkins, Carrere, and Gottman (2002) shows that couples who tend to assume the best about each other avoid conflict more and handle conflict more gracefully when it arrives on the scene.

Chapter 7 will provide you with many practical, simple ways you can develop this absolutely essential skill. You can begin right now, however, simply by doing your best to remember that the vast majority of offenses committed in marriage are not so much the result of malicious intent as they are simple clueless-ness, miscommunication, and misunderstanding, and these are all best dealt with through patience, gentleness, and understand-ing. Don't make excuses. Don't let things slide. Just be charitable. The overwhelming majority of husbands and wives simply do not enjoy antagonizing each other. No doubt, at this stage of the process, you may be convinced that your spouse is the exception. I assure you that at least one spouse in every troubled marriage believes his or her mate is that exception, and almost to a couple, they come to see that their perception was as wrong as yours most likely is. Do yourself and your marriage a favor by working hard to assume a positive intention behind your spouse's slights, offenses, and misdeeds.

Healthy-Marriage Habit #5: Caretaking in Conflict
Caretaking in Conflict Quiz

Answer true (T) or false (F) for each statement.

T F   1. My spouse and I look for ways to support each other through tense times and encourage each other to find solutions to our problems.

T F   2. My spouse and I look for ways to reassure each other of our mutual love even when we are disagreeing with each other.

T F   3. I feel as if my spouse and I are real partners when it comes to solving problems together.

T F   4. My spouse and I are really good at helping each other get back on track if either of us ever gets upset or frustrated during a disagreement.

T F   5. My spouse and I are really good at staying focused on the topic at hand when we are having a disagreement.

T F   6. Even when we can't find an answer to a problem right away, I generally feel hopeful that my spouse and I will figure things out in time.

T F   7. When my spouse has concerns about ideas I present, he or she expresses those concerns in a way that feels supportive and encouraging (as opposed to critical and undermining).

T F   8. My spouse and I work hard to avoid blaming each other for problems *even when one of us is at fault.*

T F   9. When we get stuck in an argument, my spouse and I will stop and take some time to pray together and seek God's wisdom for a solution.

T F   10. When discussing new ideas, I can almost always count on my spouse to be open and supportive.

Give yourself 1 point for each T.

You scored _____ out of a possible 10 points.

A score of 8 or higher means that practicing Caretaking in Conflict is a real strength in your relationship.

A score of 4 through 7 means that you could significantly improve your marriage by giving greater attention to increasing your ability to practice Caretaking in Conflict in your marriage.

A score of 3 or lower indicates that this is a critical area for improvement in your relationship.

Why This Habit Is Important

The most important thing in problem solving in your marriage is not actually solving the problem. Rather, it's how well you and your spouse take care of each other as you work together to find solutions to the problem. Think about it. If you manage to find a solution to a particular challenge in your life or relationship, but walk away from your conversation with your spouse feeling demoralized, resentful, exhausted, and out of sync, what good is it? Solving problems is important, but *how* you solve those problems is even more important.

I shared earlier that couples in healthy marriages work to maintain a 20:1 ratio of positive to negative interactions in their day-to-day relationship. Subsequent research shows that these same couples exhibit five times as many positive exchanges as negative ones when they are dealing with problems together and even disagreeing with each other (Gottman, 1995). You might ask, "What *planet* are these people on?"

The good news is that these happy couples have their feet planted firmly on planet Earth, and they are not that different from you. Happy couples argue. As I mentioned earlier, they argue just about as much as you do. But they remember that to get through their arguments, they have to try hard to take care of each other in the argument and encourage each other toward solutions. They do this in little ways. With little glances, touches, and words that say, "Even though this is hard, I still love you," praying together so that they check their own wills against God's will, treading carefully around each other's sore spots even when they are upset, trying hard not to pour fuel on the fire to make things worse than they need to be, and taking breaks to cool down—early and often.

This is not as crazy an idea as it seems. In any high-stress environment, taking care of your partner is job number one. A fireman might run into a burning building to save a baby, but his first job is to make sure that his partner can make it back out alive. A police officer might be charged with apprehending a dangerous and armed criminal, but her first job is to watch her partner's back so they both make it through in one piece. A soldier might need to claim that hill from the enemy, but his first job is to make sure that his comrades stick together. The second any one of these professional, high-conflict problem-solvers lose sight of this, his or her risk of failure and death escalates exponentially.

As American Founding Father Patrick Henry memorably put it, "United we stand. Divided we fall." He might as well have been talking about marriage. High-stress situations call for a high level of commitment to partnership above all. Those in healthy marriages know this, and they work hard to take care of each other, no matter what the problem. Unlike the fireman, the police officer, and the soldier, you are not contending with a burning house or someone shooting at you. Your life isn't on the line (and if it is, put down this book and call 911). If those professionals can learn to take care of their partners when the heat is on, you can too. In challenging you to learn to take care of your partner in conflict, I am not asking you to learn a marriage skill so much as I am challenging you to develop a healthy life skill.

Dr. Daniel Seigel (2013) notes that people who are good at problem solving tend to be *kinder* than people who are not good at problem solving. He notes that kindness—which happens to be one of the fruits of the Holy Spirit (Gal. 5:22)—is more than simply being nice to others; it is actually a sign that our brain is working properly and able to focus on solutions. The somewhat jarring conclusion we must draw from this is that anger is not the sign that our Solution-Focused Brain has turned off. Rather, unkindness is!

Think of how that changes your perspective on the way you and your spouse communicate. My clients often struggle with the idea of being kind to their spouses when in conflict. They often feel that their spouses don't deserve it. However, when we view kindness not as a gift we give to the other person but as a sign of our own integration, it becomes easier to see why kindness is essential in arguing and how kindness makes finding mutually satisfying solutions possible.

This is probably the skill that most couples in difficult marriages lack. Many people were not raised in homes that modeled this kind of problem solving. No matter. You can learn it. In fact, you must if you wish to be happy in any area of your life, not just in your marriage. For the Christian, this is even truer, because our ability to be kind to others is, in large part, the measure by which we will be judged (Matt. 25:31-46).

Chapter 8 will discuss simple, practical ways to improve your ability to take better care of your partner during conflict, but you can start today by simply remembering that taking care of your partner and coming out of discussions feeling connected is more important than solving whatever problem you feel must be addressed in the moment.

Healthy-Marriage Habit #6:
Mutual Respect, Accountability, and Boundaries

Mutual Respect, Accountability, and Boundaries Quiz

Answer true (T) or false (F) for each statement.

T F 1. My spouse and I actively try to appreciate and know about each other's hobbies and interests, even if we personally don't enjoy those things.

T F 2. My spouse and I genuinely respect and value each other's skills and areas of expertise.

T F   3. If my spouse knows more about something than I do, I am interested and willing to learn from him or her.

T F   4. If my spouse is more skilled at something than I am, I am willing to defer to his or her expertise.

T F   5. If my spouse tells me that I offended him or her, I am good at quickly apologizing and correcting the offense, even if I didn't mean to offend him or her.

T F   6. I am interested in listening to and learning from my spouse's opinion, especially when it is different from my own.

T F   7. When my spouse is upset, I don't try to assert that he or she shouldn't feel that way.

T F   8. My spouse and I are usually good at taking to heart each other's corrections and suggestions.

T F   9. I can learn a lot from my spouse about being a loving person.

T F   10. When we have disagreements, I am interested in listening to and learning from my spouse's perspective on what needs to change.

Give yourself 1 point for each T.

You scored _____ out of a possible 10 points.

A score of 8 or higher means that the degree of mutual respect is a real strength in your relationship.

A score of 4 through 7 means that you could significantly improve your marriage by giving greater attention to increasing your ability to exhibit mutual respect in your marriage.

A score of 3 or lower indicates that this is a critical area for improvement in your relationship.

Why This Habit Is Important

Ephesians 5:21 challenges husbands and wives to "defer to one another out of reverence for Christ." In this way, St. Paul reminds us that while both husband and wife have roles to play, Christ is the head of the home. Despite what many people think about this passage from Ephesians, the Church teaches that the heart of St. Paul's message is one of mutual respect.

Many people think that showing respect is simply being polite, but it is much, much more. As the statements in the quiz suggest, respect in marriage involves a willingness to learn from each other; to see the truth, goodness, and beauty in the things that each finds true, good, and beautiful; to defer to each other's knowledge and expertise; to accept each other's boundaries; and to listen to each other well, especially when you disagree.

The root of partnership is mutual respect, the willingness to see your spouse as a real, three-dimensional person who you believe can teach you a great deal about living a healthy, happy, loving life. This willingness to listen and even to submit to one another — especially under stress and pressure — is what marriage therapists call the *fondness and admiration system* (Gottman, 2011).

This quality covers a lot of ground in marriage. The stronger a couple's *fondness and admiration system*, the more willing they are to learn to understand and participate in each other's interests (despite not personally being drawn to those interests); to accept input, guidance, and even correction from each other (even when it's hard to hear); and to respect each other's limits and boundaries (despite not personally understanding why those boundaries or limits are important).

Fondness and admiration are not qualities that happy couples automatically possess to the same degree at all times. They work to cultivate these qualities by learning to listen and really try to understand each other's perspective and defer to each other's strengths.

Happy couples know more than how to learn from each other's positive influence; they also know how to see each other's faults and failings, not as "the other person's problem" but as opportunities for each spouse to grow. For instance, spouses who struggle with irritability may need to grow in positivity, but their mates may also see this as an opportunity to become more patient and sensitive. Spouses who tend to withdraw may need to grow in assertiveness, but their mates may also view this as an opportunity to become more nurturing. That's not to say healthy couples are always happy to learn these lessons but that they are willing to swallow their pride and learn to do it anyway.

This willingness of spouses to humble themselves enough to learn from each other, listen to each other, and seek to understand each other even when it doesn't come naturally is the heart of respect. We'll talk about simple, practical ways to facilitate mutual respect, accountability, and boundaries by cultivating the fondness and admiration system in your marriage in chapter 9, but you can begin now by realizing that your spouse is more than a cross or a curse.

Your mate is God's invitation to you to grow in ways you would never grow on your own; to grow in ways God needs you to grow in order for you to be the fully formed person he calls you to be in this life and to be able to enjoy the fullness of the eternal wedding feast with him in heaven. You could simply ignore this call and self-righteously claim that your spouse has nothing to teach you about becoming the person God needs you to be. If you did this, I have no doubt you would feel very justified. But feeling justified is a poor second to being in a healthy, rewarding marriage. That's why I encourage you to humble yourself and begin doing what you can today to start discovering what your spouse has to teach you, because chances are, the less you think your mate has to offer, the more God may think you have to learn.

Healthy-Marriage Habit #7:
Reviewing and Learning from Mistakes
Reviewing and Learning from Mistakes Quiz

Answer true (T) or false (F) for each statement.

T F 1. My spouse and I regularly share in positive discussions about how we can improve our relationship.

T F 2. After we argue, my spouse and I have productive conversations about what we could do to handle the conflict better next time.

T F 3. Rather than just venting, our problem-solving conversations usually result in practical ideas for making things better.

T F 4. We don't tend to rehash old hurts and injuries in ways that provoke new arguments.

T F 5. Even when one of us is more "at fault" for causing a problem, we both behave as if we are mutually responsible for preventing the problem from occurring again.

T F 6. My spouse and I regularly put energy into learning ways to improve our marriage.

T F 7. My spouse and I regularly ask if there is anything we can do to take better care of each other.

T F 8. When something goes wrong, we work together to seek answers.

T F   9. Our behavior shows that we see mistakes and problems as opportunities to learn and grow, not as opportunities to attack and blame.

T F   10. When we have a big argument we *do not* pretend it never happened and go back to business as usual.

Give yourself 1 point for each T.

You scored _____ out of a possible 10 points.

A score of 8 or higher means that reviewing and learning from mistakes are real strengths in your relationship.

A score of 4 through 7 means that you could significantly improve your marriage by giving greater attention to increasing your ability to review and learn from mistakes.

A score of 3 or lower indicates that this is a critical area for improvement in your relationship.

Why This Habit Is Important

I try to encourage my clients not to underestimate the human being's capacity for being consistently surprised by the same thing happening over and over again.

Healthy couples work hard to learn from their own and each other's mistakes. They do this by "returning to the scene of the crime" (i.e., a time when tension caused things to get out of hand), both with their own ideas for doing a better job of it next time. Or one of them, if unsure of what he or she could have done differently, can ask and listen.

Healthy couples do not dredge up past hurts and attack each other with them, but neither do they ignore their past. They know that their mistakes will only repeat themselves unless they take some time to process those mistakes and learn from them, preferably in a way that doesn't make the other feel blamed.

Interestingly, with both healthy and struggling couples, about 70 percent of their disagreements will never be solved (Gottman, 2011). Healthy couples do a better job of managing these so-called perpetual problems by having conversations about these issues that allow the couples to keep them from growing into bigger problems. When you marry someone, there are a certain number of quirks you just have to accept. Chances are, before you felt as if your marriage was in crisis, you were doing at least a fair job of accepting those quirks. Once things turned negative, then every problem became magnified, even the ones you were perfectly content to live with before things got bad. Part of dealing with these "perpetual problems" is developing a good sense of humor about them.

Obviously, both learning from past mistakes and finding a way to talk about perpetual problems that doesn't feel like settling can be difficult skills to get the hang of, but chapter 10 will lay out some very simple ideas and examples that anyone can follow. For now, remember what was said earlier in the book about leading with solutions, not with emotion. If a conversation goes south, take some time apart. Pray about it. Ask yourself what you could have done differently to make things go better (or at least not to make things worse), and then discuss these ideas with your spouse. Reviewing these mistakes in a respectful, solution-focused manner helps break the cycle of simply reliving the same problems over and over despite the best intentions to the contrary. And, for those problems that can't easily be solved, try to remember that you're not perfect either, and recall how much you appreciate when someone indulges you in your craziness.

Eight Marriage-Friendly Habits

Healthy-Marriage Habit #8:
Getting Good Support
Getting Good Support Quiz

Answer true (T) or false (F) for each statement.

T F   1. I share my marital problems only with spiritually mature friends who have demonstrated by their actions that they are able to tell me when I am in the wrong.

T F   2. I understand the difference between the kinds of help I can get from counseling and the kinds of help available from "talking with my pastor."

T F   3. I know the difference between a marriage-friendly therapist and any other marriage therapist.

T F   4. I *do not* share my marital problems with people who are dependent upon me in some way (employees, needy friends, family members who are emotionally or practically dependent on me).

T F   5. I *do not* discuss my marital problems with my children (whether they are young or adults).

T F   6. I know what Retrouvaille, PREP, and Third Option are and when they next meet. (Or, we have completed Retrouvaille, PREP, and/or Third Option.)

T F   7. When I seek others' help, I look for people I know who will challenge *me* to change.

T F   8. When I seek *nonprofessional* marital advice, I try to go to people who have their own, firsthand knowledge of my spouse.

T F   9. I am familiar with the qualifications that distinguish a marital therapist from a general counselor, psychologist, or psychotherapist.

T F   10. I know what distinguishes good marital advice
      from bad.

Give yourself 1 point for each T.

You scored _____ out of a possible 10 points.

A score of 8 or higher means that knowing how to get
good support is a real strength in your relationship.

A score of 4 through 7 means that your marriage
would significantly improve by increasing your ability to get good support.

A score of 3 or lower indicates that this is a critical
area for improvement in your relationship.

Why This Habit Is Important

Every couple needs support from time to time, but whom you
turn to for that support and what kind of support you get can
spell the difference between healing your marriage and tearing
it apart. Healthy couples know this and are careful about whom
they turn to for help and are discriminating about the kind of
advice they receive. Chapter 11 will discuss the best approaches
to seeking support from friends, family, pastors, and counseling
professionals. The most important thing for you to remember
in the meantime is to limit yourself to seeking support from
people who are biased toward preserving your marriage, who
know both you and your spouse, who have demonstrated that
they aren't afraid to tell you when you are doing something stupid, who are faithful Catholics, and (when seeking professional
help) who have specific graduate or post-graduate training in
marriage-friendly approaches to counseling (as opposed to most

counselors, who "do marital counseling" but have no specific training in it).

Collect Your Scores

For simplicity's sake, write down your scores for each section in the following spaces (for those couples working together, spaces for both scores are given).

____ ____ 1. Rituals of Connection

____ ____ 2. Emotional Rapport and Benevolence

____ ____ 3. Self-regulation

____ ____ 4. A Positive Intention Frame

____ ____ 5. Caretaking in Conflict

____ ____ 6. Mutual Respect, Accountability, and Boundaries

____ ____ 7. Reviewing and learning from mistakes

____ ____ 8. Getting good support

Now What?

Now that you have completed your evaluation of all eight Healthy-Marriage Habits, you should feel free to move through the rest of the book according to your needs.

As I mentioned at the start of this chapter, *if you are working with your spouse* and you identified separate areas of concern, even radically different areas of concern, don't worry. That's completely normal. You don't have to agree on the best way forward. If you can decide on one area to make a priority together, that's great. It will be wonderful to be able to support each other in the process. On the other hand, if you can't agree on the best place to start, simply begin working on the area that you feel is most vital. The important thing is not agreement on the place to start. The important thing is your mutual investment in bringing change to your marriage in whatever ways you feel it's easier to start.

If you are working through this book on your own, be not afraid! You might feel overwhelmed by how much work you feel you need to do. Remember that all things are possible through God, who strengthens you. He is rooting for your marriage, and you can create change with your faithful efforts and his abundant grace. Take one section at a time, and work to mastery.

Either way, as I mentioned earlier, I recommend starting with the habit you think would probably be the easiest to master — as opposed to the habit that might address what you feel is the most critical issue. Why? Because success builds on success. The better you are able to accomplish even a small degree of improvement in your marriage, the more inspired you will be to continue the effort. Start with the low-hanging fruit first; then climb the tree.

Are You Doomed?

What if you scored poorly in most or even all of the Healthy-Marriage Habit categories? Don't worry about it. In many cases, this book will at least help you start developing the skills you're missing. Start small. Be patient. It will come. If you feel overwhelmed or need additional support at any time, skip ahead to chapter 11 to learn more about seeking local resources. Or you may go straight to the source and contact a faithful, professional, marriage-friendly counselor at any time through the Pastoral Solutions Institute's tele-counseling practice by visiting www. CatholicCounselors.com or by calling 740-266-6461 to schedule an appointment. Regardless, you don't have to struggle through on your own. Competent, marriage-friendly therapy succeeds over 90 percent of the time (Gottman, 2011). Don't hesitate to seek help early and often.

A Beautiful Challenge

Marriage is a beautiful challenge. It is God's plan for helping you and your spouse become everything he created you to be in this life and to help you both get to heaven in the next. In seeking to preserve and heal your marriage, you are participating in God's plan for saving the world and witnessing to the constant, faithful, undying love he has for each and every one of his children. Thank you for accepting that challenge. Know that you are not alone. I invite you to commit your marital journey to God and ask for the intercession of the Holy Family.

Lord Jesus Christ, I give you my heart. I give you my spouse's heart. Help me to feel your love for me. Help me to share that love with my spouse. When I look at my spouse and my eyes fill with pain, anger, and hurt, help me to see my spouse through your eyes. When being in the presence of my spouse causes my hands to clench in anger, help me to serve my spouse with your hands. When my heart is corrupted with bitterness and resentment, help me to love my spouse with your heart. Make me anew. Make my marriage anew.

Holy Family, pray for me. I commit my marriage to your counsel and guidance. Intercede for me. Inspire me. Challenge me. Encourage me. I entrust my marriage to your intercession and to the loving care of our Lord and Savior, Jesus Christ.

Chapter 4

Rituals of Connection

Imagine that there was a completely safe pill that was all natural, had no side effects, could be easily tolerated by adults and children, and had been shown, in literally hundreds of studies over the course of sixty years to do everything from increasing the levels of life and relationship satisfaction to improving family stability, and significantly decreasing the risk of depression, substance abuse, promiscuity, and behavior problems.

There is such a thing. Only it's not a pill. And every couple can do it. Think of it as vitamin R, that is, *Rituals of Connection*.

Marital Rituals of Connection have been shown to do all of the above and more. In fact, the research on rituals and routines over six decades attributes almost miraculous powers to simple habits such as regular family meals, game night, weekly family days, regular family prayer, and regularly scheduled times to work, communicate, and play together as a family (Fiese, 2006).

Osteoporosis is a disease that causes the deterioration of a skeleton. Those who have osteoporosis can look perfectly healthy on the outside, but they are susceptible to fractures and all the disabilities that can be associated with easily broken bones. Taking calcium is one way to help maintain healthy bones. In a similar way, the times you and your spouse spend together and the activities around which you connect on a daily and weekly basis form the skeleton of your relationship.

A couple may do many kinds of things together, but vitamin R, Rituals of Connection, helps guarantee that the skeleton that supports their relationship remains strong by identifying a baseline of daily and weekly work, play, talking, and praying activities that the couple commits to, come hell or high water. In doing so, the couple makes certain that their connection remains strong, regardless of how busy they become or how frustrated they might happen to be with each other.

If you're reading this chapter, it's probably because you scored lower on the Rituals of Connection Quiz. Take a moment to review the statements you were asked to consider on pages 57 and 58.

What the Absence of Rituals of Connection Does to Marriage

Chances are, if you are lacking in this area of your marriage, you and your spouse struggle to get the time you need to be together, and the time you do get may often be, unfortunately, unpleasant. You may feel as if you don't really "get" each other, and because of that, you can become defensive with each other fairly easily. Another common problem when Rituals of Connection suffer is the complaint, "I love you, I'm just not 'in love' with you." What that usually means, practically speaking, is that you wouldn't want anything bad to happen to your partner, but it has been a while since you've felt as if you enjoyed each other's company or truly felt a heart-level connection to each other. Not every couple who struggles to maintain Rituals of Connection will report this complaint, but almost every couple who reports this dynamic has, in fact, been missing these Rituals of Connection for years if not decades.

Without the presence of strong rituals and routines, couples tend to struggle to find time to talk about anything of great significance. Because of this, issues and concerns tend to pile up. Then, when the couple finally does get a moment to be together, they are reluctant to use that time to talk about problems. Two things happen as a result. First, this can tend to put a damper on the fun times the couple manages to have. They may enjoy themselves well enough when they finally do get a date, but there's always "stuff" (unaddressed concerns) lurking in the background, so they can't ever completely relax around each other.

Second, because they don't have time to address issues when they're small concerns, and they don't want to spoil the rare couple time they do get by talking about problems, any problem "discussions" tend to be ugly and emotional. These arguments occur when one spouse or the other just can't keep things in anymore. Things blow up in a way that seems random to the other spouse, but in fact, the issue has been brewing for weeks, months, or even years. Because these arguments are so emotional and more "real," they tend to blot out the memory of any more pleasant but "less real" conversations, giving rise to the complaint, "All we ever do is talk about problems these days."

What Developing Rituals of Connection
Will Do for Your Marriage

It can be hard for couples to believe that a simple thing such as not getting regular time to *work, play, talk,* and *pray* together could have such a devastating impact on marriages. In fact, couples have such a hard time believing that it will make a difference that they will drag their feet for months on this skill. Everyone wants to believe that their problems are exotic and complicated. They want techniques that will reveal the deep-seated inner conflict that prevents them from being able to love one another and makes them "addicted to conflict" or "unable to love." You'd be surprised by the number of couples who are downright disappointed to think that something as simple as having dinner together four times a week and instituting a weekly date could really change so much. Of course, this is not a panacea; most couples in counseling need more than this—sometimes much more. But without rituals, often the other skills a couple will learn in counseling won't sustain them. Without rituals, there is no time to practice new skills, master new skills, or be accountable for keeping up new skills, so old ways reassert themselves quickly, especially when the couple discontinues their weekly counseling ritual.

Rituals bind us together. They are more than mere repetitive actions. They have the ability to release spiritual power to create community and intimacy (Pargament, 2011). Rituals of connection—regular activities that enable couples to work, play, talk, and pray together on both a daily and weekly basis—have incredible power to bind couples together.

Perhaps a nonmarital analogy will help illustrate the incredible binding power of rituals. Almost every election cycle, some politician will attempt to curry votes by claiming a deep affiliation with his Catholic faith. This politician usually holds positions that are diametrically opposed to most, if not all, of the Catholic Church's teachings, but any attempt to challenge him on this fact will result in his defensively asserting that his faith is "deeply personally important" to him and that "he was even an altar boy growing up." And often that's absolutely true. What's going on here?

Assuming the politician isn't committing an outright lie, the most likely explanation is the strong emotional connection forged between this person and the rituals he participated in as a child, and may still participate in to some degree. Rituals facilitate lasting emotional bonds that transcend reason. Although the politician can't bring himself to believe the things the Church teaches, the rituals he has participated in have bound him to the Church in deeply meaningful and personal ways that prevent his leaving the Church, even though his relationship with the Church is so intellectually and morally complex.

Highlighting this point, Colm Toibin, a Columbia University professor, poet, and novelist who has his own complicated relationship with Catholicism, had this to say about the power ritual has to bind people together: "The Roman Catholic Church and its rituals were so much part of life that, although my parents would often question a small matter of dogma and none of us seemed more religious than anyone else, no one ever questioned the rituals or the basic tenets of belief." Taken together, this powerfully illustrates how you can disagree with someone almost absolutely (in this case, the Church) but still feel a profound emotional affiliation with that person if you have participated in enough rituals with him or her.

The same is true in marriage. The more a couple makes it a priority to create rituals that enable them to work, play, talk, and pray together, the more they feel connected to each other by a bond that transcends mere reason. That bond is what couples keep coming back to work things out—especially when things get tough. Sharing rituals and routines that allow couples to connect around work, play, talk, and prayer on both a daily and weekly basis welds the hearts of couples and families in ways that are difficult to explain and hard to appreciate unless you experience it for yourself, but it is definitely worth experiencing for yourself. Rituals give couples the chance to build a body of shared experiences that make them feel like a team, enable them to develop inside jokes, finish each other's sentences, understand each other's expressions, and get to know one another inside and out. In other words, rituals enable couples to build a sense of intimacy, comfort, and familiarity.

Most couples try to squeeze marital rituals around all the different activities they and their kids are involved in. That approach never works. Smart couples *start* by defining how many and what kind of rituals make them feel closer together, enjoy each other's company more, and work better together and *then* decide what other activities they have time for after the most important activity—family life—is defined.

Putting Rituals of Connection into Practice

If you haven't had a lot of rituals in your marriage before, it can be difficult to know where to start. The rest of this chapter will offer some examples of daily and weekly Rituals of Connection around *work, play, talk,* and *prayer* that can get you thinking about the rituals you might be able to start in your marriage.

Marital Work Rituals

Work rituals are a simple but powerful way to build trust. When a relationship has deteriorated to the point at which talking about almost anything ends up in an argument, it can be incredibly healing to know that you have each other's back when it comes to working together (not separately) on household chores.

Work rituals can solve a second problem many couples have: namely, the challenge of finding time for each other. When I suggest that couples need to take more time for their marriage, they often object that their busy schedules won't allow them to fit "one more thing" into the week. If this sounds like you, don't worry. One of the best, and easiest, ways to get time together is to start sharing in the things you already do alone to take care of the life that you have created with your mate. Folding laundry, dusting, doing the dishes, bathing the baby, and grocery shopping can all be opportunities to create connection.

You might be thinking that these activities might not sound like a lot of fun. I understand, but let me share a story. When my wife and I were dating in college, we lived on a campus that had men's dorms and women's dorms, and except for a limited number of hours, men and women were not allowed in each other's rooms. Even so, the laundry facilities on campus were co-ed. With so few places to hang out as a couple, you can imagine how "exciting" doing laundry with your boyfriend or girlfriend suddenly became.

Most couples can remember a time in their relationship when it didn't matter what they did, as long as they did it together. Happy couples work hard to hold on to this habit. While other couples think that "having fun" is the only way to build intimacy, happy couples recognize the romance that is hidden within the activities that go along with maintaining the life they are creating together. There was a time when having a home together and raising kids was a romantic dream. Well, now you're living that dream. Too many couples forget this and instead treat the dream like drudgery. Taking care of their home and raising their children becomes just another chore they "have" to do. But happy couples try to see these activities as important ones that help them care for the dream they are realizing together.

Do I mean to suggest that happy couples love folding socks together as much as they enjoy a date or a weekend away? Of course not. But happy couples know that working together to care for the dream they are creating together is an opportunity to talk, to help each other, to connect, and to reflect on what they have and what they have created with each other. Going to the grocery store with your mate seems less like a chore and more like a date if you have this attitude. And while it's still important to have rituals that allow you to play together, work rituals give you the sense of being a team that allows you to enjoy those play rituals all the more. Work and play rituals build off each other by allowing you to say, "We sweat together. Now let's celebrate the work we did!"

Gabe and Marianne can't seem to talk with each other for long before the conversation devolves into an argument. The years of neglect and guerilla warfare (i.e., vicious, sudden fights that come out of nowhere followed by a hasty retreat and awkward silences) have taken a serious toll on this couple's ability to trust each other. Various communication exercises we tried failed miserably. Date nights were a miserable failure. They just didn't trust each other enough to let down their defenses to be vulnerable to each other even a bit.

I decided to try a different approach. I talked to them about creating work rituals in their marriage. They told me that they never really worked side by side anymore on any task. After a bit of negotiating, I got them to agree to clean up after dinner together every night—whether they had dinner together or not. If they ate with each other and their kids, the kids would get some time to play while Mom and Dad cleaned up the kitchen and washed the dishes. If one of them missed dinner, cleanup would wait until the other got home, at which point they would work together to straighten up.

I asked Gabe and Marianne to talk to each other as little as possible during cleanup time at first. They could exchange pleasantries, but I wanted them to focus on working together to get the task accomplished—on being a team.

In our next appointment, Gabe said, "It was really funny how much of an impact this had for us. It was awkward at first, you know? But it was nice accomplishing something together. Since you told us not to talk too much, I felt safe enough to be around her—I wasn't afraid some fight was going to break out any minute—and I kind of enjoyed working with her."

Marianne agreed: "I didn't feel as alone as I usually do. It really helped to feel like I could count on him at least this much. And there were some nights it was a real sacrifice for him to come home late and still agree to do the cleanup with me. Maybe this sounds silly, but I felt like he was making me a priority. I haven't felt that way in a long time."

Gabe and Marianne continued this for a few weeks. They argued in between—sometimes pretty seriously—but they maintained this cleanup ritual whether or not they fought, and it helped them feel as if they would be there for each other in good times and bad. After about a month of this, and after adding a few more work rituals, such as straightening the family room before bed and making the bed together every morning, we tried some of the communication exercises again with much more success. Gabe and Marianne still had work to do, but the simple act of committing to these work rituals and learning that they really could accomplish things together when they focused on being partners instead of defending themselves taught them powerful lessons in commitment and focus that they were able to apply to their efforts to be more effective communicators.

Following is a list of some common work rituals. Which of these rituals would you be willing to commit yourself to working on with your spouse? Feel free to write your own ideas in the spaces provided.

Daily Work Rituals

Set the table together.
Clean up together after dinner.
Make the bed together in the morning.
Straighten the family room together before bed.
Bathe the baby together.
Pay bills together.
Other _____
Other _____

Weekly Work Rituals

Go grocery shopping together.
Do a small home-improvement project together.
Work together in the yard or the garden.
Clean the house.
Other _____
Other _____

Try to stick to one daily and one weekly work ritual at first. It's important to have both. If you pick just a weekly ritual, you won't get enough practice, and because of the limited frequency, you'll forget to do it more often than not. If you had to choose, picking a daily ritual would be better, but adding the weekly work ritual gives you a chance to see that you can work well with a somewhat bigger task too. Remember, success builds on success. Start small and build. You can always add other rituals later once you've mastered and integrated your first choices into your marital life.

If you are working on your marriage by yourself, you can still create work rituals. Choose a work-related activity or chore that your spouse does, and join in regularly. If your spouse asks why you're there, just say that you saw how hard he or she was working and you wanted to help out. Don't try to make it anything more than what it is. Just focus on rediscovering a consistent opportunity to be helpmates to each other.

Play Rituals

Planning to have fun together is the first category most couples want to go to when I propose this exercise. Most couples think that if they can just enjoy each other a bit more, that will fix things right up, but that can be harder to accomplish than it seems at first. It can be especially difficult to keep up a play ritual when you're angry at each other or when you've had a fight. No one would want to sit down and play a game with someone who just called him or her an awful name.

Despite the common impulse that says, "We just need to have more fun together," many couples who struggle to spend time together without giving in to arguments and tension may actually need to build up to this category of rituals, but for those couples who can get past the tension to carve out regular time to enjoy each other's company, play rituals can be very beneficial.

Many couples have a hard time identifying activities to do together. They tend to think "date night," which is great, but not always possible, especially with children. Anyway, even if you do get a regular date night, if you haven't enjoyed each other at least a little each day in between, date nights can quickly become high-pressure experiences in which couples feel forced to create as much connection as possible before going back to not seeing much of each other for seven more days.

That's why it's important to have little play rituals that you take advantage of every day. Marriage should be an opportunity to make each day at least a little more pleasant. Creating daily moments of connection — even as brief as fifteen minutes — can help you and your spouse begin to see your relationship as a break from the stress instead of just one more stressor. Then, building on this, if you can carve out a little more time at least once a week, you have these pleasant daily moments to refer back to and laugh about together.

Weekly time together doesn't have to be a multiple-hour affair either. It's great when you can plan a whole-day date or a weekend away, but that's not going to be the norm for most couples. Start by just planning an hour to go for coffee or breakfast on Saturday mornings or for dessert one night a week after dinner. Take a class together. Try something new. That doesn't necessarily mean skydiving. Going to a new restaurant or even a different movie theater can count. Research shows that couples who work to share new experiences together feel that their marriages are more "relevant" and, as such, are more happy and stable over time (Lewandowski and Ackerman, 2006).

Many couples will object that they either don't have time to do anything new with each other or they don't enjoy the same things. The first objection, that they don't have time to do a new activity together, can be resolved by simply making an effort to do together the fun things they already do on their own. Even when spouses don't do things together, they often do things on their own for fun. The easiest way to create a play ritual is to start doing these things with each other. Of course, that leads to the second objection: "What if we don't both like doing those things?"

As I noted in the section on creating work rituals, happy couples actively practice the attitude that it doesn't matter what you do as long as you do it together. Happy couples realize that a particular activity is just an excuse to be in the same place at the same time so they can get a little time to connect with each other and share an experience. The activity is secondary.

As Christians, we know that the key to both holiness and a happy marriage is *self-donation. Self-donation* is a term coined by theologians to refer to a heroic kind of generosity that allows you to step outside your comfort zone to work for the good of the other person and your relationships. Interestingly, even secular psychology vouches for the relational and life benefits that come from practicing what people of faith refer to as self-donation (and secular psychologists refer to as *eudaemonia*). Research shows that people who step outside their comfort zones to connect with others are happier and healthier all the way down to the cellular level (Fredriskon, Grewen, Coffey, et al., 2013).

Judy was the only girl in a family with five boys. When she was a child, her family bonded around sports. Luis, an only child and a semiprofessional keyboard player, was not athletic at all and didn't enjoy sports. On the weekends, Luis scheduled practice with his band when Judy would be watching games on TV because he didn't enjoy sitting around watching sports. Both Luis and Judy found this to be an acceptable arrangement.

The problem was that this left little time for them to be together. When I suggested that they needed to create play rituals that would allow them to rediscover their ability to enjoy each other again, they both objected that neither enjoyed doing the things the other was most passionate about. I expressed that I understood their concern, but I shared with them the idea that the activity was secondary. The real point of doing anything as a couple was to share an experience as a couple. Enjoyment would come, not necessarily from the entertainment value of a particular activity, but from the intimacy they created by sharing the experience. Both Luis and Judy were doubtful, but they trusted me enough to try creating some play rituals by sharing their interests.

They agreed that every other week, Luis would move his band practice to their house. Judy would hang out with the band and listen to them practice — she at least liked the guys Luis played with — and Judy would DVR the games she didn't want to miss. Luis agreed to watch either a live game with Judy or one of the DVR'd games later in the week. Neither was particularly keen on doing this, but they agreed to try. I encouraged them to ask themselves how they could approach each other's activity in a way that could make it more their own.

After several weeks of trial and error and discussions in session on how to improve on their efforts, Luis and Judy were in a much better place.

Luis said, "Sports really isn't my thing, but once I got past needing to be 'the guy who didn't like sports' and could just see it as an opportunity to hang out with Judy and do something with her, it took the pressure off. I don't really enjoy sports any more than I did a month ago, but I like the snacks Judy makes, and I like having an excuse to just sit next to her on the couch and have her hold me. I can't remember the last time we actually just sat and helped each other for any extended period of time. Even with the kids hanging out with us, I caught myself thinking that it was like we were on a date. That really surprised me."

Judy added, "I really liked having Luis watch some games with me. Usually, it's just me and the kids hanging out while he goes to band practice, but it felt really special having him make that effort. And I liked getting to sit together. It was really nice. I have to say, I enjoyed having the guys from the band over too. The kids and I would dance in the family room, and I liked having the house full of energy from their music. It was fun having a beer with the guys after practice too. Some of them started bringing their wives and girlfriends, and we've totally enjoyed hanging out together. It's almost like a group date! I used to never go to Luis's gigs. I don't really like the bar scene and with the kids, it's just easier to stay home, but having made friends with the other guys in the band and the girls, I think I might get a sitter once a month so I can go to some of their shows. We did that last weekend, and we had a great time. It was so much fun seeing Luis play. He's really good. It's been a long time since I've seen him being that passionate about something."

Luis's comment about needing to get past "being 'the guy who didn't like sports'" is a tremendously important point. Too many of us build our identities around our likes and dislikes. We feel as if we are "losing ourselves" if we are ever asked to do something we don't especially enjoy. This is a tremendously weak and foolish thing to build an identity around, however. As Christians, we are not the sum of our likes and dislikes. We are known by living out the virtues that come from the heart of God. We "find" ourselves by making a gift of ourselves (Gaudium et Spes, no. 24). With a little effort, Louis and Judy found the strength to step out of their comfort zones and find each other again.

Following is a list of some common play rituals. Which of these rituals would you be willing to commit yourself to working on with your spouse? Feel free to write your own ideas in the spaces provided.

Daily Play Rituals

Play a hand or two of cards.
Take a walk.
Read a book aloud together.
Give each other a neck or shoulder rub.
Watch a favorite TV show together.
Other _____
Other _____

Weekly Play Rituals

Have dinner out.
Take a dance class together.
Join a team together.
Take a cooking class together.
Volunteer together.
Other _____
Other _____

As with work rituals, try to pick at least one daily and one weekly play ritual. This way, you are making sure you have the opportunity to connect around both smaller and larger activities. Shared experiences are the key to intimacy and long-term happiness. Creating shared experiences on a daily and weekly basis enables you and your spouse to learn to laugh together and be a source of joy in each other's lives.

If you are working on your marriage alone, you can still create play rituals. Choose an activity that your spouse enjoys, and announce (don't ask permission) that you'd like to join in. Before you announce your intention to participate, try to think of ways that you could make the time together less stressful. If the activity is a sport, read up on the rules. Think about a snack you could make. Have in mind some ways for you to make the experience more enjoyable *for your spouse*. If you encounter strong objections to your participation in some activity, back off, wait two weeks, and use the same strategy for a different activity that your spouse enjoys but perhaps is a little less passionate about.

Talk Rituals

We've all heard that communication is everything in a relationship. While most people know that, few couples are as intentional as they need to be to carve out the time they need to discuss anything beyond which kid needs to go where and which things need to be picked up at the grocery store.

In his book *The Seven Levels of Intimacy*, author Matthew Kelly illustrates the kinds of topics happy couples regularly make an effort to discuss. We'll examine these categories in more detail in chapter 5, but looking at these topics of conversation now can help you get a sense of how to get more out of your time talking together. While most unhappy couples never communicate about topics beyond intimacy levels 1 through 3 (i.e., 1. clichés, 2. facts and current events, 3. opinions), happy couples regularly make an effort to discuss topics that relate to hopes and dreams (level 4), feelings (level 5), fears, faults, and failures (level 6), and needs (level 7). Kelly makes the point that conversations that involve these deeper levels of intimacy come from the couple cultivating what he calls a spirit of "carefree timelessness." Although that quality sounds, on the face of it, impossible to achieve in our careworn, time-strapped lives, we don't have to wait until all the chores are done and we are on vacation somewhere before we can experience this. Taking a little time (even fifteen minutes) each day, and a little more time each week (at least an hour), to hang out and talk about any subject is the easiest way to cultivate opportunities to talk about the things that really matter—as you and your spouse probably did when you were first dating.

The nice thing about talk rituals is that they can often be combined with other rituals. If you have the right attitude about it, you can have intimate conversations rooted in carefree time-lessness while you clean up the kitchen together just as easily as you can on a dinner out. With talk rituals, the important thing isn't the activity you're doing while you're talking. The important thing is carving out specific time to discuss something besides what's going on and what needs to be done. The following are some examples of things you will want to make time to talk about, whether you do it simultaneously with another activity or make specific time just to talk.

Daily Talk Rituals

Ask about each other's day.
Call from work to coordinate evening expectations or plans.

Find out the best thing that happened today.
Find out the toughest thing that happened today.
Ask what you could do to make life a little easier for the other.
Share at least one honest compliment.
Other _____
Other _____

Weekly Talk Rituals

Talk about when you felt closest that week.
Discuss a personal goal or dream.
Discuss a goal or dream for your marriage.
Share something you're struggling with in
       your personal or spiritual life.
Discuss what's going on in your relationship with God.
Discuss where you hope to be five years from now.
Coordinate your schedules for the week ahead.
Other _____
Other _____

With the other rituals, I asked you to choose one from each category (daily and weekly). With talk rituals, the goal is to pick a *time* to discuss all of these topics on a regular basis. The time you choose to do this could be special time reserved just for talking together (e.g., while having a cup of coffee together after the kids go to bed), or it could be paired with another activity that still makes more intimate sharing possible (e.g., folding laundry together).

Some couples who haven't shared on this level for a while have a hard time knowing where to start. Jack and Suzanne came up with a great idea. They made up a list of questions that had to do with the topics listed in both the daily and weekly categories.

They got two jars and filled one with daily questions and one with weekly questions. Every day after dinner, they chose to clean the kitchen together as a work ritual. While they did this, they took turns drawing and answering a question from the daily-question jar. They asked as many questions as they had time to answer before they were done with the kitchen. If one of their children interrupted or needed something, one of the parents stopped working on the kitchen while the other responded to the child's needs. They resumed cleanup and talk time when they both got back together.

Once a week, on Saturdays, they got up before the kids were awake and went to breakfast together. Their kids were old enough (fourteen, twelve, and ten) to take care of themselves for the first hour or so after they woke up. Jack and Suzanne brought their weekly-question jar with them and took turns drawing and responding to questions for as long as it took to have breakfast.

Jack said, "This has become a genuinely important part of our relationship. It was a little uncomfortable at first. I'm not a big talker, per se. But we used to talk more than we do. It's been nice to get back to that and discover there's more to our relationship than bussing kids and taking care of business."

Suzanne added, "It probably seems a little odd to hear Jack say that because our daily talk ritual revolves around kitchen cleanup! But honestly, it's been great. Usually, the kids leave us alone out of fear we might ask them to help! And we get to talk about things we wouldn't normally think to discuss. Plus, I'm really grateful for our Saturday mornings. Drawing questions from the jar takes the pressure out of 'what are we going to talk about?' I really appreciate feeling like we're really getting to know each other again."

Jack and Suzanne found a creative way to make talk time easier. The Retrouvaille program uses a "dialog" exercise to help couples get used to communicating on a deeper level. For more information, visit the Retrouvaille website (www.HelpOurMarriage.com). Likewise, the Gottman Institute offers Love Map Cards, a deck of cards with somewhat deeper questions a couple may wish to ask each other to get more meaningful conversations going. Even if you're naturally tongue-tied, you can learn to create talk rituals that enable you to draw closer as husband and wife.

If you are working on your marriage by yourself, you can still create talk rituals. Be careful not to grill your spouse, but make a point of asking at least one of the questions from the daily column each day. If you have to join your spouse in a chore to do it, then so be it. Also, once a week, invite your spouse to do something he or she enjoys. During that time, ask more of the daily questions. Over the next few weeks, as you get used to this time together, start adding some of the weekly questions as well. Get Gottman's Love Map Cards for more ideas, but share only the questions, not the cards, with your spouse.

Prayer Rituals

Many couples struggle with the idea of praying together, but this can be one of the most important rituals to create. Research shows that couples who cultivate a shared spiritual life are much happier across almost every dimension of relating, from communication to partnership to sexuality (Larson and Olsen, 2004; Rushnel and DuArt, 2011).

Couples can tiptoe into praying together by saying Grace before meals or simple prayers such as the Our Father or the Hail Mary, but the key to effective couple prayer is to make it personal. Avoid the temptation to pray as if you were checking off something on a to-do list. It's against Scripture (Matt. 6:7), and it bears little practical fruit. Regardless of how simple your prayer is, be sure to mention aloud the specific reasons you are offering a particular prayer—for instance, in thanksgiving for a particular blessing that day, for a specific intention, or for the needs of someone you care about.

For those who would like to try to get a bit more out of their prayer life, I teach couples to use the PRAISE format.

P   Praise and thanksgiving

R   Repentance

A   Ask for your needs

I   Intercede for others

S   Seek God's will for your decisions

E   Express your desire to serve God until you meet again in prayer

It is flexible enough to be personal but structured enough to prevent you from feeling lost and confused about what to do. You don't have to use every step in the PRAISE format every time you pray. Just think of it as a rule of thumb for cultivating a more meaningful couple prayer habit. You and your spouse should take turns sharing something from each of the steps you would like to include in a particular prayer time.

• *Praise and thanksgiving.* Take a moment to thank God for the little blessings of the day (that unexpected parking spot near the grocery store, the kind word from your boss, the sunny day) or just to acknowledge God's goodness and love. For example: "Lord Jesus, thank you for letting our son do so well on his math test today. He was so worried. And thank you for giving me a good day at work—those happen so rarely. I'm really grateful for your love and care."

• *Repentance.* This is not the time for confessing serious sins. It is simply the time when you and your spouse acknowledge the little ways you both know you let yourselves or each other down and you ask God's help to do better tomorrow. For example: "Lord, I'm sorry for snapping at my wife when I came home from work. Help me to find ways to let go of the stress before I walk in the door. Help me behave in a way that makes her happy to see me when I come home."

• *Ask for your needs.* Simple enough. Tell God what you need. For example: "God, tomorrow I have a huge presentation that I'm stressed about. Please be with me, and help me to do well."

• *Intercede for others.* Keep the needs of others in mind. For example: "Lord, please be with my mother and her health issues. Give her a speedy recovery."

• *Seek God's will for your decisions.* This is similar to asking for your needs but includes learning to listen to God's voice and discerning his will about the decisions you face in your life. For example: "Lord, give us your grace to know what activities the kids should be involved in this year. Last year was so crazy. And please help me know if I should apply for that new position that opened up at the

office. I'd like to take it, but I'm not sure about the hours.
Let us know your will."

• *Express your desire to serve God until you meet again in
prayer.* This is your wrap-up. You conclude your prayer
with a reminder that prayer doesn't end with "Amen."
You invite God to continue pouring out his grace in your
life, and you commit to remaining open to the movements
of his spirit as you go about your day. For example: "Lord
we give you every thought and word and action, and we
ask you to be with us as we go about our day. Keep us
open to your will and listening for your voice. Fill our
hearts with your grace until we gather together again in
prayer. Amen."

The PRAISE format can take five minutes or an hour, depending upon what you want to do with it. You may also decide to
include some formal prayer, such as an Our Father or a Hail Mary
or a decade or more of the Rosary.

Some people ask me, "How much should we pray as a couple?" The answer to that question is founded on the idea that
prayer is an act of intimacy. St. John Vianney said that "prayer
is nothing less than union with God." Likewise, prayer is act of
intimate union with those you are praying with. The answer to
the question "How much should we pray?" then, is: however
much prayer allows you to experience greater closeness to each
other and God.

Of course, that assumes a serious effort on the part of you
and your spouse, but considering that, at the point you feel your
mind wandering or you feel awkward, or that you've said what
you need to say and listened as long as you can, stop. Whether
that is five minutes or longer is really dependent upon where

you are in your relationship with God. Just do what you can and enjoy what you do.

The second question is "When do we pray?" This is really up to you. At what time of day will you most likely have the time and energy to talk with God for five or ten minutes (or more)? Many couples try to pray at night, after the kids are asleep, only to find themselves conking out as well. Some couples take a few minutes every morning together. Other couples pray before or after cleaning up the dinner dishes. Pick a time you can be consistent with.

Here are some ideas for creating daily and weekly prayer rituals.

Daily Prayer Rituals
Use PRAISE together.

Pray a decade (or more) of the Rosary together (for a
  particular intention or to give thanks).

Pray a Divine Mercy Chaplet together (for a particular
  intention or to give thanks).

Reflect on a daily Scripture meditation together.

Other _____

Other _____

Weekly Prayer Rituals
Go to Sunday Mass together.

Go to a weekday Mass together.

Attend a Bible study together.

Attend a prayer group together.

Take an adult faith-formation class together.

Other _____

Other _____

Choose both a daily and at least one weekly prayer ritual *in addition* to weekly Mass, unless you are not in the habit of attending Mass together.

There are several benefits you will attain by cultivating prayer rituals in your marriage.

First, you and your spouse will experience an *influx of grace* that will make your hearts more open to learning to love each other as God loves you. Every couple, even happy, healthy couples, hit a wall at some point and feel as if they, personally, do not have enough love to sustain the marriage on their own. Secular couples have to power through this on their own, but Christians can turn to God's grace to carry them through. Meditating on how much God loves you and your partner and that he called the two of you together to challenge each other to grow in ways you would never grow if you were left to your own devices is a powerful motivator to dig down deep and find the love God gives you for your mate when your own love runs dry.

Second, couple prayer *facilitates intimacy*, both because it is an intimate activity (which is why you feel vulnerable doing it) and because when you talk to God in the presence of each other, you automatically bring up topics that address the deeper levels of intimacy we discussed in the section on talk rituals. Couples who pray together tend to enjoy more and deeper communication because they are in the habit of reflecting together on the life they are creating with each other and the direction that life is taking.

Third, couple prayer is a *powerful solution to marital conflict and a contributor to marital satisfaction.* Why? Obviously, grace is a factor. But I would argue that there is an important psychological dimension as well. Marriage researchers at Northwestern University developed an intervention they call the *Marriage Hack*

(Northwestern, 2013). The Marriage Hack is a simple process in which a couple first recalls a recent argument they had. Next, the couple imagines how an impartial third party who loves each of them would advise them to respond to that problem in the future. Finally, the couple reflects on any obstacles that might prevent them from taking this advice and how to overcome those obstacles. That's it. Couples who did this Marriage Hack exercise *only once* for twenty minutes were able to arrest the decline in marital satisfaction they were experiencing before the intervention and keep the level of satisfaction with their marriage stable for months afterward. Further, the Marriage Hack group experienced greater marital satisfaction than the control group of couples who received no intervention during the same period.

The Marriage Hack allowed couples to get an outside perspective on their marriage, forced them to check their perceptions of each other and their responses to each other, and challenged them to be loving and intentional about seeking solutions with each other. I would argue that, in addition to all the many spiritual benefits and graces provided, the Marriage Hack is built into the mechanics of sincere couple prayer. Every time a couple prays together, they are challenged to consider the perspective that God—the impartial, mutually loving third party in their marriage—has of each of them. Both spouses are encouraged by the graces they receive in prayer to see one another through God's eyes and to consider their actions in light of God's love. Further, couple prayer empowers the couple to consider ways they could do better in the future, inspired by the loving care God has for each of them.

It is not my intention to reduce couple prayer to a spiritualized marital technique. I believe there is much more to couple prayer than meets the eye. But even if this were the only benefit—and it is not—it is easy to see why couples who sincerely and intentionally pray together have, on the whole, much more stable and happy marriages than couples who don't.

Jennifer and Paulo have been married nine years. They were in a terrible place in their relationship when they came to me for counseling. They spent little time together, and the time they did spend was not enjoyable in the least. Despite having two children together and having built a home together three years before, they shared few interests and did nothing together, not even household chores. In fact, they actively avoided time together. The only thing they did was attend Sunday Mass together, but because they often fought on the way to church, they had begun to take separate cars.

By the time the couple came to me for counseling, they were opposed to trying to spend any time together outside of session, which caused progress to be painfully slow. Because they both had what they considered to be personal and meaningful relationships with God on their own, I finally got them to agree to pray together for five minutes each day after dinner and before and after any disagreements they had.

When I first made the suggestion, Paulo laughed. "If we have to pray every time we fight, all we're gonna do is pray all the time!" We all chuckled about that, but admitted that even if this were true, it would be an improvement.

It was hard in those first few days for them to follow through, but I give them both credit: they stuck with it, and of course, God responded to their efforts with his abundant faithfulness. After two weeks of consistent effort, Jennifer told me in session that they had had a run of five days without an argument. "I'm kind of afraid to jinx it, but this is the longest we've gone without fighting."

Paulo agreed. "I mean, I know that five days probably sounds pathetic, but it beats the hell out of where we were."

I asked them what they thought was different. Paulo replied, "Well, I wasn't thrilled with the idea of praying with this woman I can barely stand talking to, but I have to admit it's making a big difference. Somehow, I just don't get as upset about the things that used to bug me. She seems like she's trying harder, and I really appreciate it."

Jennifer laughed. "That's really funny to hear you say that, 'cause I was going to say that I thought *you* were trying harder. Well, either way, I do agree with Paulo that there's a difference. We've both been pretty conscientious about praying every day for the marriage, and we've both tried really hard to stop for a minute and pray when it looks like we're headed for a fight."

I asked them how they prayed when they were starting to argue. Paulo said, "It's nothing to write home about. I think the last time, I said, "God, I have no idea how to have this conversation with Jennifer. I'm so tired of fighting with her. Please help me."

"That's about right for me too," Jennifer added. "And then, regardless of how things go, we try to end any disagreement with a prayer too. I think the last time it was something like, 'God, this is really hard, I don't know how to convince Paulo that I'm not his enemy, and I don't know how to get him to not be so upset with me all the time. Help me do better in our conversations.' And he said something similar."

I complimented them on their efforts, particularly that they didn't use their prayer time to complain about each other, but rather to ask God for help improving their own behavior. Paulo agreed. "That was hard, especially when I felt like I hadn't done anything wrong, but it felt wrong to try to use my prayers to beat Jen up, so I tried to watch it."

Thankfully, Jennifer and Paulo took their prayer-ritual homework seriously. God poured out abundant grace on this couple who hadn't been able stand the sight of each other just a few weeks before. Establishing solid couple-prayer habits enabled them to experience enough peace and connection to be willing to try to do other things together as well. We had several other issues to work on besides establishing solid Rituals of Connection, but establishing couple prayer, especially as a habit before and after difficult discussions, gave us the foundation to rebuild their marriage and pursue what was ultimately a very successful counseling experience.

Jennifer and Paulo did three things that enable their couple-prayer ritual to work. First, they both took responsibility for making it happen. One spouse can do it alone, but it's always easier with two. Second, they were sincere in their desire for prayer to change their own hearts. They recognized that the most sincere prayer is: "Lord, change me," not: "Lord, change my spouse." Finally, they both stuck with it. It can take a while before your spirits begin to benefit from the grace of your efforts. Satan has a hard time letting go of hearts that have gone cold. But keep persevering. God's grace will not fail.

I have tried to present some very rudimentary approaches to couple prayer. For those who would like to learn more, I encourage you to visit www.CouplePrayer.com. There you can find a video-based home-study program for learning more about couple prayer. It is a tremendous and very helpful resource that I wish every couple would take advantage of.

If you are working on your marriage by yourself, you can still create prayer rituals. Try adding one of the daily suggestions to your mealtime prayers. Another idea is to make it known to your spouse that you are taking five minutes each evening to pray for your marriage. Invite your spouse to pray with you. If your mate refuses, don't push, but keep the prayer time. And don't hide while you're praying; be in a place that is not intrusive but where your spouse could at least notice as he or she walks by the room you're in. Even if the answer is no, continue each day to ask your spouse to join you in your five-minute prayer time for your marriage.

Incidentally, this should not replace whatever individual prayer time you have. The goal of this suggestion is to institute a placeholder for couple prayer that makes it difficult for your spouse to avoid the idea of couple prayer without your being overly aggressive or obnoxious about it. Keep this up for at least a month before deciding whether it is working. If your spouse does join you, don't criticize or critique his or her effort — even if it is willfully bad. Establish the habit; then work on the quality. Seek professional assistance if you find you are unable to make this work on your own.

Finally, regardless of how these other ideas are working, always remember to ask your guardian angel for help. The *Catechism* tells us that every person has been given a guardian angel (no. 336). Ask your guardian angel to speak with your spouse's guardian angel to smooth the path between you and your mate, to catch any uncharitably expressed works on either part, and to soften any emotional blows that either of you might try to strike. I can't tell you how effective this prayer is. The *Catechism* tells us that our guardian angels are here to be protectors and shepherd us through life. Since our sacramental marriage plays a significant role in our sanctification and in the perfection of husbands and wives in grace, it stands to reason that our guardian angels care deeply for the well-being of our marriage.

Wrapping Up

Throughout this chapter, I have focused on helping you generate ideas for creating Rituals of Connection that will help you develop a sense of intimacy, comfort, and familiarity in your marriage — the kind of intimacy that enables you to feel as if you are good partners to each other, that you "get" each other, that you can share a body of experiences that allow you to finish each other's sentences.

The presence or absence of Rituals of Connection is what largely accounts for a couple's ability to feel "in love" with each other. Rituals of connection serve as the skeleton of the relationship and enable a couple to feel like a couple instead of just two individuals living under the same roof.

As I have counseled throughout the chapter, if Rituals of Connection are new to you, start small. Pick one area to begin with. Choose one daily and one weekly ritual, and work on it for a few weeks until it feels like a natural part of your life. Then build from there. Of course, if you are struggling to establish Rituals of Connection in your relationship, or encountering insurmountable resistance from your partner, counseling can help you overcome these challenges. Take advantage of opportunities to work with a marriage-friendly therapist in your area, or contact the Pastoral Solutions Institute to learn more about our marital tele-counseling services.

With a little effort, you can create Rituals of Connection that strengthen the foundation of your marriage and bind you together in the good times and bad for the rest of your lives.

As this chapter draws to a close, I hope you will keep the following prayer close to your heart over the weeks you are working — either alone or with your spouse — to create the Rituals of Connection around work, play, talk, and prayer that will serve as the bones of your healthy marriage.

Pray

Lord Jesus Christ, you bind your family, the Church, together with rituals that allow us to work to build your kingdom, celebrate the joys of life, talk with you, and listen to your voice. In the same way, bless our home, our domestic church. Help my spouse and me to create the Rituals of Connection that help us work, play, talk, and pray together so that we might have the strength to remain bound to one another despite the busyness and frustrations of our everyday life. Give us the courage to say no to all the outside activities, pressures, and commitments that seek to tear us apart and empower us to say, "I do" to each other by committing to the daily and weekly activities that help the two of us create one life.

Discuss

• List the three most important points you took from this chapter.

• What type of Rituals of Connection (work, play, talk, or prayer) would be simplest to begin cultivating? Why do you think so?

• What specific daily and weekly Rituals of Connection will you seek to establish in the coming weeks?

• What resistance or obstacles do you anticipate having to overcome on the road to establishing these rituals?

• What plans do you need to make or resources must you acquire to overcome these obstacles?

• Once you have established the above rituals, what will be your next step?

• How will you know if you need to seek professional help?

Chapter 5

Emotional Rapport and Benevolence

Love one another with brotherly affection;
outdo one another in showing honor.
—Romans 12:10

Marriage masters know that happy couples do not say, "I do" only on their wedding day. They know that every single time they interact with each other, they are saying either, "I do" or "I don't" to their marriage. These couples know that when they look for ways to make each other's lives a little easier or more pleasant, when they take the time to learn about each other's lives, when they do things that make their partner feel cared for and attended to, they are saying, "I do." They also understand that when they ignore each other, become so caught up in their own lives that the relationship exhibits an "everyone for himself" dynamic, or refuse to leave their comfort zone for the sake of their partner, they are saying, "I don't" to the marriage.

Emotional Rapport and Benevolence is the source of trust in marriage—trust that enables the couple to open up honestly with each other, to bear wrongs patiently, and to assume the best about a partner even when that partner is sometimes at his or her worst. Having good emotional rapport with your spouse means that you generally feel cared for by each other. You understand what each other's days are like. You are good at sharing and celebrating each other's successes, and you turn to each other for support. Benevolence refers to a couple's ability to know how to please each other and their active efforts to try to please each other, even when it comes at some small sacrifice to themselves.

If you are reading this chapter, you probably received a lower score on the quiz on this topic in chapter 3. Take a moment to review the statements you were asked to consider on pages 60 and 61.

What the Absence of Emotional Rapport
Does to Marriage

Having low levels of Emotional Rapport and Benevolence often leads to a culture of suspicion or wariness between a husband and wife in which the couple habitually misreads each other's intentions and reacts defensively to each other even when no offense was intended. The lack of Emotional Rapport and Benevolence tends to increase the likelihood of secrecy between a husband and wife, as they will often not share things for fear of being misunderstood, criticized, or shamed. These couples tend to limit their interactions to conversations about facts, current events, and opinions, rarely sharing deeper feelings, hopes and dreams, fears, struggles, or needs with each other. Because of the culture of suspicion or wariness that exists in these relationships, these couples are at a fairly high risk for conflict; they may be prone to assuming the worst about each other's behavior since negative actions tend significantly to outweigh any positive caretaking that would soften the blow of slights and offenses (Gottman, 2011).

Couples who exhibit low levels of Emotional Rapport and Benevolence tend to love their own comfort zones more than they love their partner. In healthy marriages, couples try to be generous regarding each other's requests. Assuming a spouse is not being asked to do something that is not objectively immoral or demeaning, a healthy spouse will try his best to say yes to the request, even if it is difficult for him to do or not something that he usually prefers to do. A less healthy couple will regularly say no to such requests on the ground that "that's just not who I am" or "you know I don't like that."

Often husbands and wives in marriages where there is low Emotional Rapport and Benevolence complain of feeling profoundly lonely in their marriage or in life in general, especially if they do not have other close friends to share with. Or one spouse feels abandoned as the other spouse spends more and more time with those friends (or with God in church).

At best, marriages displaying low levels of Emotional Rapport and Benevolence tend to limit themselves to a quiet life of unsatisfying, superficial interactions where both the husband and wife have learned to avoid conflict by not risking too much vulnerability with each other and doing their best to seek emotional support outside the marriage. This tendency can lead to the unintentional development of "work-spouse" or "church-spouse" relationships (or full-out infidelity), in which the spouse seeking emotional support outside the marriage makes a strong connection with a friend of the opposite sex, with whom they may be required by their work or circumstances to spend a great deal of time (Dorsett, 2011).

What Developing Emotional Rapport and Benevolence Will Do for Your Marriage

When couples work to increase their experience of Emotional Rapport and Benevolence, they become true friends to one another. They are able to avoid potential conflicts more gracefully, engage in more intimate sharing, and turn toward each other to share joys when they are happy and get support when they are stressed. Let's look briefly at each of these benefits.

Avoid Conflicts

Couples with higher levels of emotional support and benevolence take excellent care of each other. As I shared above, they look for ways to make each other's lives a little easier and more pleasant and try hard to respond generously to each other's requests, even when it challenges them to leave their comfort zone. Surprisingly, this has a direct impact on the couple's ability to avoid conflict when possible and manage conflict more gracefully when it does come.

Research from the Gottman Institute found that healthy couples exhibit a 20:1 ratio of positive to negative interactions when they are not in conflict (neutral interactions don't count) (2011). Gottman found that maintaining this high level of caretaking made couples much more likely to give each other the benefit of the doubt when they accidentally offended each other and much gentler to each other when they had disagreements. The research also found that these couples did not get along with each other simply because they were more compatible with each other. Rather, they avoided and managed conflict more efficiently because of the little things they did to take care of each other during the day.

Remember, if thirty-eight times out of forty, your spouse is doing concrete things to look out for your best interests, make your life less difficult, and take the time to understand and care about what you go through in the course of your day, then chances are you'd be willing to let slide the two out of forty times your spouse muffs things up. Likewise, if you had a disagreement with such a spouse, chances are you could easily remember all the little ways your mate tried to lighten your load, share your burdens, let you know he or she cared. Because of those recent memories, you'd be much more likely to be gentle with your spouse during disagreements; you'd probably feel awful attacking someone who worked so hard to take care of you!

That's exactly what the Gottman research found. Couples who worked hard to do the concrete things that increased Emotional Rapport and Benevolence had less inclination to argue in the first place and handled their disagreements more respectfully when they did.

Increase Intimate Sharing

The second benefit of increased Emotional Rapport and Benevolence is an increased trust that leads to deeper emotional sharing. Research has shown that benevolence (along with integrity and competence) is an essential ingredient to trust (McKnight and Chervany, 2001). The more a person is willing to put himself out for the sake of doing things to make your life easier or more pleasant, the more you are likely to trust that person, because you see how much he values you and his relationship with you. You know you are important to such a person. You tend to assume that the things you care about are going to be important to such a person—even if he or she doesn't have the same feelings or experiences as you do—so you are more likely to share those feelings and experiences with such a benevolent person.

All of this leads to a willingness to risk deeper intimacy. In my book *For Better . . . FOREVER!*, I note that it can be helpful to think of intimacy as love's "unit of measure." In other words, as inches and feet are units of measure for distance and cups and gallons are units of measure for volume, intimacy tends to tell you how much love is present and how deep it is. It's good to know that someone loves you, but it's even better to know whether the love that person has for you is a puddle or an ocean.

In his book *The Seven Levels of Intimacy*, Matthew Kelly notes that in the healthiest relationships, couples are comfortable relating to each other regarding each of the following:

- *Clichés*: Healthy couples are comfortable sharing social conventions, such as "Good morning"; "How was your day?"; "How are you?"; "Can I get you something?" This is not a deep level of intimacy, and it can be shared with anyone, but I know couples who struggle to connect even on this level as a result of the lack of effort they have put into tending to Emotional Rapport and Benevolence.

- *Facts*: At this level of intimacy, couples regularly discuss current events, schedules, plans, and so forth. Again, this is a level of intimacy that can be shared in any relationship, but couples who do not try to come even close to a 20:1 ratio of positive to negative interactions often are stingy about sharing the events of the day and treat even their schedules as a state secret.

- *Opinions*: This is the first level of intimacy that risks something personal. In sharing my opinions, I let you know something about my values, priorities, and goals. We can share this level of intimacy in most relationships, but if a couple does not work to take care of each other, they can become reluctant to share opinions out of fear that they will be made fun of or shamed for thinking differently from their mate.

• *Hopes and dreams:* This is the level of intimacy usually reserved for better friendships. At this level, couples share their hopes and dreams for the future and discuss their plans for their relationship and lives together. Couples who struggle with Emotional Rapport and Benevolence will have a very difficult time sharing hopes and dreams for fear of being judged or criticized.

• *Feelings:* This is different from "sharing" emotional reactions. Everyone does that at any level of relationship. This is the level of intimacy where a couple is comfortable sitting down and intentionally talking through how they really feel about the things that are going on their life. Couples at this level of intimacy display sufficient care-taking in their day-to-day relationship to know they can count on their partner to help them work through difficult emotions and celebrate joys together.

• *Faults, fears, and failures:* At this level of intimacy, couples display a high enough degree of gentleness, caretaking, and thoughtfulness in their day-to-day interactions to feel safe in asking for their partners' help to deal with personal struggles and fears, and to discuss how to recover and learn from failures without feeling shamed or criticized or hearing, "I told you so."

• *Psycho-spiritual needs:* This level of intimacy refers to a couple's ability to talk about what both the husband and wife need from life and their relationship to be genuinely fulfilled. They don't just talk *at* each other about these things. Rather, they share and plan together and reassure each other that the things that are important to one will be important to both. These conversations help create an intentional life plan that is ordered toward helping the husband and wife become everything God created them to be in this life and helping each other get to heaven in the next. This is a very deep level of sharing that can safely occur only when couples are consistently approaching the 20:1 ratio of positive to negative interactions.

Regardless of the level of intimacy at which you usually relate to your partner, the point of this section is to show that the level of intimacy you achieve is driven by how well you and your spouse take care of each other. The more you think of little ways to make your partner's life easier and more pleasant, work for your mate's good, and willingly step outside your comfort zone for the sake of your partner's happiness and well-being, the more likely it is that you will find yourself at a deeper level of intimacy without even trying. Achieving deeper intimacy isn't something you can force. It is something you nurture. The fruit of intimacy grows in the rich soil of emotional connection and caretaking.

Share joys and gain support

As you might imagine from our discussion on intimacy, couples who work hard to maintain healthy levels of Emotional Rapport and Benevolence are much more comfortable coming to each other both to celebrate successes and to gain support in times of trial.

When a couple consistently works to get as close as possible to the 20:1 ratio of day-to-day caretaking, their relationship develops two superpowers. The first is the power to synergize joy. Synergy is the ability for two things to create more energy than either thing could on its own. When a couple exhibits good Emotional Rapport and Benevolence, and they share joys and successes with each other, their mutual joy harmonizes and resonates between the two of them.

When you have good rapport with someone, the mirror neurons in your brain allow you to feel a little bit of what that person feels (Cozolino, 2014). If you have a good rapport with your spouse and he or she feels something good, your mirror neurons send signals to your brain that you should feel good too. In response, the mirror neurons in your spouse's brain register the good feelings you "caught" from him or her as if they were original good feelings. This enables your spouse to feel even better for having shared how good he or she feels with you!

By contrast, when you are in good rapport with your spouse and he or she shares sad news with you, your mirror neurons give you a taste of what your spouse is feeling, which provokes a caretaking response in you. You immediately and automatically turn to the repertoire of caretaking activities you've cultivated that you know make your spouse's life easier or more pleasant, and your spouse is buoyed up by your loving response.

If you haven't worked hard to maintain your Emotional Rapport and Benevolence through daily caretaking activities, then something quite different happens. When your partner shares a joy with you, you might genuinely feel happy for him or her at the moment, but since you don't have a repertoire of caretaking activities, a ready list of small ways to enhance that joyful feeling, it basically dies there. You move on, and your spouse feels deflated for having shared good news with you.

Likewise, if you don't have good Emotional Rapport and Benevolence established and your partner shares bad news with you, your mirror neurons will cause you to feel a bit of your spouse's sadness, but because you don't know what to do to make him or her feel better, the sad feeling in you provokes your fight, flight, or freeze response. Perhaps you react angrily that he or she is dragging you down. Or you just ignore your spouse and look for the earliest opportunity to get out of the conversation, if not the room. Or you just stare dumbly at your spouse, hoping awkwardly that he or she will go away. Of course, all of this just makes you both feel worse to be around each other.

Many husbands and wives think this dynamic is terminal and that there is nothing short of a personality transplant that can fix it. The reality is much simpler for most couples. Practicing Emotional Rapport and Benevolence habits—working to take care of each other in little ways every day, especially when there is not something particularly significant (either good or bad) going on in either partner's life—enables couples to develop the skills to enhance their good feelings and mediate the bad ones.

Putting Emotional Rapport and Benevolence into Practice

In his Theology of the Body, Pope St. John Paul the Great asserted that we were made to give ourselves to each other and that happiness and love both prosper when people are committed to using whatever they have at their disposal to work for the good of those around them. This quality, known as *self-donation*, is a radical form of generosity that encourages all people, but especially married people, to look for both big and small ways to be a blessing to each other. Self-donation isn't just a technique for making relationships better, however. It is ultimately the engine that drives God's plan of perfecting us into the generous, loving, caring, grace-filled saints we are destined to be.

This might seem like a big job, but even the smallest gestures can convey the greatest degrees of Emotional Rapport and

Benevolence. Marriage experts refer to simple acts like smiling at your partner when she walks in the room, meeting your mate's gaze, intentionally brushing your hand against your spouse's shoulder as a gesture of support, and really listening when your mate speaks as ways of "turning toward" each other, and all of these—and other simple behaviors like them—count toward that 20:1 caretaking ratio I've referred to so often (Gottman, 2011). As in life, it is the little things that spell the difference between marital bliss and marital miss. The good news is that the presence or absence of these small actions is entirely within your control. It can be challenging to make yourself do them, especially if you and your mate are at loggerheads, and it will probably feel forced to do these things at first, but if you push through this initial resistance, you may be surprised to see a dramatic change in the quality of your relationships in as little as three or four weeks.

To get started, do the Love List Exercise on page 279.

Turning Toward

As you practice this exercise over the next several weeks with or without your spouse, you may occasionally feel some resentment. That's just a sign that you've lost focus on how God is calling you to grow (unless this has been going on for several weeks, in which case, you will need to say something or seek counseling). If this happens, refocus on God's personal call in your heart and redouble your effort.

Practicing the Love List Exercise will help you and your spouse learn to turn *toward* each other for support, counsel, and celebration. This is a key aspect of benevolence—the tendency to turn toward another person and work to repair or improve upon the relationship even when you don't necessarily feel like it. Benevolence fertilizes the soil that allows the tree of intimacy to bear fruit.

Pray

As you conclude this chapter, take a moment to pray the following prayer. Remember to keep this prayer in mind over the next few weeks.

> Lord Jesus Christ, help us to learn to love each other more than we love our comfort zones, and give me the grace to lead the way. Help us to value equity over equality in our efforts, but prevent us from using or being used by each other. Help me to respond to the call in my heart to become the person you created me to be, and help my spouse and me enjoy the intimacy that comes from trying to make each day more of a gift for each other. Amen.

Discuss

• Are you nervous about the Love List Exercise? If so, what are you nervous about?

• What are the ways you tend to love your comfort zone more than your spouse? How can you use this exercise to overcome this?

• What level of intimacy (according to Matthew Kelly's seven levels) are you most comfortable relating on? What would it be like for you and your spouse to take good enough care of each other to go to at least the next level of intimacy?

Chapter 6

Self-Regulation

The Lord has given me a well-trained tongue.
—Isaiah 50:4

In chapter 2, we discussed the difference between the Solution-Focused Brain and the Misery-Making Mindset. Recall that when we are in the Solution-Focused Brain state, we're able to feel whatever emotions are appropriate to the situation (including anger, frustration, sadness, fear, etc.), but our intellect is still running the show, so our focus is not so much on the problem as it is on gathering resources to help solve the problem. By contrast, when we allow ourselves to fall into the Misery-Making Mindset, we become stuck in our emotions, we ruminate about our problems rather than thinking through them, and we often fall into one of three reactive personas that cause us to *pout or withdraw*, *tantrum*, or put on the airs of a *Contemptuous Expert*. These personas cause us to get stuck in unhealthy ways of thinking about our problems and cause us to act in ways that ultimately make a bad situation worse.

Self-regulation is the skill that enables husbands and wives to respond rather than react to an argument or another stressful situation. Although it does involve having the "well-trained" tongue referred to in Isaiah 50:4, it goes far beyond this. More than knowing how to watch what you say, good self-regulation gives you the ability to control both how long and how intensely your body and mind react when conflict occurs.

If you're reading this chapter, you most likely received a score on the Self-Regulation Quiz indicating that you could use some improvement in this area. Take a moment to review the statements you were asked to consider on pages 63 and 64.

What the Absence of Self-Regulation Does to Marriage

When a couple lacks good self-regulation, they "flood" easily in conflict. *Flooding* refers to the tendency to fall into the Misery-Making Mindset and adopt one of the three Misery-Making Personas (*Pouting/Withdrawing, Tantrumming, Contemptuous Expert*). When we flood, our bloodstream is literally pumped full of stress hormones such as adrenaline and cortisol that cause us to rev up and feel stuck at the same time. Once these chemicals reach a certain level, our logical, problem-solving cortex goes offline and the emotional-reactive limbic system takes over.

Once this happens, you are incapable of solving problems. The only thing you are concerned with in this limbic-controlled, stressed-out state is either getting your spouse to shut up and go away or manipulating your spouse into giving in, by overpowering him or her with the force of your emotions (tantrumming) or a tidal wave of words and "reasonable arguments" (Contemptuous Expert).

The practical effect of all of this is that you end up simultaneously making your problems infinitely worse and making it infinitely more difficult to identify solutions because the very part of your brain dedicated to finding solutions is offline.

What Developing Self-Regulation
Will Do for Your Marriage

In addition to making it much easier to find your own way through conflict and also use any new ideas that you might learn along the way (instead of losing all your new ideas and repeating the same old patterns when your cortex—the place that stores all your new ideas—goes offline and your limbic system takes over) developing good self-regulation is the most important way to maintain a sense of confidence and personal power when you are in conflict.

Why would you want to maintain a sense of "personal power"? How does that square with God's call for humility and for husbands' and wives' willingness to "defer to one another out of reverence for Christ" (Eph. 5:21)? To clarify, I don't mean "power" in the sense of trying to force your spouse to accept your arguments. I mean it in the sense of feeling confident that, regardless of the circumstances, your stress-level, or even your spouse's hostility, you will be able to work through all that to find a mutually satisfying solution. When you lose a sense of personal power, you feel threatened and vulnerable, and you tend to react defensively, producing a hostile, defensive reaction in return.

Research on happy couples shows that learning to avoid flooding is essential to effective conflict management (Gottman, 2011). People in healthy marriages learned in their families of origin how to regulate this physiological and psychological stress response in the presence of conflict both by seeing their parents engage in conflict that was safe, short, and productive and by engaging in similar disagreements with parents and siblings themselves. Being raised in such an environment allows a person to keep a cool head even when the person he or she is speaking with is being either hostile or unreasonable in some way. People raised in households who never witnessed their parents argue—or who rarely engaged in arguments themselves growing up—tend to flood very easily (usually falling into pouting or withdrawing) because they are not used to experiencing any tension at all in relationships and are easily shocked by it. By contrast, people who witnessed constant tension or regularly high levels of conflict also tend to flood easily because their brains are primed to assume every conflict means going to war.

Adults raised in families in which conflict was infrequent and productive (more or less) tend to learn through observation that every relationship involves at least some degree of disagreement, that disagreements can be held safely, and that conflict, while unpleasant, tends to produce positive results. This enables husbands and wives raised.in such families to learn unconsciously how to regulate their body's stress response in the presence of conflict and naturally tend to stay in their Solution-Focused Brain, which accounts for their ability to manage marital conflict much more effectively than those who did not naturally learn self-regulation in childhood.

The good news is that no matter how poorly developed your ability to self-regulate is, you can learn this essential conflict-management skill using these steps.

Step 1: Become aware of the Stress Temperature Scale.

Many people and in particular, many husbands and wives in troubled marriages, simply don't pay attention to how stressed they are—either overall or from moment to moment. We may feel our stress or become vaguely aware of it, but most of us don't *attend* to it. Attending to your stress level means semi-actively monitoring how stressed you are at any given moment and knowing how to take appropriate steps to lower that stress level when it is *beginning* to elevate, but *before* it causes your Misery-Making Mindset to become activated.

People raised in households that displayed healthy conflict tend to learn this process naturally, which enables them to be *emotionally engaged* in conflict. Being *emotionally engaged* means knowing how to let yourself get just stressed enough to process information quickly and think on your feet but not so stressed that you trip over your own feet and fall into the fireplace. If you haven't learned how to do this unconsciously by observing your parents do it, you will need to learn to calibrate your psychological and behavioral cues to an objective standard that will help you know when you're getting too close to the Misery-Making Mindset and to pull back. I call this standard the Stress Temperature Scale.

The Stress Temperature Scale runs from 1 (completely relaxed) to 10 (completely reactive). Each point along the scale tends to correspond with certain states of mind, behaviors, and modes of thinking about your situation and the person you're talking with. Let's look at each point on the scale.

1-2: *Completely relaxed.* At this moment, you are completely relaxed and at peace. You feel good about your circumstances, yourself, and the people you are interacting with. You are more peaceful than normal and probably a little disengaged from your circumstances. Your heart and respiration rates are low-normal. You are probably not involved in much, if any, problem solving of any kind at this stage.

3-4: *Relaxed/alert.* You are engaged in your surroundings and interacting well with the people around you. You are in a good mood, and you are good company. You are enjoying what you are doing in the moment, and even the challenges you might be encountering feel good because they feel like opportunities to show just how competent you are.

5: *Alert/focused.* You are engaged in your surroundings and interacting well with the people around you. You are in a decent mood, although your mind may be wandering to certain concerns that, while not critical, are demanding more of your attention. You have to work a little harder at the challenges that present themselves, but overall you are feeling good about the work, roles, or tasks you are in the middle of.

6: *Alert/stressed.* You are handling the challenges in your environment and interacting well with the people around you, but it is taking more effort to feel as if you are on top of things. You are more conscious of the effort it takes not to be terse in your comments to others. Your body has begun to notice an increase of stress chemicals in your system, although at this point, it is not problematic. You feel somewhat pressured, and although you are able to control your reactions, you are obviously harried and irritable below the surface. Others notice that you seem a little tense, but since you seem to be mostly in control of your reactions, few people aside from close friends are likely to call attention to it. This is usually the point where others, if they say anything, may say, "Is everything all right? You seem a little off."

7: *Irritable.* Your bloodstream has begun to flood with stress chemicals, and your heart and respiration rates are increasing. You are still able to problem-solve effectively at this stage, but you are no longer trying to hide your irritation or — at the higher end of 7 (say, 7.6 to 7.9) — your disgust. Your brain is beginning to respond to the presence of stress hormones, and you are increasingly losing your ability to control your nonverbal signs of stress and frustration. This is the point where you may find yourself rolling your eyes at the (to you) unbelievably dumb things people say. You may occasionally let out a disgusted sigh to show the people around you how put upon you are beginning to feel. You may also start feeling fidgety and struggling to stay put. At the higher end of 7, you may struggle to look people in the eye and instead find yourself staring at the door and wishing you could leave. Inside your head, you are starting to think how ridiculous it is that you are having to put up with whatever is going on. Even so, you don't exactly feel angry, per se, and would object if anyone said you were. At this stage, if someone asked if you were okay, you'd probably respond, "I'm fine. What? I'm *fine.*"

This is the highest level you can get on the Stress Temperature Scale and still effectively solve problems. The conversation is still primarily focused on generating ideas for working together to solve the problem at hand. That said, if one more frustrating thing happens, or if one more annoying thing is said, your problem-solving resources will most likely be all but completely offline. People who have good self-regulation skills automatically know that they need to take a break at this level — even if only for a few moments — so that they can bring their temperature back down again.

8: *Angry*. At this point, the nonverbal filters in your brain have shut down, and your verbal filters are under assault. You are not yelling or calling names, but the tone of the conversation has changed. In the case of a marital conflict, instead of trying to discuss ways to identify resources and solve the problem together, you are now focused on trying to convince your spouse that he or she *is* the problem, unless you are the pouting or withdrawing type, in which case you may find yourself agreeing with your spouse just to shut him or her up. At any rate, you are openly scowling now. You may also find yourself lecturing and unable to stop yourself from running off at the mouth for relatively long periods, during which you try patiently (you think) to explain to your spouse why he or she is wrong, wrong, wrong, and would be doing the world a huge favor if he or she would just admit to being wrong already. Your Misery-Making Mindset is now fully engaged, and your respective Misery-Making persona (Pouting/Withdrawing, Tantrumming, Contemptuous Expert) is quickly walking to center stage. Regardless of which persona is emerging, this is the first point where you are most likely to admit that you are angry, although it's really — as far as you are concerned — your spouse's fault.

People with good self-regulation skills rarely go past this point, usually choosing to end the conversation for several hours while they take time to pray or think through what was said, remind themselves that their spouse really is a good and loving person who is similarly struggling through things, and try to generate new ideas for solving the problem so that, when they come back to the conversation later, they can begin on a better, more productive note.

9: Very angry/feeling like a victim. Now your verbal filters have completely collapsed. You are furious. If you tend toward pouting or withdrawing, you have most likely shut down and will not be speaking for the rest of the day. Otherwise, this is the point where the yelling, hurtful comments, and name-calling start. Even so, these cruel and hurtful comments seem perfectly defensible to you because your spouse is just being *so mean/thoughtless/irresponsible/obnoxious that how could anyone possibly expect me to respond in any other way?!*" Because you feel like a victim of your mate's inexcusable behavior, you feel completely justified using whatever emotional slash-and-burn tactics are at your disposal to get your partner either to agree with you or to go away. To your mind, either would be fine at this point.

People tend not to mean literally the things they say at this stage. Rather, the words that come out are meant to express the deep level of emotional pain they are feeling inside. They genuinely think they are crying out, "I'm hurt and angry, and I don't know what to do about it." Unfortunately, what actually gets said is something that sounds a bit more like, "You're a crazy, horrible person, and I hate every agonizing moment I spend watching you breathe."

10: *Outraged/abusive.* Now the physical filters are collapsing. This is the point where people slam doors, throw objects, and sometimes hurt each other physically. People at this stage are completely reactive and can be said to be high on their own neurochemistry. Although they must be held responsible for their actions, they are completely past the point of being able to control themselves. Any marriage that regularly makes it to this stage almost certainly requires immediate and intensive professional help.

By now, you should be getting a clearer sense of the importance of self-regulation in managing conflict. The most important thing to take from this is that, although it can feel as if your spouse has driven your stress temperature higher, you are the only person who can decide how high you let your emotional temperature go. No one but you can allow it to rise. No one but you can control it.

It is unquestionably possible to learn to keep yourself at a 7 or lower. Soldiers, police officers, firemen, and, yes, happily married couples have learned to keep their stress temperature lower under much worse circumstances than you currently have to contend with. No matter how upsetting or offensive your spouse is, there is absolutely no excuse for allowing your temperature to rise above an 8 — ever. In fact, doing so constitutes the deadly sin of wrath (i.e., anger that does not work toward the good of each other but instead works to harm the other). If you allow yourself to rise to this level, I urge you to go to confession to seek God's grace and cultivate the humility that will allow you to see that, despite how you feel, your partner is not your enemy.

Assuming you are ready to take responsibility for getting your own reactions under control, let's look at the next step in cultivating good self-regulation.

Step 2: Establish your baseline.

People tend to focus on the specific offenses and irritations that cause their stress temperature to spike. We'll get to that in a minute. First, I need you to take stock of how high your emotional temperature is at rest. Sometimes people tell me that they go from a 0 to 10 in no time flat. This is never the case. The body doesn't work that way. More likely, people who feel this way live at or around a high 6 (6.5 to 6.9) or 7 all the time and have been living at that level for so long that it feels like someone else's 4 or 5. Unpleasant experiences and offenses tend to cause our stress temperatures to spike by at least a point or two. If your baseline temperature is a 4 or 5, that's not a problem. You have some wiggle room. But if you live at a 7, you have no place to go but crazy at the first sign of an offense. Trying to learn to control your response at the trigger point is useless, because by the time you become aware that you're offended it's too late to get control of yourself. You have to focus on prevention by lowering your stress temperature when you are not feeling under attack.

How do you do this? You can't avoid stress. So what do you do? You become mindful of monitoring your temperature throughout the day. You take small steps to pace yourself and lower your temperature when it is still relatively (for you at least) low. The following three tips can get you started. I recommend using them whether or not you feel a critical need to do so. The lower your baseline stress temperature, the more peaceful you will feel and the more effective you will be. Who doesn't want more of both?

First, get a notebook and, using the earlier description of the individual points on the Stress Temperature Scale, record your stress temperature in the morning when you wake, at lunchtime, at midday, at dinnertime, and before bed. Simply becoming aware of how hot you are running will engage whatever natural "calm down" resources you have at your disposal but tend not to use because you mistakenly think it's normal to be this upset all the time.

Second, pray. Take regular time throughout the day to stop and bring whatever stressors you're facing before God. You don't have to make a production out of it. Just a simple, "Lord, help me to respond to my frustrations with a more peaceful heart. Help me see my life and the people in it through your eyes" will do. Meditate on Scripture verses such as Proverbs 19:11: "Those with good sense are slow to anger, and it is their glory to overlook an offense." Do an Internet search of Scripture verses on anger for more examples. Bringing your stress and irritability to the Lord at regular intervals throughout the day will help slow you down enough and give you grace enough to keep things in perspective.

Third, speaking of slowing down, *slow down*. Literally. When your stress temperature starts to increase, you'll notice that you talk faster and do everything else faster too. Slow. It. Down. Not to the point that you look strange to the people around you. Just enough to let your mouth keep up with your brain and for you to pay attention to what you're doing. Throughout the day, force yourself to speak a little more slowly than you want to. Walk across the room a beat slower than is usual for you. Do the things you do a touch more intentionally than normal. Concentrating and being intentional about your actions and rate of speech, even the slightest bit, will lower your emotional temperature by a full point or two, which can make all the difference in the world.

There are many other strategies I could suggest if I had the space. Start with these, but if you find you need additional help in bringing down your baseline stress temperature, contact the Pastoral Solutions Institute for additional support.

Step 3: Identify your spikes.

Now that you are taking steps to get your baseline temperature under control, it's time to learn to handle a little better the offenses that cause your temperature to spike. Spikes are sudden and significant rises in one's stress level due to some irritating external event.

In the same notebook you are using to record your stress temperature throughout the day, divide a page into three columns. In the first column, as you go about your day, list the situations (especially those in your marriage but also in general) that bring out a strong negative emotional reaction in you (including the times when you shut down or freeze up). In the second column, next to those items, write down how you usually respond to those frustrations. What do you usually say and do? Chances are these responses will be consistent with one of the Misery-Making Personas, but they may not be. Regardless, this is where you will write down the responses you would like to improve upon — the responses that do not represent you at your best. Finally, in the third column, write down how you would like to respond differently from the way you usually do. Script it out. What will you say? How will you act? If you aren't sure, reflect on the virtues you are lacking that, if present, would help you be more effective in this situation.

Notice I did not say, "What virtues would make you nicer?" People tend to think that the virtuous response is the "nice" response. This is not the case at all. The word *virtue* comes from the Latin for "strength" or "manliness." Virtue isn't the ability to be "nice" at all costs. It is the ability to be strong, effective, and competent and keep your head about you under pressure. Yes, sometimes that might require you to be more patient, understanding, or sensitive. But it could just as easily require you to be courageous, strong, assertive, and forceful. So again, if you are stuck for what to do as an alternative to your usual response, ask yourself, "What are the virtues that would help me be more effective, but are missing from my usual response?" Then ask yourself what those virtues would ask you to do in this situation. If you aren't sure, prayerfully reflect on times in your life when you have exhibited those virtues under pressure. How did you act then? Adapt those responses to fit this new challenge.

Bringing the question of virtue into play is a powerful reminder that God wants to use every aspect of your life to refine you and make you into your best self. Sometimes we forget, when we are upset with our spouse, that marital conflict is as much about our need to grow and change as it is our spouse's. You may feel that your spouse is the biggest idiot who ever had the misfortune of drawing breath, but that doesn't change the fact that God wants to use every situation in your life — including, no, *especially* the challenges you face in your marriage — to enable you to become the saint you were meant to be. Not in that self-righteous, "God is making me a saint by making me put up with *you*" sense, either. But in a genuine sense like this: "I realize that I am far from perfect and that, as a Christian, I am grateful for the opportunity God is giving me to grow in my marriage, despite the difficulty and frustration of the process of perfection in grace." I realize this will sound horrifically pious to some readers, but I promise that if you can wrap your head and your heart around this idea, it will make the difficulties in your marriage so much easier to bear. Your marriage will seem much less like something you have to endure because you had the misfortune of marrying a moron and more like the process by which two sincere but broken people are being given the chance to grow, sometimes because of each other, sometimes in spite of each other, but always in light of each other.

In addition to being aware of the opportunities to grow in virtue that your marriage offers you, don't forget to be realistic in the way you approach this Three-Column Spike Exercise. Inevitably, in response to the question, "In the future, how would you like to respond differently to X?" my clients often say, "I shouldn't get so upset about it." That isn't an answer. You should assume that you will get as upset as you always do. The degree to which you become upset is, at least for now, your automatic reaction, and while reactions can change with time, you can't prevent yourself from feeling this way at the outset. Assume that you will be as upset as you usually are, but ask yourself, "Even though I will probably be as upset as ever the next time this happens, what will I do to behave more gracefully? What could I say or do that would not have me pretending that I wasn't upset, but still allow me to be respectful and effective?"

Often just answering this question generates a wealth of ideas. Even so, if you're stuck, contact a professional for additional support. It is simply too important not to. Why? Because if you don't develop self-regulation, you will never be able to make any changes in your relationship at all. You will never be able to use any of the advice or techniques you learn from any source, and you will be doomed to repeat the same responses over and over again, no matter what you do. Again, why? Because all new information, tips, techniques, and ideas are stored in your cortex, and what part of the brain is inaccessible when you slip into your Misery-Making Mindset? You guessed it. Your cortex. Without self-regulation, the very techniques you learn to improve your marriage when you are calm become frustratingly unavailable to you when you are in the middle of a stressful marital situation and you need them most! You will be able to remember them. You will be able to criticize yourself for not using them. But you will not be able to employ them, no matter what you do. Self-regulation is the skill that makes mindfulness possible. Mindfulness is the ability to keep your cortex turned on while you are under stress so that you can choose the best course of action, despite the emotional storm raging inside of you.

One final word on this Three-Column Spike Exercise before we move on: Don't cheat. Actually write this exercise down. Clients who attempt to do this in their heads are inevitably in therapy at least twice as long as those who write it out. This is because the act of writing engages your whole brain, while "doing it in your head" limits the activity to your right brain. Writing out therapy exercises in general, and this one in particular, will be essential to your efficient progress. Believe me, I know that the majority of you will nod as you read this and then try to do it in your head anyway. Fine. But four weeks from now, when you are frustrated that "none of the things Popcak said in that stupid book are working," I want you to remember this paragraph, go back to the exercise, and do it properly. I predict that you will be suddenly amazed to see things coming together in ways that they couldn't when you were doing it in your head.

Step 4: Be Prepared!

Okay. You now have a list of the common frustrations, marital and otherwise, that cause your temperature to spike, your usual responses, and the responses you would like to make despite what your feelings tell you to do. Now what? Well, there are many strategies for getting more conscious control of the tendency to spike, but the tip many of my clients seem to find useful is "Be prepared."

No, I'm not suggesting you join the Boy Scouts. What I mean to say is that too many times, our stress temperatures spike because we allow ourselves to be consistently surprised by the same thing happening over and over again. "Sure, my husband forgot to pick up his socks yesterday, and the day before that, and the day before that, and, now that I think of it, the day before that. But it *never occurred to me* that he would forget to pick up his socks *today* of all days! Who'daTHUNKit?!" Seriously. We all do this. But that doesn't make it smart.

More often than not, it is the surprise that makes offenses so offensive. Someone randomly jumping out at me and yelling, "Boo!" will get a reaction from me. By contrast, someone jumping out and yelling, "Boo!" at me immediately after I told him to do it won't. I am not suggesting that you tell your spouse to be offensive. I simply mean that we tend not to be shocked or appalled by whatever we are prepared for. Ergo, be prepared. Your best bet is to assume that the way your spouse behaved yesterday, and the day before that, and the day before that, is probably about the same way he or she is going to behave today.

That might sound depressing on the face of it, but it is actually incredibly empowering, because if you know what's going to happen before it happens, you can prepare for it and even take charge of the direction of it. How often have you fantasized about being able to predict the future? How many movies have been produced about how wonderful it would be to have special knowledge that prevented some future calamity from taking place? Well, here is a real-life opportunity to do just that.

Every morning, take out the Three-Column Spike Exercise. Review it. Take a moment to imagine the day ahead. Imagine that many of the things that are on that list of frustrations will probably happen today. Imagine when those things would most likely happen. Imagine feeling those strong emotions bubbling up inside, but this time, imagine doing something different. Despite that same old situation bringing up the same old angry feelings, see how you will respond differently. Watch yourself do the things you've written in the third column of your exercise. See yourself handling this situation with grace. Imagine how you will feel about yourself to have done something different, something more effective, something virtuous.

Now bring this vision to God.

Lord, I give you this day, and I ask you to give me the grace to respond to both its blessings and its challenges as you would have me do. I know I can accomplish all things if you are my strength. Be my strength, Lord. Let me be a man/woman after your own heart. Help the changes I am making heal my heart and the heart of my marriage, and help me to persevere even if things get worse before they get better, but help them get better soon through your grace.

Which brings us to the final step.

Step 5: Persevere.

Often a client will tell me, "It won't matter if I do something different because my spouse won't change." Or, "I know the right thing to do, but I can't do it because my spouse will get angry or it will just make things worse."

I want you to take to heart what I am about to tell you. Although I want your marriage to be saved, your first job is not to save your marriage. Although I hope that one day your spouse will be pleased with you, your first job is not to please your spouse. Although I want you to have a peaceful marriage, your first job is not to avoid conflict. Your first job is always and everywhere to do God's will and not count the cost. Period. End of story.

If you prayerfully discern that a particular response to a specific frustration is the truly godly response — especially if you discern this in consultation with a mature, faithful spiritual director or counselor — then that is what you must do, regardless of how you imagine your spouse will respond or whether you think it will make your marriage better or not. Let me give you an example. If your spouse asked you to do something immoral and you refused and your spouse got angry or even threatened to leave you, would you be wrong to continue to refuse to do that thing? Of course not. Why? Because your duty to God is greater.

The same principle applies for lesser marital dilemmas. You must never act in a way that is contrary to your spouse's good. And you must never intentionally do anything to offend your spouse's dignity or jeopardize your marriage. However, if your sincere and prayerful attempts to work for your spouse's good and the good of your marriage result in your spouse's behaving in an unhealthy or ungodly manner, that is not your fault. If this happens, you should, by all means, take your spouse's response back to prayer and consultation with a faithful, mature spiritual adviser, but bearing this in mind, it should not make you feel that you've done the wrong thing. We must do what we believe is the godly thing, regardless of the response we get and the effect it has. While we must never intend to threaten the integrity of our marriage, we must be willing to accept that sometimes, doing the godly thing may cause our spouse to threaten it.

This can be hard to understand. We tend to think something is "working" if it makes our spouse happy and decreases conflict. But sometimes doing the godly thing will have the opposite effect. Never mind. If we want God to heal our hearts and our marriage, we still must do what we prayerfully and with consultation believe is the godly thing to do, even if that angers or inadvertently alienates our spouse.

Jesus says, "He who loves his life loses it" (John 12:25). Life is the greatest gift. And yet, if we love our life more than we love God, we will lose it. In the same way, if we love the idea of marriage more than we love God's call to behave in a godly manner within our marriage, no matter what the cost, we will lose our marriage as the accommodations we make destroy our heart, our spouse's heart, and the heart of the marriage.

When you ask yourself, "What should I do differently when X offense occurs?" The answer is not necessarily, "Whatever will make my spouse stop stomping around and being mad at me." The answer is, "Whatever I prayerfully (and with consultation) believe God would have me do. Whatever is the most virtuous and right response I can imagine." If we do this, we will become more effective instruments of God's grace, and even if the initial signs suggest that our choices are making things worse, we must persevere.

That said, if your actions are making things subjectively worse, then it is time to work with a faithful, marriage-friendly counseling professional to make sure that you are getting your math right. Just as it is easy to fool yourself into not doing God's will out of fear of getting a negative response from your spouse, it is far too easy to convince yourself that you are doing God's will despite actively engaging in behavior that is offensive to either your spouse's dignity or your marriage itself. If you find that your best efforts to respond to your spouse in a godly, virtuous way are causing your spouse to become angrier, or to threaten divorce, it is time to seek professional, marriage-friendly therapy for the relationship or at least for yourself, if your spouse refuses to join you.

Too often, when we don't immediately get the reaction we hoped for out of our spouse, we suspend our attempts to do the right thing. This is nothing less than playing into Satan's hands. We can never stop trying to do the right thing, the virtuous thing, the godly thing.

Ideally, your efforts will inspire your spouse to do the same. If they don't, that may not mean you've got it wrong. It may only mean that your spouse is inclined to resist your efforts to have a more godly marriage. If that's the case, you can't exactly agree to conspire with your spouse to have an *un*godly marriage, can you? You can only seek consultation to make certain that your understanding of what is godly and virtuous in your circumstances is, in fact, godly and virtuous, but either way, you must persevere in your efforts to make yourself and your marriage more godly and virtuous, even if that risks your spouse's displeasure.

Wrapping Up

Committing to the process of the Three-Column Spike Exercise and the other suggestions in this chapter will help you develop your capacity for self-regulation, which will enable you to be intentional about your responses to difficult situations, to learn from your mistakes, and to use even the worst experiences in your marriage as opportunities to grow in virtue. It will give you clarity of the best and most godly path to walk even in the face of resistance, conflict, and internal emotional storms. It will allow you to remember and employ new techniques and avoid old patterns of destructive behavior that undermine your progress and your dignity as a person.

The capacity for self-regulation is a fundamental skill. If you don't have it, it is impossible ever to be happy in any relationship. Doing the work to develop good self-regulation will enable you to feel powerful, confident, and effective, even when your spouse and your marriage seem to be falling apart around you. It will allow you to respond to even the most difficult circumstances with grace and enable you to chart a path toward marital healing and personal holiness, even when your spouse isn't exactly on board with the project. It is a powerful, powerful skill and well worth the time it takes to master it.

Pray

Lord Jesus Christ, I give you my will. I give you my pride. I give you my passions and emotions. Take them all and transform me according to your will. Grant me the serenity that comes from mastering myself, so that I can always choose the godly path in my marriage. Give me a peaceful heart and a courageous spirit, so that even when the storms that cause my marital tension rage around me and within me, I can feel safe in your arms, confident in your plan for my life, and resolved to do your will, no matter what the cost. Jesus, I trust in you. Help my lack of trust. Amen.

Discuss

• What was your experience of conflict in your family of origin? How did your family's approach to conflict affect your capacity for self-regulation?

• When you fail to regulate yourself, do you tend to shut down and become quiet and withdrawn? Do you tantrum? Or do you tend to self-righteously lecture others about their wrongdoing? Who exhibited this response in your family of origin?

• What do you think is your baseline stress temperature? List three things you could do to help bring it down throughout the day.

• What are the top three irritating things that happen between you and your spouse that cause your stress temperature to spike? How will you respond differently in the future?

• Do you think you are more likely to fail to persevere in doing what you know to be right out of fear of your spouse's reaction, or do you think you are more likely to convince yourself mistakenly that you are doing the right thing out of misplaced confidence in your discernment? What steps will you take to correct for these tendencies? To whom can you turn to keep you accountable?

Chapter 7

A Positive Intention Frame

"One of the things I like about the way we handle problems is that we work hard to give each other the benefit of the doubt," says Jennifer of her relationship with Tommy. "It's almost impossible not to step on each other's toes in marriage, even when you don't mean to. I really appreciate that Tommy tries to assume the best about me even when I'm not at my best. I try to do the same for him."

"We're far from perfect at it, but we certainly try," says Tommy. "Even on those days when we're not getting along or I don't feel the connection between us, I try to remind myself that it doesn't make sense that she would go out of her way to be hurtful or offensive. I mean, what would she have to gain by intentionally trying to alienate me? It's the same for me. We tick each other off all the time, and sometimes it can seem like it's even on purpose, but it never is. If we can give each other the benefit of the doubt and try to assume a positive intention from each other even in the absence of evidence to the contrary, we do a lot better than if we react to every little slight."

Tommy and Jennifer are a smart couple. It is so easy to assume that your spouse is out to get you, especially when the rapport between you and your mate is at an all-time low—and sometimes, even when it's not. We're all afraid of being taken advantage of, and the more we experience this fear — either because of our backgrounds or because of the way we perceive having been treated in the marriage — the more likely it is that we will assume a negative intention on the part of our spouse and feel justified in doing so.

That said, research shows that happy couples do not do this. You may say that this is because in happy marriages, one spouse genuinely does not intend to offend the other, and while this is true, the same research shows that couples in unhappy marriages do not intend to offend each other either. No one benefits by intentionally setting out to hurt his or her mate. As I point out in my book *For Better ... FOREVER!*, it makes no sense to go out of your way to offend your mate because, well, your spouse knows where you sleep — so to speak. Anything you do to irritate your spouse will inevitably come back to haunt you, and you know it. By this simple logic, it is obvious that if your spouse offends you, there is something going on besides the desire to be offensive.

Positive Intention Frame is the term relationship experts use to describe the skill happy couples practice whereby they intentionally and willfully choose to assume that their partners are not trying to hurt them, even when it seems as if they are. It refers to whether your natural tendency is to "frame" another person's behavior in more of a positive or negative way. Having a Positive Intention Frame is not the same as making excuses for bad behavior or letting one's mate off the hook for inappropriate actions. Happy couples do not justify and excuse each other's offenses. They address them directly. But they do so in a way that assumes the best about their partner; attributes these offenses to either misunderstanding or miscommunication; and allows their spouse to save face.

A Positive Intention Frame

Chances are, if you are reading this chapter, it is because you received a low score on the Positive Intention Frame Quiz in chapter 3. Take a moment to review the statements you were asked to consider on pages 65 and 66.

What the Absence of a
Positive Intention Frame Does to Marriage

More than any other habit, the absence of a Positive Intention Frame is the catalyst for the collapse of marital communication. Marriage researchers have identified four stages of marital communication collapse: *criticism, defensiveness, contempt,* and *stonewalling* (Gottman, 1995). It is true that every couple engages in some degree of each of these behaviors, but there is a difference, for instance, between being defensive with your spouse once in a while on a bad day and being defensive as a matter of habit. When one of these qualities tends to define almost all your interactions, especially during disagreements, you can be said to be in that particular stage. Let's briefly look at each.

Criticism is the stage when couples talk about their problems as if they were the result of flaws in their mate's character. Criticisms are different from marital complaints in that marital complaints are actually healthy and more neutrally stated. For instance, imagine that at a dinner out with friends, one spouse thoughtlessly said something that embarrassed the other. If, later, in a private moment, the offended spouse said, "You really hurt my feelings at dinner," that would be a complaint. By contrast, if the offended spouse said, "You can be such a thoughtless jerk sometimes," that would be a criticism. Do you see the difference? Both address the offense, but *complaints* address the offense by stating it in a way that allows for clarification, discussion, and hopefully, resolution of the issue. Criticism begins with one spouse trying and convicting the other in marital kangaroo court and goes downhill from there. While all spouses criticize each other from time to time, a couple has entered the Criticism Stage of marital collapse when most of their communications, especially conversations about their concerns, are characterized by this trait.

Defensiveness is the tendency to shift blame or responsibility in response to a spouse's unjust criticism. "Don't blame me"; "Well, what about you?"; "That's not my fault"; and "I *would* have done that if you hadn't" are all common examples of defensive statements. As I just mentioned, all spouses are defensive with their mate once in a while, but couples who are in the Defensiveness Stage of marital collapse respond defensively to even innocuous exchanges. For instance, imagine that you misplaced your keys and you muttered quite innocently, "Where the heck did my keys go?" Imagine further, that your spouse, from the other room, piped up to say, "Don't blame me. I didn't take them!" It wasn't your intention to accuse your spouse. You weren't even speaking to him or her. But there have been so many accusatory conversations in the past that your spouse is now primed to respond to almost every comment you make as if you were personally attacking him or her. If situations like this happen once in a while, you're probably fine. But if this exchange characterizes the normal interactions between you and your spouse more often than not, you are probably in the Defensiveness Stage of marital collapse.

Couples end up in the Defensiveness Stage when they have gotten so used to criticizing each other (as per the Criticism Stage above) that they just reactively assume that their spouse is attacking them, even if he or she is not. Incidentally, some spouses who grew up in families in which criticism and defensiveness were the norm can be naturally defensive, but this would be present from the early stages of the relationship. Most couples get here honestly through their own hard work to alienate one another.

The *Contempt Stage* is what happens when defensiveness becomes expected and pervasive. A couple is in the Contempt Stage when they *habitually* dig at each other, at first, in the middle of their disagreements and later, any time. Name-calling, attacking each other's soft spots (e.g., negatively referring to each other's weight, family of origin, or past failings in the middle of conversations), diagnosing (e.g., "Why do you have to be so obsessive-compulsive?"), cruel comments disguised as "humor" ("What? I was just kidding!"), and contemptuously correcting each other's grammar or facts in the middle of an argument are a few examples of common expressions of contempt. Remember, every couple has bad moments when they forget themselves and let the odd contemptuous comment slip. But when a couple habitually criticizes, digs, or picks at each other, they can be said to be in the Contempt Stage of marital collapse. After living in a perpetual state of defensiveness, a couple is driven to contempt by the need to say, "You think you're better than me, that you never do anything wrong, and that everything's my fault all the time. Well, let me show you that you're not all you think you are!" Although the behavior is negative and offensive, the intention behind contempt is actually quite positive. It is a flawed and deeply disordered attempt to say, "Both of us are responsible for the mess we're in, not just me, you know." Unfortunately, this invitation to share the burden of healing the marriage comes out more like this: "I think you're an idiot and an ass." So it can be—*ahem*—difficult to read the intended positive subtext in the heat of the moment.

Finally, *stonewalling* is the stage where at least one spouse (at first) and sometimes both (later on) decide, "We know how this conversation is going to end, so why start it in the first place?" Direct questions are met with stony silence, a change of subject, or even with the other spouse leaving the room. Couples at this stage look outwardly peaceful. They aren't fighting, after all, but they are in a perpetual state of cold war. Research suggests that without professional assistance, the vast majority of these couples will divorce within five years (Gottman, 1995).

What a Positive Intention Frame Will Do for Your Marriage

The skill that prevents this slow grinding down of the marriage is the couple's ability to adopt a Positive Intention Frame, which is the assumption that marital offenses are the results of miscommunication, misunderstanding, or simple ignorance of a better way to meet a need, *not* the maliciousness of one's partner.

The more a husband and wife—or even one or the other—practices viewing offenses through a Positive Intention Frame, the more easily they remain in their Solution-Focused Brain and can productively address the problems they are experiencing. Recall that the first stage of marital communication collapse was represented by the tendency to criticize instead of complain. Remember that while criticisms are ineffective ways to raise a problem because they make problems personal, complaints are actually healthy because they help the couple focus more objectively on a problem that they need to overcome together. Spouses who use a Positive Intention Frame are good at making complaints rather than criticisms. Because of this, they tend to get a more positive response from their spouse when they bring up issues and are more likely to resolve those challenges.

A Positive Intention Frame

Ultimately the ability to use a Positive Intention Frame is an insurance policy against the marriage's falling prey to the four stages of marital collapse, which represent the most common process by which most marriages fall apart.

Readers for whom faith is an important part of life might appreciate knowing that while developing a Positive Intention Frame is a psychological concept rooted in empirical data, there is a spiritual corollary to this concept that Christians refer to as the art of charitable interpretation—a way of applying the spiritual work of mercy "to bear wrongs patiently." It should not come as a surprise that marriage is full of opportunities for spiritual growth. While many couples never begin to scratch the surface of the spiritually transformative power of marriage, that shouldn't stop you. Practicing the art of charitable interpretation, or using a Positive Intention Frame, is a great way to learn how to be both kind and effective as a problem solver. This is a skill that will make your spouse happy to sit down and work through issues with you, which would, I'm guessing, be both a novel and rewarding experience for you.

How to Develop a Positive Intention Frame

As I mentioned earlier, practicing the art of charitable interpretation or using a Positive Intention Frame does not mean letting the offender off the hook or explaining away offenses (although this is a common misunderstanding that leads to a lot of poor decisions by well-meaning, faithful people). Rather, this practice asks you willfully to assume that the things your partner does to offend you are the result of miscommunication, misunderstanding, or simple ignorance about a better way to meet a need or positive intention. It is founded on the principle that everything that people do is, to their mind at least, an attempt to meet some need or fulfill some positive intention. If we can approach people as if this is true—even when it feels as if it isn't—they will be much more willing to work with us to create change together.

The largest objection I encounter to using a Positive Intention Frame is the sincere belief that one's spouse genuinely intends to be hurtful. It is especially difficult to believe that there is really a positive intention behind one's spouse's behavior when that behavior is hostile or belligerent. I should also say that even though, strictly speaking, there is a "positive intention" behind even physically abusive behavior, it is beyond any spouse's ability to work through this with a mate. In the event that your spouse is abusive, your first course of action must not be to try to analyze or justify your mate's behavior; rather, you must get yourself to safety and seek professional help.

That said, assuming we are not talking about physical abuse, just about every other kind of behavior can be successfully dealt with via charitable interpretation/positive intention framing. While this can be hard to accept, I'd like you to reflect on those times when someone told you that you seriously hurt him or her. On at least most occasions, were these offenses the results of some specific intention to go out of your way to hurt this person, or were they the results of some kind of misunderstanding? Some people will tell me that they did, indeed, set out to hurt someone for having hurt them, but even in these instances, was the intention actually to hurt the other person, or was it a horribly flawed attempt to right a wrong, address an injustice, or get the other person to see how much pain he was causing by his actions after many other less offensive attempts to address these problems failed? It is very rare for anyone's true intention to be offensive. We are offensive, often, but if you look closely at those offenses, they are almost always the result of either misunderstanding, miscommunication, or simple ignorance about a better way to meet a need or right a wrong.

If you still struggle to accept this, you may be dealing with the cognitive distortion known as *labeling* (Burns, 2008). A cognitive distortion is a kind of false thinking pattern that research has shown tends to lead to poor emotional, relational, and mental health. Spiritually speaking, this is akin to what St. Ignatius of Loyola would call a *desolation*; that is, a thought, or movement of the spirit that attempts to pull us away from God or the ways God would have us think or act.

There are about a dozen cognitive distortions, and each one is associated with a problem, such as depression or anxiety or poor impulse control or relational dissatisfaction. The more you tend to allow real problems to make you even more miserable than you have a right to be and prevent you from finding efficient, lasting solutions to those problems, the more your own thinking will tend to reflect these cognitive distortions.

Labeling is the cognitive distortion that lets us off the hook for dealing with people we don't like. Labeling asserts that So-and-so is "that sort of person" (a jerk, a narcissist, a user, a control freak, selfish, thoughtless, etc.) and therefore is unworthy of my time and effort. We may lecture such a person. We may ignore such a person, and we may certainly treat him with contempt and scorn, but heaven forbid we actually deal honestly with that person. In short, labeling makes us self-righteous and judgmental and allows us to feel proud of ourselves for both. Labeling is a kind of modern "Thank heavens I am not like that tax collector!" (cf. Luke 19:9-14) sort of pharisaism that Jesus was fond of calling out. It makes us feel good for looking down our nose at someone else who is obviously so much less enlightened and put together than we are.

In fact, Jesus was consistently hard on those who gave themselves a pass on their own bad behavior but were hard on others. The parable of the unmerciful servant (Matt. 18:21-35) speaks powerfully to the lesson of this chapter.

> Then Peter came up and said to him, "Lord, how often shall my brother sin against me, and I forgive him? As many as seven times?" Jesus said to him, "I do not say to you seven times, but seventy times seven.
>
> "Therefore the kingdom of heaven may be compared to a king who wished to settle accounts with his servants. When he began the reckoning, one was brought to him who owed him ten thousand talents; and as he could not pay, his lord ordered him to be sold, with his wife and children and all that he had, and payment to be made. So the servant fell on his knees, imploring him, 'Lord, have patience with me, and I will pay you everything.' And out of pity for him the lord of that servant released him and forgave him the debt. But that same servant, as he went out, came upon one of his fellow servants who owed him a hundred denarii; and seizing him by the throat he said, 'Pay what you owe.' So his fellow servant fell down and besought him, 'Have patience with me, and I will pay you.' He refused and went and put him in prison till he should pay the debt. When his fellow servants saw what had taken place, they were greatly distressed, and they went and reported to their lord all that had taken place. Then his lord summoned him and said to him, 'You wicked servant! I forgave you all that debt because you besought me; and should not you have had mercy on your fellow servant, as I had mercy on you?' And in

anger his lord delivered him to the jailers, till he should pay all his debt. So also my heavenly Father will do to every one of you, if you do not forgive your brother from your heart."

Charitable interpretation/positive intention framing is an extension of the generous, forgiving heart of which this parable speaks. I've said again and again in this chapter that charitably interpreting your spouse's words and behavior does not mean letting him or her off the hook. It just means refusing to respond unkindly to your spouse's perceived unkindness. St. Augustine said that forgiveness was merely our willingness to surrender our desire to hurt someone for having hurt us. It doesn't mean that all is well or all is forgotten. Even once you have extended forgiveness, the work of reconciling—the (usually) two-person effort of healing the hurt—may still be in front of you. Practicing the forgiveness that is behind making charitable interpretations of your spouse's behavior does not mean setting yourself up to be hurt again. It means being mature enough to address your spouse's offenses without your justifying being offensive, self-righteous, petty, and nasty in return.

If you are having difficulty accepting that your spouse is the sort of person who could possibly have a positive intention behind his or her offensive behavior, you will need to speak with a counselor to learn strategies for overcoming this tendency within yourself. You may also use the strategies identified in this chapter, but unless you can get control of the tendency to label your spouse, you may not be able to use them consistently, because it is much easier simply to wash your hands of your spouse and his or her behavior than it will be to take responsibility for being a catalyst for change.

Assuming you can accept that there is at least a chance that the things your spouse does to drive you crazy are actually rooted in miscommunication, misunderstanding, or simple ignorance about a better way to address a need, the following suggestions will help. First, we'll look at a strategy to help you develop a Positive Intention Frame for those offenses caused by misunderstandings or miscommunication. Then we'll look at ways to develop a Positive Intention Frame for offenses caused by simple ignorance or confusion about the best way to meet a need.

Positive Intention Framing and Misunderstandings

As a matter of habit, to develop your ability to use charitable interpretation, you will need to practice telling yourself that any time it feels as if your spouse is intentionally trying to offend you, hurt you, or upset you, you are incorrect in that assumption — that, in fact, the offensive behavior is not caused by malicious intent but most likely by miscommunication or misunderstanding. Instead of attacking your spouse or defending yourself, as you will most likely want to do (and will do unless you remind yourself about the truth of the intention behind the offense), you will need to use the Clarification Exercise on page 287.

An additional benefit to using a Positive Intention Frame is that it makes it safe for you and your spouse to make mistakes in each other's presence. When a couple who do not know the art of charitable interpretation come to counseling, it can be a nightmare because they are practically obliged to get everything I teach them perfectly correctly the very first time *or else*. If couples don't know how to use positive intention framing, they tend to react to every little mistake the other makes: "You *promised* you would do it differently next time! You didn't listen to *anything* Dr. Popcak said!" It's impossible to create change in such a high-pressure environment.

In order to learn, you need to be able to learn from mistakes. If you can't make mistakes without having your head handed to you because you are *obviously* not trying hard enough to be practically perfect in every way *every single time*, it can be hard to learn to make a marriage work. While practicing the art of charitable interpretation does not require making excuses for bad behavior, it allows enough room for error so couples can find their way to healthier responses that don't feel forced or canned.

The process is similar for managing times when your spouse behaves offensively and you are trying to assume a positive intention. As above, you will begin by pausing and taking a breath. Give your brain the split second it needs to overcome its initial desire to fight, flee, or freeze.

Next, ask your spouse, "How were you hoping I would respond when you did that?"

This is a terrifically disarming question. Most likely you will see your spouse stop short, blink a couple of times, and look at you a little funny before either telling you what his or her intention was or saying, "I don't know."

If your spouse tells you the response he or she was hoping to get by acting "that way," you have now discovered the intention behind the action. At this point, you will need to suggest other ways your spouse can meet that intention or need. Namely, what could your mate do that would be more likely to generate the response he or she was looking for? Ask your spouse to please do that in the future. Be polite but firm.

If, on the other hand, your spouse says, "I don't know" in response to your question, press a little bit harder. Again, be polite but firm. "Well, you must have been hoping I would respond somehow to that. What would you imagine as my ideal response to that?" At this point, your spouse will either be able to tell you what the intention was or come face-to-face with the fact that he or she has been behaving poorly—sometimes both. If your spouse tells you the intention behind the behavior, follow the directions above. Alternatively, if your mate just shuts down and either refuses to say anything or mutters something unintelligible, simply say, "Well, look, I don't know how to respond to that, so when you figure out what you were trying to get me to do, please tell me. I would really like to know." Then drop it.

This technique is very powerful because it challenges your spouse's actions without your having to say a single cross word. Likewise, once you do get down to the intention behind your spouse's behavior, you will be able to identify more respectful ways he or she could get that response from you in the future.

If it happens again, use the same strategy, but also remind your spouse that the last time he or she behaved that way, you both decided that he or she would approach you differently. Don't lecture. Be as calm and matter of fact as possible. Your mate will either be forced to apologize for the lapse in memory or at least try again, and you will have reinforced that there are just some behaviors you can't respond to. As a bonus, your spouse doesn't have to be a willing participant for this to work. Asking this question forces your mate into a more Solution-Focused Brain by making him or her think about the desired outcome of his or her behavior and the likelihood that that specific behavior will generate that outcome. Once your spouse is back in a more logical mindset, it will become much easier to solve problems.

Assuming a positive intention behind your spouse's words and actions—especially hostile words and actions—is never easy, but the practice has the advantage both of bearing terrific spiritual fruit for you and creating real change in your marriage. Even so, if you find these techniques too difficult for you to follow through on or if they are not working for you, please know that there are many other ways to make this work; there just isn't enough space to discuss them in this book. Whether you ultimately find these specific ideas useful or not, the most important thing to realize is that there is a healthier option available to you besides blowing up or shutting down when your spouse says offensive things or behaves offensively.

In addition to empowering you to heal your marriage, developing your capacity for using Positive Intention Frames will help you become a kinder and more compassionate person in general. It will enable you to see others, even difficult people, as human beings who, just like you, are broken but struggling to do their best through the pain and challenges of everyday life. Developing this skill will help you experience greater peace and confidence in your life and marriage because it will enable you not to fear conflict, having developed the power to see—and work to fulfill—the humanity and good intentions hidden behind others' offensive behaviors.

Pray

Lord Jesus Christ, give me a heart of compassion. Help me to see my spouse as you see him or her, through eyes of charity. Give me the wisdom to see the good intentions behind my mate's frustrating, irritating, and hurtful actions, as well as the strength to set charitable boundaries and limits with those actions so that the weakest parts of our marriage might soon become the strongest. I know that I can accomplish all things if you are my strength. Help me, then, to accomplish the impossible and see the good in my spouse in spite of myself. I give my judgmentalism and bitterness to you, Lord. Make me anew. Amen.

Discuss

• Think of a time someone was mistakenly convinced that you hurt him intentionally. What were the true intentions behind your actions?

• Imagine that you were able to see the positive intentions behind your spouse's behavior, be more compassionate toward your mate, and use the goodwill you cultivated to change those irritating behaviors. How would you begin to treat your spouse differently? How would this change your attitude toward your spouse?

• How do you think you would benefit personally by learning how to use charitable interpretation/positive intention framing in all of your relationships, including your marriage?

• Think of a time someone else was more forgiving of you than you deserved. What happened? How did it feel to be the recipient of such generosity? What would it be like to be able to extend this gift to your spouse?

Chapter 8

Caretaking in Conflict

I say to you, "Love your enemies and
pray for those who persecute you."
—Matthew 5:44

I mentioned earlier that the most important thing about problem solving isn't actually solving the problem. It's taking care of your partner so that you can solve the problem in the first place and become closer together for having solved it in the second place.

A couple's ability to be Caretaking in Conflict is what drives the sense that one's spouse is actually a partner in problem solving as opposed to an obstacle to be overcome. Caretaking in Conflict represents the degree to which you and your spouse know how to nurture each other through the tension and toward mutually satisfying and lasting solutions. Despite how it may sound, becoming good caretakers of each other in conflict doesn't mean that you don't argue or have passionate discussions. It doesn't mean that you are always perfectly polite. It doesn't mean that you never say a cross word to each other, that you are living saints, or that you float on a cloud of Zen-like peace and enlightenment. Likewise, taking care of each other during conflict doesn't mean trying to keep a lid on challenging topics or tiptoeing around each other for fear of setting off some emotional bomb. Rather, mastering the ability to be Caretaking in Conflict enables couples to have difficult conversations that feel less like boxing matches and more like a deep-tissue massage, in that it can be a bit uncomfortable to go through it, but the experience leaves you feeling more flexible, energized, and healthy.

If you're reading this chapter, you probably received a lower score on the Caretaking in Conflict Quiz in chapter 3. Take a moment to review the statements you were asked to consider on pages 68 and 69.

What the Absence of Caretaking in Conflict Does to Marriage

There are three basic problems associated with a limited ability to take care of your partner during conflict: rapid escalation of conflict, difficulty in finding lasting solutions, and a culture of suspicion and resentment.

Rapid Escalation of Conflict

Peter and Daniella have been married for eight years. They have been struggling in their marriage for a while. Their biggest complaint is the way their arguments spin out of control so quickly.

"He doesn't listen to anything I say," says Daniella. "He just keeps talking and won't let me get a word in edgewise. It drives me crazy. I might as well be a piece of furniture for all he cares. Eventually I just give up trying to talk because he doesn't want to hear me anyway, but then, when he finally comes up for air, he pushes me for an answer—but only the answer he wants to hear—and then I blow up because I can't take it anymore."

"That's such a crock," replies Peter. "She doesn't even try to listen to me. I can tell from the look on her face the moment I open my mouth that she doesn't agree and isn't open to what I have to say. What she calls not listening is really me just trying to give her more information so she actually can hear what I'm talking about before she tells me no. Then she freaks out and accuses me of not listening. I don't have to listen any more than I do to know she's going to say no before she even hears me out."

Clearly Peter and Daniella don't feel that they are being especially well cared for during their discussions with one another. Their focus on their own feelings, their own agendas, and their own needs is preventing them from truly listening, attending, and responding supportively to each other. Because neither feels heard or cared for, both slip into their Misery-Making Mindset. Notice that Daniella's first response is to pout and withdraw ("Eventually, I just give up trying to talk ..."), and then, when pushed, she tantrums ("... and then I blow up because I can't take it anymore"). Peter, for his part, sees what he believes is Daniella's negative expression, and he immediately launches into his lecturing Contemptuous Expert Persona ("What she calls not listening is really me just trying to give her more information"). Poor self-regulation (see chapter 6) and a failure to caretake in conflict often go hand in hand and deliver a one-two punch to any possibility of having respectful conversations. Recall the Stress Temperature Scale we discussed in the self-regulation chapter. Peter and Daniella's conversation begins at a 7 (Peter's observation of the disgusted look on Daniella's face is the giveaway; remember, a 7 represents the shutdown of nonverbal filters in the brain and the emergence of nonverbal signs of disgust and irritation). Peter's not feeling cared for immediately pushes him to an 8 (verbal filters starting to fall, as evidenced by a change in tone to blaming and lecturing). Peter's lecture pushes Daniella to an 8, but because her initial stress response is to pout and withdraw, she doesn't vocalize her blaming and lecturing. She starts having an internal conversation, thinking that he isn't interested in listening to her, so why should she bother talking? When Peter pushes her for an answer, she gets to a 9 (verbal filters in brain are completely fallen; yelling and possible name-calling emerge), and the discussion has now completely fallen apart. Neither spouse is to blame, really. The problem is that their mutual lack of Caretaking in Conflict inevitably pushes them both toward failure in a rapid and virtually unstoppable way. If this seems even remotely familiar to you, the skills presented in this chapter will help you get control of this tendency of your arguments to escalate toward disaster.

Difficulty Finding Lasting Solutions

Jerilyn is fed up with what she considers to be PJ's "constant betrayals."

> "I can't trust him. We'll have a discussion, get it all out there, come to some mutual decision, and then he just does whatever he wants to do! It hurts me to the core that he never follows through on our agreements."
>
> PJ responds, "I guess I know where she's coming from, but her version of 'getting it all out there' is beating a conversation to death. I tell her what I think, but she usually doesn't like what I have to say, so she tries to refute everything. It's exhausting, so I just tell her what she wants to hear. What kills me is she knows that's

exactly what I'm doing, but she cares so little to learn what I really think about things that she pretends that I've actually agreed to something. Then she gets to act all put out and self-righteous when I don't live up to our 'agreement.'"

PJ and Jerilyn's failure to take care of each other during conflict leads to false or flimsy agreements that aren't really meant to solve the problem so much as escape a difficult conversation. In this example, Jerilyn is unaware of her tendency to fall into the Contemptuous Expert Persona, and PJ is unaware of his tendency to pout and withdraw. With both of their Misery-Making Mindsets activated, they make quick work of destroying any chance at a lasting solution, as Jerilyn, too exhausted by the drama to care enough for PJ to press for a real solution and a real commitment, settles for verbally painting PJ into a corner. For his part, PJ escalates and fails to caretake by essentially lying to Jerilyn so he can get out of dealing with her concerns. Both PJ and Jerilyn become so focused on their own feelings and agendas that they don't even consider taking care of each other. Because of this, their partnership suffers and the "agreements" they come to end up being one-sided, underdeveloped, and doomed to fail.

A Culture of Suspicion and Resentment

Jorge and Melinda came to counseling complaining about a lack of respect.

"Jorge does whatever he wants," Melinda complained. "He doesn't talk to me about anything. I had to find out from my friends that he bought a new truck. Can you believe it? He was keeping it at the office so I wouldn't find out.

He thinks I'm an idiot. I got a call from my friend, saying that she liked our new vehicle. I'm like, 'What new vehicle?', and she's like, 'I saw Jorge in a new pickup.' So I said, 'I don't know what you're talking about," and then I drive down to the office, and, sure enough, there's this brand-new bright-red pickup parked in front of the store. I *flipped out.*"

Jorge smiled sheepishly. "It's just easier to ask forgiveness than permission with her. I've tried to tell her that I needed a new truck for months, but she's always saying, 'You don't need a new truck now. We need this. We need that.' Well, sure. We need a lot of things, but I also need a new truck, and if she isn't going to have a reasonable conversation about it, then I'm gonna get myself a truck. I work hard. It's my money. If I need it, I need it. I don't need to get her permission. She's not my mother."

Melinda looked as if she were ready to kill Jorge. "I can't believe I married someone so selfish."

Melinda and Jorge's failure to attempt to work together in general, but especially on this issue, has resulted in a marital culture of suspicion and resentment. Because neither knows how to truly make the other feel as if his or her needs and concerns matter, Jorge sneaks around behind Melinda's back, choosing to think that her need to be included is akin to requiring him to "ask permission" to get his needs met. To be fair, Melinda plays into this characterization by reacting to his ideas and naysaying rather than listening and working with him to make a plan. Together, they create an atmosphere of suspicion and resentment in the marriage that colors, not just conflict, but their entire marriage.

How Developing Caretaking in Conflict
Will Help Your Marriage

Where the lack of this skill manifests itself in the rapid escalation of conflict, the failure to create lasting, workable solutions, and a marital culture of suspicion and resentment, cultivating Caretaking in Conflict benefits marriage in three related ways. First, it enables a couple to keep their stress temperature low even in disagreements. Second, it empowers a couple to hash out real, workable solutions that are designed to reflect the realities of their lives and mutual concerns. Third, it allows a couple always to trust that each will be open to the other's ideas and goals and that their attempts to address concerns about each other's ideas will not make it seem as if they are trying to kill each other's dreams. This allows the couple to have the "sustainable marriage" we discussed in an earlier chapter as they challenge each other to learn new things, encounter new experiences, and grow closer because of their mutual willingness to leave behind their comfort zone for the sake of their spouse.

Caretaking in Conflict is the marital embodiment of Jesus' exhortation in Matthew 5:44 to "love your enemies." It represents the godly husband's and wife's good-faith efforts to grow in virtue by practicing these spiritual works of mercy: to comfort the afflicted, to bear wrongs patiently, and to forgive willingly.

In an earlier chapter, I discussed research that showed that couples who are in solid marriages maintain a positive to negative interaction ratio of 20:1 when they are not in conflict with each other. I explained how maintaining this ratio outside of conflict helps couples to be more resistant to conflict in the first place and do a better job of giving each other the benefit of the doubt when offenses occur. What you also need to know is that similar research demonstrated that couples who are good at managing conflict also maintain a 5:1 ratio of positive to nega-tive interactions when they are in conflict (Gottman, 1993). Usually, when I share this bit of information, the couples I counsel act as if this must be impossible. Don't worry. As you'll soon see, it isn't as hard as it sounds. Couples who know how to take care of each other in conflict are still honest and direct with each other. Sometimes they step on each other's toes and make mistakes and say things they shouldn't. Being a good caretaker in conflict does not mean you have to be a saint. But it does mean that while your agenda is always important and deserves to be heard and responded to, you are committed to demonstrating that you love your spouse even more than you love your agenda. This isn't easy, but with practice, anyone can do it.

How to Develop the Ability to Caretake in Conflict

There are four simple ways you and your spouse can begin to practice taking better care of each other in conflict: *team-building gestures, mini-breaks, prayer,* and *negotiating the "how and when" but not the "what."*

Team-Building Gestures

Happy couples know that they are, and must be, a team. Even good teams are not perfect. Sometimes teammates irritate each other. Sometimes their egos get in the way. Sometimes they accidentally hurt each other on the field, but they always realize that even when these things happen, the teammates are not the problem. Winning the game is the problem. Sometimes they win (or lose) *because* of each other. Sometimes they win (or lose) *in spite* of each other. But they always win or lose together, *as a team*. If they are going to fight anyone, they fight the opposing team, but you will never — even under the worst circumstances — see teammates attack each other on the field.

Too many couples are like a grown-up marital version of the team that starts brawling with each other every time one of them drops the ball. "You did it again!" "You're an idiot!" "You're just like your mother!" These couples forget that messing up is part of the game. Sure, messing up is unfortunate, and hopefully, over time, you'll learn from your mistakes, but even the best teams know that every game is going to involve some successes and some failures. Someone is going to drop the ball, have a foul called on him, get sacked, tagged out, or checked, or ruin the play. What do good teams do when this happens? They encourage each other. "It's okay, man." "You'll get it next time." "Let me give you a hand." "We got this." "Don't sweat it. It's over." "Shake it off." "Next play!"

Married couples have to have the same attitude, and the best couples do. They recognize that the only way they can "win the game" (i.e., solve the problem they are struggling with) is by encouraging each other through the tension and toward the solution. Here are some examples of how you can do this.

• *Complain, don't criticize.* In the chapter on rapport, we discussed the difference between complaints and criticisms. Remember that complaints focus on the problem that has to be solved. They are impersonal. Examples include the following statements:

"I hate being late."

"It really bothers me when you leave socks and underwear all over the floor."

"It really hurts when you forget to do the things you promise to do."

"I get so upset when you criticize me — especially in front of other people."

All of these statements articulate real problems in straightforward, impersonal ways. Criticisms, on the other hand, are personal and antagonistic. All of the following address the same problems as the previous statements, only they are worded as criticisms.

"You're so thoughtless. You couldn't care less if you make us late all the time."

"Why do you have to be such a pig? Stop leaving your crap all around the house for me to pick up like I'm your mother or something."

"I can't trust you as far as I can throw you. Why can't you ever follow through with anything you say you're going to do?"

"If you ever criticize me in public again I'll pack your bags so fast you won't know what happened."

See the difference? Caretaking in Conflict at its minimum respects the fact that dropping the ball is part of the game. You can address problems, even problems caused by your spouse, without making your spouse the problem.

• *Offer simple, supportive comments.* They can make a huge difference in the tension level. Here are a few examples:

"I know this is a tough topic, but thanks for hanging in there with me."

"I can't tell you how much it means that you're willing to talk this through."

"I know it's hard, but I'm glad I can count on you to work through this kind of stuff with me."

"I really love you, y'know."

"Hey, it's going to be okay. We've been through so much already. This is nothing."

"Remember when [some bad thing] happened and we thought we were going to be crushed by the stress? We made it through that. I know we can handle this if we stick together."

"Thanks for being willing to work through this together. I know not everyone would. It means a lot."

"I know we need to talk through this, but it's okay by me if we take a little break if you need to."

"I'm really thirsty. I'm going to get a drink from the kitchen. Can I get you something while I'm in there?"

Even simple nonverbal gestures of support — the occasional knowing smile, that small hug, giving your spouse's hand a supportive squeeze, and other small gestures of supportive affection (as opposed to anything more romantic in nature) — can do so much to make your spouse feel loved and supported. The more supportive you can be along these lines, the more likely it is that you and your spouse can learn to encourage each other through the tension and toward mutually acceptable solutions.

Sometimes, when I share these examples with my clients, they scoff. Inevitably, that's because they think of trying to use these ideas when they're already in an argument that has gotten to an 8 or 9 on the Stress Temperature Scale. These couples are correct in thinking that these ideas would be laughably ineffective at that level of tension. Supportive comments and gestures are used by happy couples at a 5, 6, or 7 to keep discussions at or below a 7 (when nonverbal signs of disgust emerge). Couples who are practiced can also use these strategies when the stress temperature rises to an 8 (the tone of the conversation has become accusatory, lecturing, and blaming but not aggressive). Novices who attempt these strategies at an 8, or any other couple who tries to inject these comments into a conversation at a 9 or 10, will get these supportive comments or gestures thrown back in their faces. People at that level are simply not receptive to loving gestures, since their brains have already convinced them that you are the enemy. Use supportive comments and gestures to keep the temperature low in the first place or to bring it back down if it starts rising.

Mini-Breaks

Mini-breaks are five- to ten-minute interruptions in the conversation that give both husband and wife a chance to step away from each other to accomplish some mundane task and calm down. Like supportive comments and gestures, mini-breaks will not work at a score of 8 or higher on the Stress Temperature Scale for newbies or a 9 or higher for anyone, but they go a long way to keeping the temperature lower in the first place or getting the temperature back down to a manageable level if it is. Please note that the goal of a mini-break is bigger than avoiding the conflict for a minute or two. The real goal is to take the time you need to calm down enough to refocus yourself and the conversation.

Here are examples of ways to introduce a mini-break:

"Listen, I know we need to keep talking, but I need to grab a drink from the kitchen. Can I get you something?"

"I need to use the bathroom. I promise I'll be right back. Don't go anywhere, okay?"

"I feel a little nervous 'cause I don't hear any noise. Let me go check on the kids, and I'll be right back."

Then, when you step out of the room, do two things. First, shift your thoughts and emotions to where you can be sympathetic to your spouse. Regardless of what you think of your emotional state, *you are not actually calm unless you can be sympathetic toward your partner's position (whether or not you agree with it)*. Anything less is just simmering, and if you have not done whatever you have to do to get yourself into a more sympathetic mindset, you will be right back to being irritated and disgusted with your mate the second you rejoin the discussion. What can you appreciate about your spouse's position? What can you appreciate about your spouse? How do you know—on an emotional level (as opposed to a merely intellectual one)—that your spouse loves you? When you can answer these questions, you're halfway ready to return.

Second, ask yourself what you might need to do to refocus the conversation on a possible solution to the problem. Start by asking some version of the question, "Do you have any thoughts about how you'd like to handle situations like this in the future?" The goal is to go back to the conversation in a more sympathetic and solution-focused mindset than when you left. If you can't manage it, then when you return, simply say something like, "Listen, I do think we need to keep talking about this, but I need some time to think and pray about what we've said already. Can we come back to this [insert specific time here]?" Suggesting a specific time (that evening, at breakfast the next morning, etc.) will keep you from looking as if you're trying to get out of the conversation altogether.

A second way breaks can be useful is to give your spouse a *heads-up*. That's when you say to your spouse at one time that you'd like to have a conversation about something at a later time. For instance, imagine approaching your spouse in the morning and saying, "Hey, listen. I don't want to talk about this now, but this evening I'd like to get some time to go over our budget [or other problem]. I know that's a tough conversation for us. Can you just spend some time thinking about how you'd like to handle it? I'd really like to know your thoughts."

This is a great way to stop your spouse from feeling ambushed by a conversation, especially if your spouse isn't great at thinking on his or her feet. This is also a great way to let any initial tension that might appear just at the mention of a hot topic dissipate before you have to discuss it. Finally, because you have not just said that you want to discuss the topic, but also that you specifically want to know what your spouse thinks about it, it is less likely that your mate will respond to you as if he or she has been called to the principal's office.

Mini-breaks are great ways to maintain the marital stress temperature. They are simple and friendly ways for you and your spouse to give each other the time you need to get in and stay in the sympathetic, solution-focused mindset couples need to be in to find real solutions.

Prayer

In chapter 4, I shared a technique called the "Marriage Hack," in which couples imagine a third party who loves them both suggesting ways to resolve disputes between them. This technique had a powerful impact on couples who used it to manage conflict and stabilized their overall experience of satisfaction in the marriage. I also said that Christians don't have to imagine this. There is a third party who loves you both and wants to have a say in your arguments—God! Ask God for help at the beginning, middle, and end of your difficult discussions. Anytime you feel the conversation is starting to go off the rails, pray. But don't just pray yourself. Pray out loud. Invite your partner to pray with you. If your spouse doesn't pray, then ask if you could please just take a minute to give the conversation to God so you can be a better, calmer listener. Here are some examples of brief prayers that you can use before, during, and after difficult conversations.

BEFORE

Lord, we both feel pretty strongly about this issue, and neither of us is very good at talking about it without getting upset. Please help us really to listen and care for one another and look to find your will instead of just fighting for ours. Amen.

Lord, we give this problem to you. Help us figure out the best way to handle it. We don't know what to do, but we trust in you, Lord Jesus. Lead us and guide us. Amen.

Lord, open our hearts to each other and to your will. Help us really listen and care about each other's feelings and thoughts in this discussion, but help us care most about your will. Amen.

DURING

If you feel like a conversation is starting to get heated, say to your mate, "Would you mind taking a minute just to check in with God? I really feel like if we keep this up, we're not going to get anywhere. Could we just ask him for some help?" Then say something like this:

> Lord, this is hard. We're both frustrated and worn out, and we don't know what to do. Help us remember we're in this together. Help us remember to love each other through the worst of it. But most of all, make it obvious—somehow—what you want us to do. Amen.

> Lord, neither of us is really feeling very loved or cared for right now. We don't want to hurt each other. This is so hard. Please show us the way to solve the problem and care better for each other while we do it. Amen.

> Lord, we both want to be done with this problem already, but we need to solve it. Please help. Tell us what you want. And lend us some of the love you have in your heart for each of us because we're both feeling pretty tired and emotionally wrung out. We love you, Lord. Amen.

AFTER

Whether you have solved the problem, or are just taking a break, the following simple prayers are a great way to end discussions.

> Lord, thank you for getting us this far. Help us to follow through on the things we've agreed to do but to be open to your grace as we move forward. Let this conversation and the things we've decided to do about this problem draw us closer together and help us be more in love with each other. Amen.

Lord, we need a break from this conversation, but please use this time to soften our hearts to each other and to your will. Amen.

Lord, we still need more time to work all this out. We're pretty burned out right now. But we trust that you will see us through to a great solution and to a better relationship. Help our lack of trust. Make us a couple after your own heart. Amen.

Lord, thank you for giving us some new ideas for moving forward. Help us to be faithful to our plan, and let us look back on this time as a moment we really worked well together and learned how to love each other better. Amen.

Obviously these are all just suggestions. Feel free to change the language to whatever you are comfortable with or add some traditional prayers or other spiritual exercises that help you focus on God's love for your mate and a desire to be open to his will more than your own. Just keep it short and personal and use the grace you are given to get back to work in a more sympathetic and solution-focused manner.

Negotiating the "How and When" but Not the "What"

This is the most challenging of the suggestions in this chapter, but it is a tremendously powerful technique for you and your spouse, because it will change both your attitude toward each other and the entire dynamic of your arguments.

Most couples' arguments break down because of fear. Couples are afraid they won't be heard, won't get their needs met, won't be taken care of. If you could eliminate that fear, you could have almost any difficult conversation and feel confident that your mate was willing to hear you out, meet your needs, and make sure you felt taken care of! What would that be worth to you? That's what I thought.

Most couples act more like parents than partners toward each other. We end up arguing about whether our spouse should or should not want something or whether he or she can or cannot have or do something. This is not our place. We are each other's partners, not each other's parents.

It is a parent's job to help a child—who cannot discern for himself what is good for him—do what is best. By the time we reach adulthood, we have all the faculties we need to figure out what is good and desirable all by ourselves. What we really need is a partner to help us figure out how to get what we want and when we can best get it. That doesn't mean we always get what we want—even Mick Jagger knows that. It does mean, though, that we ultimately base our decisions on what we get by how difficult it would be to attain (and whether those difficulties make it worthwhile or not) and not upon whether our spouse approves or disapproves.

That doesn't mean your spouse has no say in your decision. Your spouse has quite a lot of say, actually. But your mate's (and your) comments need to be limited to other considerations and needs that must be taken into account on the road to meeting the need or desire you've expressed. In other words, when it comes to discussing your desires and needs with each other in a way that makes you feel cared for, the rule of thumb is: *never* negotiate the "what." Always negotiate the "how and when." That is, it should never be a question that you are willing to support even your spouse's somewhat "out there" hopes, dreams, and needs as long as the two of you can work through the other needs or considerations that have to be taken into account on the road to fulfilling that desire.

For instance, Jim and Elizabeth were arguing because Jim dreamed about owning a boat and Elizabeth thought it was silly to spend that kind of money on something they wouldn't be able to use as often as she felt would be necessary to justify the expense. Jim felt disrespected and parented by Elizabeth, and he responded by pouting like the child Elizabeth felt he was, reinforcing Elizabeth's sense that Jim didn't have the sense God gave him to decide much of anything, much less whether to buy a boat.

Instead of arguing back and forth about the issue, I asked Elizabeth what needs or desires she felt would be jeopardized if Jim decided to get a boat. She explained that she was concerned about the money in the first place. Second, she was worried about the time it would take to maintain a boat. I asked her to explain more about her money concerns. What was it that she wanted to do with the money that she was afraid she wouldn't be able to do if Jim got a boat? She explained that saving for the kids' college was important, and she wasn't sure they were saving enough. I also asked what she was afraid she wouldn't get to do if they spent as much time maintaining the boat as she imagined it would take. She explained that it was really important to her to have time to enjoy the family on the weekends. She liked going with the kids to museums and to parks and on hikes, and she liked having time to play board games and such. She was worried that if they got a boat, all their family time would be taken up cleaning and maintaining the boat or sitting around missing Jim while he did those things. Then I asked two follow-up questions. First, did either of them know how much money they needed to save for college, and second, did they actually know how much time and money it takes to maintain the boat?

After some back-and-forth, they admitted that they didn't have any hard information on either point.

At this point, I suggested reframing the discussion so that it wasn't a conversation about whether Jim could or could not get the boat, but rather, how might it be possible to get a boat and still be able to save enough for college and protect the current family-time rituals they had. I asked Elizabeth if she would be open to at least looking into the boat if, at all times, they were exploring how to do it in a manner that respected both her savings and family-time needs. She agreed that seemed reasonable. Jim was also okay with needing to respect Elizabeth's concerns.

Since neither of them knew how much money they'd actually need to save and how much time it would take to maintain the boat, I suggested they meet with a financial planner to work out a saving plan for their kids' schooling and also either talk to boat owners or visit various boat-owner websites to get a sense of what kind of time boat ownership entailed. Based on the information they got, they could figure out how much money they might have left to put toward saving for a boat—whether they got it now or much later—and they would have an idea whether they had time for a boat now or whether getting a boat at a different point in their marriage and family life might make more sense. They both agreed that this was a sensible approach to the question.

Whether they got the boat or not is beside the point. What I am illustrating here is that there is another way to have these difficult conversations that is actually supportive and caretaking. Instead of arguing about whether Jim should get the boat or not, Elizabeth needed to be clearer about the needs and desires she wanted to make certain were included in any plan moving forward. Instead of pouting because "Mommy said no," Jim needed to man up and ask Elizabeth directly what her specific concerns might be and reassure her that he thought her needs were important enough to prevent him from going after his dreams without respecting those needs.

Taking this approach, the situation could play out in three ways. First, Jim and Elizabeth might be surprised to find that the boat took neither as much time nor as much money as they thought and they could move ahead with getting a boat sooner rather than later. Second, they might discover that they didn't have enough time or money at the moment to make this happen, but they could make a plan for starting to save for the boat and identify a time in the future when having a boat could be a good thing for their family—even if it still wasn't really Elizabeth's favorite activity. Finally, after seeing how little they really did have left over after saving properly for college and or how much time it really took to maintain a boat, Jim himself might decide—honestly and sincerely—that boat ownership was one of those things that is more fun and doable in theory than in reality, and instead of buying a boat, bought a subscription to a boating magazine that allowed him to indulge his fantasy while keeping reality in the forefront of his mind. All of these possibilities would be acceptable because (1) at no time would Elizabeth be anything but supportive of the process; (2) both of their needs and desires were being taken into account in the formulation of any potential plan; (3) Jim would ultimately have the freedom to decide how much time and financial sacrifice a boat was really worth to him and decide on whether to pursue this dream based on facts (which Elizabeth played an important part in helping him get) rather than on emotion. Regardless of which of these options played out, Jim and Elizabeth would grow closer together because each would feel throughout the entire planning process that the other was supporting his or her needs and desires.

This is one example of how to negotiate the "how and when" but not the "what." Through this process, Jim and Elizabeth's "what" (i.e., what they each wanted) was not only not called into question, but was cherished. Even so, both were willing to consider the "how" (i.e., the means by which their needs and desires might be met) and the "when" (i.e., the timetable that made the most sense) to get what they both wanted. Finally, they could make a mutual decision based both on facts and how much the "what" was important to both of them, not based on how one or the other felt about it.

The example I gave here is fairly straightforward. This rule of thumb can be used with considerably more complicated situations as well, but it isn't possible to go into these variations on the theme in the space we have. For now, it is enough to say that couples who care enough to convey that they will always support what each wants—just as long as a "how and when" (i.e., a practical plan) can be decided upon that respects the other's needs—will always be more successful in overcoming their disagreements in a manner that makes them grow closer together than those who get into arguments about what the other should or shouldn't want. Practicing the habit of *never* negotiating the "what" but always being willing to negotiate the "how and when" allows couples to feel safe and supported and talk about their hopes, dreams, and deepest needs in confidence, knowing that one's mate really cares about even the silly and inconvenient things we might wish to go after in life.

If You Are Working on Your Marriage Alone

The good news is that most of the strategies presented in this chapter don't require your spouse's cooperation to work. Everyone likes to feel taken care of, and chances are your spouse will respond positively to your unilateral efforts to be a better caretaker in conflict. The only difficulty may be in getting your spouse to take care of you as well as you take care of him or her.

If you find that your spouse is not responding in kind to your efforts to be a better caretaker in conflict, give it a few weeks. Keep working to develop your skill in this area. After about a month has passed without your making the lack of reciprocity an issue, ask your spouse if he or she has noticed that you have been trying to be more caretaking and generous in your disagreements. Assuming he or she has, simply say that while you plan on continuing to do this for your spouse, it would really help if your mate could try a little harder to respond in kind so that you could both feel better cared for in your disagreements. If your spouse agrees, you can begin to share the ideas in this chapter with your mate and move forward together. If your mate verbally agrees but fails to follow through, or balks at the suggestion altogether even after being a beneficiary of your efforts for several weeks, it is probably time to seek professional help for the marriage with a marriage-friendly therapist, whether your spouse is willing to join you or not. A professional could help you identify additional ways to overcome obstacles that we simply don't have time to cover in this book. Keep in mind that regardless of the specific response your spouse makes, there is almost always a way forward. Seek the support that will help you find that path that connects you with the desires of your heart for a happier marriage.

Wrapping Up

Throughout this chapter, we looked at various ways for you and your spouse to be better caretakers of each other in conflict.

Developing this skill does not mean that you and your spouse cannot be frank with each other or that your disagreements will ever be pinky-finger-extended tea parties with crumpets and frilly manners. Probably not. Rather, taking better care of each other during conflict will enable you to encourage each other through the tension toward mutually satisfying solutions, even when the stakes are high. You will learn to grow closer to each other, not in spite of your disagreements, but because of them. You will learn to be true partners to each other, even when the going gets tough, and you will feel safe to trust your partner with even your silly or most personal hopes and dreams because you will know that they will always get a generous and supportive reception from your mate.

Pray

Lord Jesus Christ, you taught us that we should do good to those who frustrate us and always be loving even to those we are angry with or hurt by. Sometimes, Lord, we are so far from this in our marriage. Help us to know how to put into place those habits that will make us feel loved, supported, and understood even when the tensions rise. Give us your grace to overcome our injured pride, emotional reactions, addiction to our preferences, and tendency to be parents to each other instead of partners. Empower us to encourage each other through the tension by exhibiting your love for each other when our own love runs dry. Most importantly, help us to pursue the solutions that respect your will more than ours so that we can have the marriage you have in mind for us — the marriage that will lead us closer to each other and to you. We ask this through Christ our Lord. Amen.

Discuss

♦ Which of the strategies for Caretaking in Conflict most appeals to you? Why?

♦ Which of the strategies for Caretaking in Conflict would your spouse most appreciate? Why?

♦ Which of the strategies for Caretaking in Conflict do you think might be the most difficult for you to employ? Why?

♦ What would you need to do to overcome these obstacles to successfully employing the strategy you identified in the previous question?

Chapter 9

Mutual Respect, Accountability, and Boundaries

Be subject to one another out of reverence for Christ.
—Ephesians 5:21

For marriage to be a true partnership, a couple must be willing to listen to and learn from each other especially in those times when they don't want to or even when they believe they know better. In both *For Better . . . FOREVER!* and *The Exceptional Seven Percent: Nine Secrets of the World's Happiest Couples*, I argue that a couple needs to have a shared mission, a set of virtues, beliefs, or principles they attempt to live out as they strive to help each other become everything God created them to be in this life and help each other get to heaven in the next.

There is considerable research that suggests that, believers or not, couples who have a shared mission exhibit stronger commitment to each other and the marriage than those who don't (Stanley, 2005). For that to occur, however, a couple needs to have an even more basic skill in place. The spouses have to be willing to listen to and learn from each other. They must exhibit mutual respect, accountability, and boundaries.

Many people think that respect is about being polite, and of course, it is, but it involves so much more. Beyond basic politeness, respect involves the willingness to see the truth, goodness, and beauty in the things another person finds true, good, and beautiful. I may not personally share your passion for sports, or stamp collecting, your religion, your profession, or your widgets, but if I respect you, I understand that there is value in the things you have chosen to pursue, and I want to see those things through your eyes. I am, in a sense, drawn to your interests. Additionally, I want to learn from you, be challenged by your insights, and benefit from your experience and perspective. I understand that there are different ways to view the world from the way I do, and because I respect you, I value the way you see things.

Applied to marriage, researchers call this kind of respect a *fondness and admiration system* (Gottman, 2011). A fondness and admiration system in a marriage allows a couple to be receptive to what each has to share with the other. Because I feel fondly toward you and admire you, I want to learn from you and turn to you for advice and even correction when necessary. I see you as a person who can help me stay on course, especially when I am blind to my own lapses and errors in judgment.

Mutual respect—a regard that allows you to listen to and learn from each other—is the best term for what I have been describing. And if you and your spouse have mutual respect, then two other related qualities will develop: accountability and boundaries.

Accountability refers to my willingness to consider seriously your constructive criticisms. All of us have blind spots. We all do our best to live up to our values and beliefs, whatever they may be, but all of us tend to think we're doing better than we actually are. We all need someone who can—*gently and lovingly*—help keep us honest. My wife helps me be true to my values. She encourages me to keep trying to be the man God wants me to be, even on the days I don't feel like being a loving, generous person. She lovingly challenges me when I make choices that betray those values—for instance, if I am short-tempered or thoughtless in some way. She lets me see myself through someone else's eyes besides my own, which helps me make certain that the way I think I am living and relating to others is, in fact, consistent with that self-perception. As the Scripture passage at the beginning of this chapter illustrates, my willingness to be accountable to my wife—rooted in my respect for her—is what helps me be truly faithful (as opposed to self-deludingly faithful) to the call of Jesus Christ in my life.

Boundaries refers to my willingness to hear when I have crossed a line. As we discussed in the chapter on Positive Intention Frames, it is very rare that anyone ever tries to offend his or her spouse on purpose. Still, we manage it often enough. In those times, I need my wife to—*lovingly and gently*—let me know that I have hurt her in some way. I may not understand why she is hurt, and I may not have meant to hurt her, but that is irrelevant. Because I respect her, I want to try to understand my behavior through her eyes. I may attempt to clarify my intention if I feel she misunderstood what I meant to say or do, but that clarification is not an excuse or a dismissal. If my attempt to clarify fails to improve things, my respect for her motivates me to say that this is a line I must not cross, not only to refrain from offending her but because crossing that line stops me from being the man God is calling me to be. This is the difference between accepting my wife's boundaries because she is "too sensitive" or "can't take a joke" and accepting my wife's boundaries because they represent a valid perspective on right and wrong behavior.

If you are reading this chapter, you may have received a lower score on the quiz examining this skill in chapter 3. Take a moment to review the statements you were asked to consider on pages 72 and 73. Regardless of your score, every couple can benefit from increasing their level of mutual respect, accountability, and willingness to learn appropriate boundaries. This chapter will help you develop those skills.

How the Absence of Mutual Respect, Accountability, and Boundaries Affects Marriage

A couple who struggles in this area will have difficulty in most areas of their life together. Because of the lack of mutual respect, they will have a hard time sharing interests. A lack of mutual respect tends to be isolating because I don't care to learn anything about you that I am not personally interested in. Generally speaking, if I don't find a thing true, good, or beautiful myself, I would prefer you not talk about it. I may even find certain things you love boring or offensive. I won't try to see them through your eyes. I don't want to be bothered with leaving my comfort zone to really understand your work, interests, or beliefs.

Many couples who argue about religion, for instance, are really suffering from a lack of mutual respect. This can play out in two ways. The nonreligious spouse, instead of trying to appreciate religion from his or her mate's perspective, may act bored, put upon, or offended when his or her mate discusses faith issues, tries to share prayer, or expresses excitement over encountering the sacred. Alternatively, the religious spouse may think of his or her nonreligious mate as a godless materialist with no values and nothing to teach him or her about living a rich and meaningful life. In this case, the nonreligious spouse — whether personally antagonistic to faith or not — may come to feel that he or she is more of a project than a mate.

Although this problem centers on religious themes, it is not a religious problem. It is rooted in an unwillingness to see value in the way one's mate sees the world. In fact, while religion tends to be the most dramatic manifestation of this problem, couples who deal with this issue usually have similar problems in other areas of the marriage where one partner has a passion or interest the other fails to share.

This lack of mutual respect can, at the extreme, lead the couple to live mostly separate lives except in instances where they either both agree with each other or are forced to interact with each other (e.g., kids, household responsibilities). Mutual respect is what allows a couple to move from mere tolerance and tentative coexistence to a real partnership in which they learn and grow together.

When mutual respect suffers, the couple has little ability to be accountable to each other. Both spouses may struggle with self-delusion, believing that, regardless of what their mate says, they are doing just fine — thank you very much — as far as living out their values and beliefs. I have often had the experience of being in session with a couple and listening to one spouse offer complaint after complaint and describe offense after offense, only to have the other spouse respond, "I'm a great husband [or wife]. I don't know what she [or he] is talking about."

Because of this lack of accountability, the marriage loses its ability to work for each spouse's good, to help each spouse become what God created him or her to be and to help each other get to heaven. In essence, this is a marriage that has lost its soul. The couple can't meaningfully discuss any topics related to how they live out their values, principles, or beliefs—whether or not they are shared. As a result, the couple tends to relate little and only around relatively superficial topics.

Finally, the lack of mutual accountability leads to the absence of consistent boundaries in arguing and problem solving. If I don't believe that your perspective is valid, I am disinclined to listen when you tell me that I've hurt you, crossed a line, or betrayed my values. I will not attempt to clarify my intentions. Why would I bother, since your opinion doesn't matter anyway? Rather, I will either ignore your complaint, justify myself (daring you to disagree), or add insult to injury by accusing you of being too sensitive, unable to take a joke, or even crazy for thinking that anything I do could possibly be hurtful to you or inconsistent with my stated values. I am practically perfect in every way, and I'll thank you to keep your differing opinions to yourself.

When a couple can't agree on boundaries, it often happens that at least one spouse—if not both—tiptoes or avoids difficult topics for fear of experiencing what feels like emotional abuse from the other. If you don't respect my boundaries, I don't feel safe around you, so I don't want to get too close or talk about anything too difficult. If we do end up discussing some hot-button topic, it will usually end with me getting hurt, you accusing me of trying to manipulate you for having the audacity to be hurt, and neither of us resolving anything. Who could blame us for trying to live superficial and tangential lives?

What Developing Mutual Respect, Accountability, and Boundaries Will Do for Your Marriage

There are three things that mutual respect, accountability, and boundaries do for marriage.

First, mutual respect allows us to enter into each other's worlds. We can learn from each other, benefit from each other's experiences, feel supported by each other, and experience true intimacy because we are willing to share with each other on all seven levels of intimacy (which we discussed in chapter 5), knowing that we will be accepted and supported. Topics, interests, and pursuits that we don't have in common become an adventure as we learn to open up and share our worlds, perspectives, and beliefs with one another. Because we work hard to see the truth, goodness, and beauty in the things each other finds true, good, and beautiful, we see each other as best friends. When you have a success in some area of your life, you know that I understand enough about that thing you do to enable me to appreciate and celebrate that success with you. When you are struggling in some area of your life, even if I am not an expert, you know that I understand enough about that part of your life to allow me at least to ask some intelligent questions and get you thinking in new ways about the problem. We can now grow closer together because of our differences rather than in spite of them. This extends even to differences of opinion about how we perceive each other's behavior.

Second, since I am interested in your world and you in mine, I value your take on my actions and choices. I want to see myself reflected through your eyes and get your input regarding how I come across to you and others. I value you as a trusted person who helps keep me accountable to my values and prevents me from making or repeating mistakes in my relationship with you and others. While we don't automatically accept every bit of feedback without question, the questions we ask each other are more of an attempt to clarify misunderstandings, not an attempt to justify, defend, shift blame, or discount our respective actions over and above each other's concerns. I am willing to apologize if you tell me that I've hurt you even when it wasn't my intention to be hurtful. I am willing to adjust my behavior to please you even if doing so doesn't always make complete sense—assuming the change helps me do a better job of communicating the values, beliefs, and principles I claim to uphold. In other words, because we are willing to be accountable to each other, we don't just learn to expand our horizons because of each other; we learn to be better people because of each other. This leads to our ability to create more of a sense of shared mission and purpose in life.

Finally, our willingness to learn from each other helps clarify the boundaries that dictate the terms of safe discussions and arguments. We know the lines we can't cross, the things we should never say. It doesn't matter if those things are fine with one of us. We want each other to be comfortable, so we accommodate each other's sensitivities—assuming that we still give each other ways to discuss difficult topics or share difficult observations with each other (as opposed to someone's being so sensitive about certain topics that entire subjects are off limits; this is actually every bit as controlling as verbally abusive behavior). Because of this, we feel safe discussing a wide variety of topics, issues, and challenges, and we usually experience those discussions as edifying and productive. We develop a strong sense of confidence in our partnership and a certainty that we can weather storms well.

Taken together, our ability to practice solid mutual respect, accountability, and boundaries enables us to have a rich, deep, safe and intimate marital life.

How to Develop Mutual Respect, Accountability, and Boundaries

For the remainder of the chapter, I'll discuss some simple ways you can begin to build greater respect, accountability, and boundaries in your marriage. Keep in mind these are only a few techniques of dozens that are available. If you find that you need additional support or other ideas, don't hesitate to reach out for professional assistance. Regardless, these ideas can get you started. We'll look at three basic ways to improve your capacity for mutual respect, accountability, and boundaries: *reframing values*, *increasing accountability*, and *boundary clarification*. Let's look at each of these exercises.

Reframing Values

As you may remember from the chapter on Positive Intention Frames, *reframing* means looking at something in a new, more approachable way. It doesn't always mean thinking positively about something. There are some things—sickness, serious problems, losses, activities you find boring and uninteresting—you just can't put a smiley face on. Rather, reframing makes a problem that seemed too huge to handle seem more manageable. It's still a problem, and you may not like it, but having reframed it, you now have a perspective about the problem that makes it seem workable at least. Likewise, if your spouse is interested in something you don't care about, you may never come to love it as much as your mate. You don't have to. But through the reframing that healthy couples tend to do naturally because of their mutual respect for one another, you could come to see the value of both the activity itself and of understanding something about it—at least objectively—even if it isn't something you ever really see yourself doing. (The Reframing Exercise on page 291 will help you develop this habit.)

This is what happy couples intuitively do with the things their spouses enjoy that they don't. They either find an approximate emotional equivalent to the benefit their spouse receives from doing that thing, so they can relate to it and appreciate it for what it is or, realizing that this a benefit that they don't currently know how to enjoy in their own life, they try to participate in their spouse's activity at least a bit more so that they can develop the taste for that benefit and share new experiences with their spouse. In this way, happy couples let their mutual respect be the means by which their marriage both draws them closer together and expands their horizons.

Even *if you are the only one working on your marriage*, you can begin to develop a greater respect and appreciation for your spouse's interests by means of this exercise. Your generosity might inspire your spouse to respond in kind. If not, keep up your effort as a way of building credibility and rapport. After a few weeks of this, go to your spouse and say, "I don't know if you've noticed, but I've really been making more effort to respect and appreciate the things that are important to you. I was wondering if you might be willing to do [such and such] with me. I'm not looking for payback, and I plan on continuing to do the things I've been doing one way or the other, but I would love to be able to share more of my life with you. The next time I do [such and such], would you be willing to do it with me?"

One way or the other, your attempts to develop a new appreciation and respect for the things your spouse does that you have tended to run down in the past will help your mate feel more appreciated, give you more experiences to share, and broaden your horizons as a person. A little generosity on your part can bring numerous benefits to your life and your relationship.

Increasing Accountability

As I mentioned earlier, increasing accountability allows you to see your own behavior through your spouse's eyes so that you can be sure that what you are trying to communicate with your words and actions is actually coming across.

This can be terrifying for some of us, especially if your spouse is hostile toward you or has an overwhelmingly negative picture of you. If this is the case, you may need to seek professional assistance to overcome this problem effectively. It can be inappropriate or even dangerous to increase your accountability to your spouse if your mate is abusive or openly hates you.

For those of you who are not in quite such a difficult position, the Increasing Accountability Exercise on page 298 can help you open your heart to your spouse's feedback without subjecting yourself to abuse or control.

Boundary Clarification

The third and final area we'll look at is the need for healthy boundaries. Couples argue differently. Some couples are more comfortable with slightly more volatile styles of arguing than others. Regardless, every healthy couple has boundaries that determine whether the discussion will continue to feel safe for both spouses. No matter how volatile a particular couple's arguing style might be, if they are a healthy couple, there will always be certain things that they understand they must never do or say, no matter what. These are the boundaries that keep the couple feeling safe, as if they can trust one another even when the going gets tough. In healthy couples, if one spouse attempts to set a boundary that the other spouse doesn't agree with, there might be some discussion about why the boundary needs to be set there, but the boundary will not be called into serious question unless there are so many conversational rules being put into place that there is no way to move forward. If this is the case, it is time to seek professional help.

Less healthy couples are not as attentive to respecting each other's boundaries in conflict. Often, one spouse will attempt to set a boundary while the other tries to plow through it, explain it away, or shame the other spouse (either by direct criticism or indirect pouting). The result is that the couple — or at least one of the spouses — does not feel safe in the marriage.

Research shows that even when healthy couples don't agree that boundaries must be set where they are, these couples respect those boundaries (Gottman, 2011). Like couples in these stable marriages, you will need to learn how to respect even the boundaries you don't understand. The Boundary Clarification Exercise on page 309 will help you with this skill.

Wrapping Up

We've looked at the various ways respect manifests itself in healthy relationships. Respecting your spouse means much more than just trying to be polite. It means trying to find the truth, goodness, and beauty in all the things your mate finds true, good, and beautiful. It means that you and your spouse should be willing to submit to one another out of reverence for Christ (Eph. 5:21) and be accountable to each other even when you don't necessarily see eye to eye. Finally, it means wanting to make each other feel safe, even when you are arguing and even if that means willfully restricting your behavior and speech out of consideration for your spouse's needs. Cultivating respect in your marriage is a foundational skill that allows many other blessings — joy and discovery, wisdom, safety, and security — to flow in your marriage.

If You Are Working on Your Marriage Alone

If you are working on your marriage alone, you can make use of all of these exercises. Depending upon your circumstances, and especially if you think it might backfire in some way, you may decide to eliminate the last step, in which you openly and directly commit to certain actions toward your spouse. Otherwise, you should be able to experience many of the same benefits other couples encounter as a result of practicing these skills. As always, though, if you find it is too difficult to do this on your own, a marriage-friendly professional therapist can be of great assistance to you. You can contact the Pastoral Solutions Institute at www. ExceptionalMarriages.com to learn more.

Pray

Lord Jesus Christ, give us a spirit of respect and humility. Help us to see each other as persons whose interests, opinions, and needs are valuable and worthy of being accepted and responded to generously. Take my pride. Give me ears to hear, a heart to care, and a mind to understand. Fill our marriage with the genuine respect that allows us to acknowledge that we are each deserving of love and consideration even in the face of conflict and disagreement. Amen.

Discuss

• How would living out this vision of respect (as a quality that allows you to appreciate the things your spouse values, learn from each other, and respect each other's boundaries) change your relationship?

• If you could learn to value the things each other appreciates, how would you be better people?

• How would the willingness to listen to each other's opinions about each other change you for the better?

• How would respecting each other's boundaries in conflict improve your ability to solve problems?

• If you could live this vision of respect, how would it change you as a person?

Chapter 10

Reviewing and Learning
from Mistakes

I mentioned in chapter 3 that human beings have an almost limitless capacity to be consistently surprised by the same thing happening over and over again. This is especially true in marriage. Rather than learning from past mistakes, many couples are simply glad to have escaped the last problem or argument they had to endure. Having made it out of the experience in one piece, more or less, many couples try to think about the unpleasant situation as little as possible.

This is completely understandable, of course. Who wants to dwell on the negative? But George Santayana's famous saying that those who cannot remember the past are doomed to repeat it is instructive. Healthy couples don't enjoy their arguments, but they reflect on them and learn from them. Less healthy couples simply survive their arguments, tell themselves to move on, and let it go, only to live out their own version of the movie *Groundhog Day*—but with fewer laughs.

If you're reading this chapter, chances are you had a lower score on the Reviewing and Learning from Mistakes Quiz in chapter 3. Take a moment to review the statements you were asked to consider on pages 76 and 77.

What the Absence of Reviewing and Learning from Mistakes Does to Marriage

We are all works in progress, and marriage is, very much, on-the-job training. As with any job, in marriage, regular performance reviews of one sort or another are essential—not sessions during which you rake each other over the coals again and again, but times when you thoughtfully and, ideally, prayerfully, reflect on what happened and what both of you could do better next time to avoid a similar breakdown.

Many couples have no idea how to begin doing this. They either tend to pick up arguments exactly where they left off and fight them out all over again—over and over again—or they pretend nothing ever happened and move on, hoping it will never happen again, no matter how many times it has happened before. Either way, the cost to the marriage is astronomical as fewer and fewer topics feel safe to discuss and the couple begins to feel hopeless that anything will ever get any better.

What Reviewing and Learning from Mistakes Will Do for Your Marriage

Couples who know how to review and learn from their mistakes don't enjoy their arguments, but they can at least look at them with some degree of hope because they see that with each conflict, improvement follows. Healthy couples look at their arguments as opportunities to learn from each other and grow closer together. Of course, they try hard not to fight in the first place, but when they do, they are able to take some time apart, reflect on what they *each personally* did to escalate things, identify things they *each personally* should have done differently, and return to discuss those insights thoughtfully and sensitively with each other.

In *For Better . . . FOREVER!*, I propose a "spirituality of marital conflict." That is, I suggest that while God may not wish for his couples to argue with each other, he makes good use of the conflicts couples experience.

The biblical book of Esther details what it was like to wed a king. The bride-to-be would be brought to the palace an entire year before the wedding day. For the first six months, every inch of her body would be rubbed with spices to remove any blemish and make her skin perfectly smooth and sweet-smelling. For the next six months, she would be trained in cosmetics and hair design. All of this so that, on the day of her wedding, she could stand confidently under the gaze of her king.

Christians recognize heaven as an eternal wedding feast (cf. Rev. 19:9) where we, the bride, are united to our Bridegroom, Christ. For us to stand confidently under the gaze of our King on the day we enter that wedding feast, every blemish, bump, crease, and wrinkle of our emotional, spiritual, and psychological being must be removed, for nothing that is imperfect can enter the Kingdom of Heaven (cf. Rev. 21:27). Christian Marriage is a sacrament, and a sacrament is, above all, one of the instruments God uses to perfect us so that we might be ready to enter heaven. Every part of a sacrament is used to perfect the recipient of that sacramental grace. Think of marital conflict, then, as the "spiritual exfoliation treatment" that removes the bumps and blemishes from our spiritual, emotional, and psychological being so that we might arrive, properly prepared and attired, for the wedding supper of the Lamb.

Granted, this is a rather exalted view of marital conflict, and I don't mean to suggest that all — or even most — healthy couples are consciously aware that this is what is going on in their disagreements. But I can tell you that while unhappy couples tend to roll their eyes or stare at me with a wistful lack of comprehension when I describe this spirituality of marital conflict, healthy couples usually experience a light-bulb moment. They nod their heads. They say, "Yes!" as if they are finally able to put words to the grace they have been experiencing all along.

This grace can be yours as well. You have only to learn to cooperate with it. Many less healthy couples think that there are only two "postures" when it comes to conflict: blow up and rage or hide and avoid. There is a third path; do your best to take care of each other in conflict (as per chapter 8) and both review and learn from any mistakes so that you can do a better job of taking care of each other the next time. The rest of this chapter will show you how any couple can develop this skill.

How to Develop the Skill of Reviewing and Learning from Mistakes

This skill tends to draw from strengths associated with self-regulation (chapter 6) and your capacity for respecting and being accountable to each other (chapter 9). Spouses with poor self-regulation skills tend to walk away from arguments only to stew about them. They never really calm down. They can appear superficially calm, but the catalog of injuries is always just below the surface, and as soon as the couple re-engages in any kind of difficult conversation, all the negative emotions—and sometimes an exhaustive list of historical offenses as well—erupt from a deep chasm of emotional pain. Spouses who do not work to develop better self-regulation will struggle with this habit too, because in order to be able to review and learn from mistakes without simply reopening the wound, you need to be able to stop fixating on the wound and see different ways you might have responded that would have made things better. Spouses with poor self-regulation simply can't do this. Every time they think of an argument, they simply ruminate over how they were done wrong. It never occurs to them that there could be more to the picture besides the hurt they incurred. They might be willing to admit that they are "not perfect" in some vague, general sense, but if pressed, they know that everything they did and said was entirely justified because of their spouse's behavior.

If this sounds like you, be sure to visit the exercises in chapter 6 to see how you might learn to truly calm down after a conflict and gain some perspective so that even in those times when you are not at fault, you can see how you could share the responsibility for improving the situation next time.

By contrast, spouses who struggle with respecting and being accountable to each other tend to return to arguments wanting to get their spouse to give perfect agreement on exactly what happened and who did what to whom. They know what really happened, and if you see it differently, then you are "lying" or "trying to manipulate" the story. Spouses who struggle with respecting and being accountable to their mate believe fiercely in their ability to be perfectly accurate reporters and will not brook any version of the story that differs from their own. Any deviation from their mental record of events is a clear sign, not of a differing perspective, but of malicious intent. Period.

The twofold truth is much different and much more freeing. In the first place, there is a vast body of literature demonstrating that no two people ever see the same event exactly the same way, and most of what we choose to remember (and how we choose to recall it) is highly subjective and variable (Toglia, Reed, and Ross, 2006). Secondly, the good news is that husbands and wives don't ever actually have to agree on what exactly happened in order to do better next time.

Some readers may be shocked, if not appalled, by this last statement. Clients will regularly object, "How can we ever hope to find a solution if we can't even agree on the problem?" The truth is, the only thing two people have to agree on to make a productive change is that they didn't like what happened last time. If they at least agree about this (they don't even have to agree why they didn't like what happened last time, only that they are unhappy with it), then they can begin to discuss how they would like next time to go. Since next time hasn't happened yet, they can script it however they like!

This is how couples who are good at reviewing and learning from mistakes handle their conflicts. They recognize that they may not agree on what happened, but they agree that they want to do better next time. To that end, when they get a break from a difficult conversation, both the husband and the wife spend a little time in reflection—and ideally, in prayer—asking themselves (and God) what they might personally do better the next time a similar problem comes up. Then, at their first opportunity after the disagreement, they return to the topic—not to rehash things—but to share their own ideas for how they each might do better in the future. Then they discuss those ideas and fine-tune them, so that the couple can go forward feeling hopeful that, despite the last conversation about widgets going so badly, the next one might be more productive. In fact, they might even look forward to it.

If this skill doesn't come naturally to you or your spouse, there are three exercises that can help you: *building on the Three-Column Spike Exercise* from chapter 6, *Solution-Focused Thinking*, and *Exceptional Thinking*.

Building on the Three-Column Spike Exercise

The first way to develop the ability to review and learn from mistakes is to build on the Three-Column Spike Exercise from chapter 6. You might recall that the original exercise asked you to divide a piece of paper into three columns. In the first column, you were asked to write down various "trigger events," that is, the upsetting situations and problems that happen between you and your spouse. In the second column, you were asked to write down the things you typically say and do in response to each trigger event. Chances are you find these responses to be problematic in some way. Finally, in the third column, you were to identify what you might like to do differently, even assuming that you would feel as upset as you usually do. To help you arrive at the answer to this question, you were asked to consider what virtues might have been missing from your default response, where you might have displayed similar virtues, and how you might adapt those more virtuous responses to this new situation.

In order to use this exercise to review and learn from mistakes in a healthy way, you will add a fourth step. Having had an argument that left you unhappy with how you responded to the trigger event, both you and your spouse should take a break and do the Three-Column Spike Exercise separately. When at least one of you is done (it is ideal for both of you to do it, but not necessary; solo spouses can use this same approach even if their mate refuses to do the exercise), come back together. Say something like the following to your spouse: "I was really upset when you did [trigger event], but that didn't give me the right to do [column 2 response]. If I had it to do over again, I think I would have [column 3 response]. If I did that in the future, would that change anything for you?"

What is terrific about this format is that it enables you both to go back to the discussion and pick it up where you left off in a more productive, solution-focused manner. This approach allows you to acknowledge the offense without beating it to death, to take responsibility for your part in the breakdown without feeling as if you are taking on all the blame, and to move forward from this point to discuss the possible solutions a change in your approach might make possible both now and in the future.

Sometimes couples get stuck because they don't know what they might have done differently. On those occasions, one small adjustment can still enable you to use this exercise to learn from your mistakes and move past the breakdown. Instead of saying, "If I had it to do over again, I think I would have [column 3 response]." Say something like, "If I had it to do over again, I'm not sure how I could have responded differently, though. Can you help me figure something out?" Then describe the response you would like to get from the other person. For instance:

> If I had it to do over again, I'm not sure what I could have done to have you be a little more sympathetic. I know that I didn't handle things well, but honestly, that's what I was hoping would happen when I did what I did. Could you help me figure out what I could say or do to have you be a little more sympathetic?"

Or

> I'd like to handle it better next time if something like this comes up again, but I really need your help. I know I handled it badly, but I was honestly just trying to get some feedback or input from you. You were silent. What

can I do next time to get more of a response from you? Obviously doing what I did didn't work.

Note the solution-focused, matter-of-fact nature of these statements. While the speaker in these examples isn't glossing over the frustration or the problem, he is also not dwelling on it. He references it just enough for the listener to know what he's talking about; he clarifies—not excuses—his behavior and asks for help in meeting his intention.

This is a process that couples who are naturally good at reviewing and learning from mistakes intuitively follow. They understand that ripping the scabs off old wounds does no good, but they also recognize that important wisdom can be gained by going over their past experiences together. They approach these experiences delicately, and rather than re-arguing what happened, they focus on what could be done differently to avoid similar unpleasant discussions. This way, couples are able to benefit from their experience without becoming bogged down in their past frustrations.

Sometimes couples struggle to identify new ideas. In those times, the other two ideas I mentioned at the beginning of this section, *Solution-Focused Thinking* and *Exceptional Thinking* can be helpful tools.

Solution-Focused Thinking

Solution-Focused Thinking is developed by constantly asking yourself three questions:

1. How are things?
2. How would I like things to be?
3. What's one small thing I can do now to move how things are to how I might like them to be?

These questions might seem tremendously obvious to some readers, but you would be surprised how many people never think of asking these questions under any circumstances, much less under pressure. Many people have been taught—either explicitly by their parents or implicitly by being beaten down in life—simply to accept what comes. These individuals have a hard time hoping things could be different than they are, much less making a plan to effect change. But the truth is, we can accomplish all things through Christ, who strengthens us (cf. Phil. 4:13). Accomplished solution-focused thinkers almost constantly ask themselves these three questions. They are always assessing how things are or how they feel, how they might like things to be or how they might like to feel differently, and what small things they might do—right now—to try to draw closer to the preferred state.

When I present this idea to my clients, many respond by saying how exhausting it must be always to have to think this way. The opposite is true. Imagine being tossed into a river with a strong current and not knowing how to swim. You are told, before you are thrown in, that it is your job to make it to the opposite shore. Before you know it, you are being pulled along by the current. You are scarcely able to keep your head above water, much less make it across. The river carries you downstream. All you can do is hope the current might wash you up on the opposite shore before you wear out and drown as you float off into the distance.

Now a slightly different scenario: imagine that you are a strong, practiced swimmer. You are told that you must swim across the same river and make it to the opposite shore, but this time, instead of being thrown in, you step confidently into the river and begin swimming hard. The current is pulling you.

You can feel your muscles burning, but you keep adjusting your stroke, kicking harder, reorienting yourself to the exit point on the opposite shore. Eventually, your feet hit the shallow water on the opposite bank of the river. You stand. Your legs are wobbly. You are a little farther downriver than you had hoped you'd be, but you made it to dry land—tired but with a sense of accomplishment.

Which person would you rather be? Most people would choose the second person, the strong swimmer. The truth is, life is like the river in this scenario. If you want to get anywhere, if you want to get anything good out of it, you have to be intentional about your journey. You have to swim and swim hard. You will be tired whether you swim or not, but if you don't swim, you'll get tired and most likely drown. If you do swim, you'll be tired but have a sense of accomplishment and strength. Asking the three questions associated with Solution-Focused Thinking will teach you how to swim instead of being pulled along by the current of your life and marriage.

Obviously, the third question, "What is one small thing I can do to move closer to where I'd like to be?" is the most important. The key to this question are the words *one small thing*. Most people exhaust themselves with *all-or-nothing thinking*—an unhealthy, distorted thinking pattern that makes people believe that unless they can figure out the one perfect answer that will solve the problem once and for all, they are powerless to change anything. Research in cognitive psychology has shown all-or-nothing thinking to be associated with passivity, depression, and other emotional problems (Burns, 2008).

It is true that it is almost impossible to find the one answer that will solve your problem for good, but there may be a million things that can help you make things a little bit better if you can dare to ask yourself what is "one small thing" you can do to make your situation a little bit better. For example:

> Jennifer says, "I was feeling really taken advantage of. My husband and kids would just get up from the table and scatter about the house after dinner, leaving all the cleanup to me. I know the kids have homework and Chuck has paperwork to do, but I just resent getting stuck with everything. Normally, I just suck it up and do it, but the other day, I asked myself, 'What's one small thing I could do to make things better?' Right at the end of dinner, I asked everyone if, on their way out of the kitchen, they could please at least scrape their own plate and take it to the sink. They didn't bat an eye! They all did it. I was shocked. I made it a new rule. Sometimes, my husband even volunteers to help rinse and load the dishwasher. I *never* saw that coming.

And for another example:

> Alex called my radio program to complain that his wife never had any time for him. "She's always running off to do her mother's bidding, and she is super-overcommitted. I can't get her to give me thirty seconds. I'm so tired of her putting me and our marriage last all the time. Any time I try to bring it up, she just gets defensive. I'm sick of being in a marriage with someone who doesn't love me or doesn't want to spend any time with me."
>
> The key to solving Alex's problem was his comment that his wife got defensive when he tried to talk to her about his concerns. Her defensiveness suggested to me that he was not complaining to her so much as criticizing her (see chapter 7). This was confirmed when I asked how

he tried to talk to her about his desire to spend more time together. "I tell her that her priorities are all screwed up and I'm sick and tired of getting the short end of the stick."

I said, "Alex, it seems to me that your desire to spend time with your wife is getting lost in your criticisms of her, which are making her defensive. I know you feel hopeless about finding the big answer that could make your wife get her priorities right and give you the time you want with her."

"That's right. She's never going to change."

"Well," I said, "that may be. But what if you could do one small thing that could at least get your wife to be a little more open to meeting your needs? Would you be willing to do it?"

"Of course."

"The next time you feel resentful about your wife not spending time with you, instead of criticizing her, I want you to go online and find three different things you might like to do with her that are going on in town over the weekend. Then I want you to go to her and say, 'Honey, I know you're awfully busy, but I miss you. I would love to get some time with you this weekend. I found three things that I thought we could really enjoy together. How would you like to do X, Y, or Z, with me sometime over the weekend?' If you did that, how do you think she would respond?"

"I think she'd be okay with that."

"And Alex," I said, "do you think that would meet your need to get more time with your wife?"

"It would. I feel a little silly, but it never occurred to me that I could just plan a date and ask her to do something."

"Well, I want you to do this every time you start feeling the slightest bit resentful about her not giving you the time you want for your marriage, and I want you to let me know what happens."

I heard from Alex in an e-mail about a month later: "Dr. Greg, you wouldn't believe how much different things are from when we spoke before. I've been asking my wife to do things, and she's been great about it. The other day, her mom called to ask her to go to the store right when we were about to go see a movie, and she told her mom that she'd have to wait until we got back! I never thought she'd choose me. The other day, she told me she really liked that I was asking her out. She said she didn't know I wanted to spend time with her! Thanks for your advice. It's really turned things around."

Not every situation can improve this dramatically from ideas as simple as these, but both examples illustrate the power of asking what "one small thing" can be done to improve a situation. Often a small change can have an unexpected ripple effect that can lead to more profound change. This technique can certainly work if you are seeking to improve your marriage on your own, but couples can use it as well. Try not to get caught up in all-or-nothing thinking. Instead, ask each other what one small thing can make a difference the next time the problem comes up. By using Solution-Focused Thinking, you can identify "the difference that makes a difference" (Weiner-Davis, 1993).

Exceptional Thinking

This leads to the third technique that can help you revisit and learn from mistakes: *Exceptional Thinking*. This involves asking yourself to look for exceptions to the rule. For instance, your wife usually may not be interested in sex, but sometimes she is at least less resistant to the idea. *What is different in these times when she has more interest than usual?* Another example: your husband may not be very communicative, but sometimes he is more communicative than at other times. *What is the difference that enables him to open up more than usual?* One final example: you might not enjoy spending time with your spouse, but some times are at least a little more pleasant than other times. *What is the difference that enables you to get along better in those times?*

When I ask what makes the difference in my attempt to explore these exceptions — which almost always exist to at least some degree — most couples' first impulse is to shrug, say, "I don't know," and return immediately to criticizing their spouse and bemoaning their fate. Resist this temptation with all your might. Force yourself to identify as many differences as you can that *occur around the time* the exception to your usual way of relating occurs. Did you get more sleep? Were you around other people? Did you ask differently somehow? Was your spouse in a better mood? If so, why? What contributed to that difference? Don't think in terms of cause and effect. That is, don't ask yourself, "What specific thing *caused* my spouse to act more in the manner I would prefer?" That's the quickest way to get stuck. Instead, ask *what differences attended or occurred around the same time as the more desirable behaviors?* Focus on identifying differences that you can have an influence over or even directly control. For instance, you can't control whether your spouse is in a better mood or not, but you might have some influence over the circumstances that attended that better mood. In any problem situation, you can almost always identify at least two or three specific factors that account for the exception and are almost entirely within your control. Once you have identified these factors, you have your key to success.

You can use this technique even if you are working on your marriage by yourself because you are reviewing your past experiences with an eye toward identifying the things that are within your control to change, which, in turn, increase the likelihood that your spouse will do more of the things you like. This is usually the point where some people ask if this isn't manipulative. Isn't it somehow wrong to consciously try to do things to influence our spouse in a positive way? The answer is no. It is loving. To love someone is to work for that person's good. Intentionally doing things to make it easier for a person to do his or her best and be his or her best is practically the definition of loving someone. That you may benefit from it too is a happy consequence, but it is hardly manipulative.

With everything we do, we influence those around us for good or ill. Whether that influence is loving or manipulative depends on the intention and the focus of the effort. If I am trying to be manipulative, I am trying to influence you (consciously or unconsciously) to give me something I want, whether it is good for you or not. If I am being loving, I am trying to influence you (consciously or unconsciously) to be your best self, and in the process, I happen to benefit. There is a profound difference between the two. Some people are not used to being conscious about their relationships, but just because you aren't used to thinking of love in these terms doesn't mean that intentionally trying to influence your spouse in ways that bring out his or her best self isn't loving. In fact, as I noted above, the very definition of loving someone is working for that person's good.

If you have the good fortune of being able to engage in Exceptional Thinking with your spouse, this can be a very powerful way to learn from your past and improve your future interactions. Instead of complaining to each other that you don't seem to get any time together, you could begin a conversation by saying, "I've really missed you this week. What's different in those weeks when we're able to get more time together?" Instead of arguing about how little affection or communication or anything else you are experiencing in your marriage, you can begin a conversation by saying, "I really like those time when we are more affectionate [or communicative or whatever]. What's different between those times and lately? I'd like to get back to being more like we were in those times."

Do you see the difference? Setting up a conversation based upon these questions that lead to Exceptional Thinking—that is, thinking about positive exceptions—enables you to have positive, solution-focused, productive discussions that actually help you identify steps to get your needs met instead of just criticizing, arguing, and becoming defensive that your needs aren't being met. Think about the difference in your marriage if you were able to replace your current criticizing and defensive discussions with conversations like this.

Couples who use what I call Exceptional Thinking learn from their past in a way that enables them to grow closer, for they use all of their experiences—good or bad—to build a brighter future together.

Wrapping Up

In this chapter, I presented ways that you and your spouse can benefit from your history without being doomed to repeat it. If you are working on your marriage alone, you can use these same approaches. The only difference is that you would not expect your spouse to initiate conversations like the ones I described in the chapter. Instead your mate will learn from your example. You may need to work a little harder to keep the conversation solution-focused, since your spouse may naturally tend to default to trying to ignore the past or get lost in the pain of your past exchanges, but by concentrating on the techniques on self-regulation we discussed in chapter 6, you will confidently be able to lead the process of reviewing and learning from your mistakes as a couple.

Whether you are working with your spouse or alone, if you find that you cannot discuss past frustrations and failures without getting mired in the pain and anger of those situations, or if you find that your spouse just refuses to speak about the past, then you will know it is time to seek professional assistance. The good news is that regardless of how successful you are cultivating these habits between you and your spouse, a competent marriage-friendly therapist can help you remove the psychological, emotional, and relational obstacles that stand between you and marital healing. By all means, you should use the suggestions contained in this chapter to develop this skill on your own, but if you need additional assistance, don't ever hesitate to contact the Pastoral Solutions Institute or seek out local resources for additional assistance.

Pray

Lord Jesus Christ, it is your intention that everything you give us should be used as a gift to work for the good of others, help us become the people you created us to be, and draw us closer to you. Help us to see our struggles as a gift that enables us to make these things happen in our lives. Give us the patience and gentleness we need to review our mistakes with an eye toward doing a better job of cooperating with your grace in the future. Give us the wisdom we need to learn the important lessons you are trying to teach us about love, life, and ourselves. Give us the fortitude we need to use these lessons to handle future problems and conflicts more effectively. But above all, give us your grace, that our marriage might become our best hope for becoming the people you created us to be and celebrating the eternal wedding feast with you in heaven. Amen.

Discuss

• How are the processes outlined in this chapter different from the way you and your spouse usually discuss past hurts, problems, or frustrations?

• What would be different if you and your spouse were able to learn from your mistakes without dwelling on the hurts or injuries you have inflicted on each other in the past?

• What would be the biggest challenges to applying the recommendations in this chapter?

• What would you need to do to overcome the challenges you identified in the previous question?

• Have there been times when you and your spouse were able to review and learn from mistakes without reigniting the argument? What did you do differently in those times?

Chapter 11

Getting Good Support

When we are in pain, we have a tendency to reach out for the easiest and most convenient sources of support. Unfortunately, many of these sources are the worst ones to turn to for help in resolving marital conflict. Despite our best intentions, the advice we get from these sources often makes a bad marital situation worse. Our friends often see the world as we do. They aren't in the best position to give objective and informed advice. That goes double for our family, who may have taught us the very habits and ways of seeing things that have caused our marital problems in the first place! Our pastor is a good person to turn to, but pastors aren't counselors, and they are often not equipped with the latest information and research to help heal our marriage in the most efficient way possible. Even beyond this there are very important differences in the nature of the discussions we would expect to have with our pastor and a counselor. While both are important, they serve different functions for the person in pain. Likewise, not every counselor is competent to help couples who are struggling; unfortunately, many counselors either will not admit or do not acknowledge their incompetence as marital therapists.

As a result, people either tend to fail to seek help at all or go from place to place seeking help with the best of intentions but failing to get adequate assistance, making them erroneously feel that their marital cause is a lost one. If you are reading this chapter, you may have received a lower score on the quiz in chapter 3 examining your ability to get good marital support. Take a moment to review the statements you were asked to consider on pages 79 and 80.

It surprises many couples to think that knowing how to get good support is actually a skill in and of itself, but it shouldn't. Not all information is created equal. Whether you are seeking medical advice, car-repair advice, or marital help, some sources are better than others, and some advice is better than others. Throughout this chapter, I will help you understand the difference between good and bad marital advice and help you know the best sources to turn to for assistance.

What the Absence of Knowing How to Get Good Support Does to Marriage

When a couple does not know how to seek good support, they exhaust themselves trying to save their marriage, using ideas that may either not work for them or may not work at all. Research shows that willpower is a limited resource (Gropel and Kehr, 2013). Like money and time, willpower gets used up as we apply ourselves to various tasks. The more stress we face, the quicker our willpower reserves are depleted. When we get bad marital advice or turn to people who aren't capable of helping us in the way we need to be helped, we become more stressed about our marriage. We cycle through hope and depression over and over as we go from thinking that this next person, this next bit of advice, will be the thing that does the trick, only to be crushed when it doesn't work—usually because the advice we received was too generic, too one-sided, or not based on any evidence that it could ever work in the first place. When we get bad advice, our willpower to stay in the marriage and keep fighting for our marriage can evaporate even more quickly than if we were struggling through things on our own.

No one sets out to destroy their relationship, but I cannot tell you the number of hours I have had to spend with couples cleaning up messes that were made from bad advice they had received. Often, my clients will spend weeks undoing the problems caused by bad advice or poor support before we can even get to the original problem. The trouble is, much bad advice can sound—or even sometimes be—good ("It's important to get a date night"); or scriptural ("Do not let the sun go down on your anger" [Eph. 4:26]); or affirming ("You have to do what works best for you").

The problem is that all of these examples are true only as far as they go. They are not true for everyone in every situation, even though these, and a few other common examples, are trotted out for almost all people in every situation. For instance, date nights are important, but if you and your spouse aren't finding at least some way to work, play, talk, and pray on a daily basis, date nights can also be a disaster because you won't have anything to talk about and you'll end up spending date night either fighting or in tense silence. Not going to bed angry is great scriptural advice, but I somehow doubt that St. Paul intended for couples to wear themselves out by staying up fighting until four o'clock in the morning. And finally, while it is absolutely true that we can do only what we think works best, what if we are working with incomplete information or poorly developed skills? What if what works best for us now isn't what would actually work much better if we only took the time to get better information and skills than we currently have?

Getting good help and knowing how to separate good advice from bad is an essential skill for healthy marriages.

What Learning How to Get Good Support Can Do for Your Marriage

A wise professor of mine once said, "You don't need to know everything. You just need to know where to look up what you need to know when you need to know it." There is tremendous freedom in the ability to know where to go to get good information when you need it. Getting good support and information can help you work more efficiently at almost anything, but especially at either saving or improving your marriage. It will spare you countless hours of frustration pursuing useless leads. It will preserve your desire to keep working on your marriage because you haven't burned through all the willpower you need to keep trying even when things move more slowly than you'd like. Most importantly, because people giving good support actually tailor their advice to your unique situation, you will cultivate real hope as you come to see what is possible in your marriage.

How to Find Good Support

Couples who are good at seeking competent support and quality information:

- know the difference between help-seeking and venting;
- seek informed peer support;
- seek marriage-friendly advice;
- know who is good at what;
- know how to choose a competent professional.

Let's look at each of these.

234

They know the difference between help-seeking and venting.

We all know a friend who loves to take up our time complaining about everything that is wrong in his or her life but who hates to do anything we suggest. This is venting, and it is not just our friends who do it. Anyone who has ever had a problem and talked to someone else about it is probably guilty of this. Talking about our troubles garners sympathy, and sympathy feels good. In fact, it feels good enough to, in a sense, become addicting. Sympathy can make us feel loved. It can make us feel special. If a person isn't careful, a weird dynamic can develop in which he actually holds on to his marital problems — out of a belief that he can't do anything about them anyway — as a way of getting sympathy and special treatment from the people he likes to complain to. No one does this consciously, but many, many people do it. Venting and seeking sympathy from friends comes to be a sad but acceptable substitute for the marital intimacy they don't believe they'll ever get anyway. If they don't believe they have viable options, they'll settle for what they can get.

That's not to say talking to others about our marital difficulties is a problem. It can be quite useful if we know the difference between help seeking and mere venting. Help seeking takes two forms:

• *A sounding board.* This is when I need someone to listen to me talk out loud so that I can hear myself think. Listening to oneself talk out loud stimulates the brain's left, logical hemisphere. My brain listens to my own voice as if someone else is talking, so I can be more critical of and objective about what is being said than I could if I kept it all in my head. This is different from mere venting because there is an ending point. Using you as my sounding board does not mean that I complain to you about different versions of the same problem over and over again. Rather, it means talking out loud to you in a way that generates new ideas that I then attempt to apply in my relationship. Using someone as a sounding board is an active process whose goal is solutions, not sympathy. This is not to say that sympathy is bad. In its place, sympathy greases the help-seeking wheels. It lets me know that you "get" me and care about my problems. But when sympathy becomes the focus, talking about problems becomes enabling and antithetical to marital healing.

◆ *Advice seeking.* This is where I go to someone whose life experience or expertise I respect, in an attempt to get new insights or skills. Again, sympathy can certainly help grease the help-seeking wheels, but it cannot be the focus of my help-seeking. Talking about problems is unquestionably helpful as long as you do it correctly. A survey of the available research shows that how you talk about your problems matters. Generally speaking, venting about your problems is useful only to the point where the other person understands the nature of the problem and how deeply you are affected by the problem. Once you've adequately communicated this to another person, venting has to stop and problem solving must begin. If venting continues past this point, the conversation becomes sympathy seeking instead of help seeking and these conversations actually become part of the problem.

They seek informed peer support.

Long before pastors or professional counselors come onto the scene, couples talk to friends and family about marital issues. Seeking informed peer support is perfectly acceptable, but the key words here are *informed* and *peer*.

◆ *Informed.* Healthy couples do talk to other people about marital struggles, but they tend to be careful about whom they speak to. They don't blab their problems to anyone with ears. Rather, they selectively and carefully look to mature friends or family who are people of proven virtue and good character. Less healthy husbands and wives talk to people who can "relate" to them (because they have similar attitudes and are going through similar problems). Healthier husbands and wives talk to people who will *challenge* them. Seeking *informed* peer support does not mean gossiping about your spouse at your scrapbooking club or complaining about your mate to your drinking buddies. It means talking to someone whose character you would like to emulate and whose marriage you admire. If the person you're talking to about your marital troubles doesn't fit this description, stop. You're probably settling for sympathy seeking instead of help seeking, and you're only hurting your chances of healing your relationship.

◆ *Peer.* The word *peer* means someone on the same level as you. Healthy couples do not talk about their marital problems to people who are emotionally or temporally dependent upon them. Talking about your marital problems to your children, your employees, your crazy friend who couldn't live without you, or anyone else who is emotionally or temporally dependent upon you is a huge no-no. You will not get good, objective marital advice from these sources. If you are talking about your marital problems to anyone you needs you—financially, emotionally, or both—stop. Now. You are actively ruining your chances of healing your relationship.

There are sources of informed peer support that are much better places to turn to than friends or family. Retrouvaille, Third

Option, and PREP each have a strong and proven record of being able to assist even the most seriously struggling couples.

- *Retrouvaille*, from the French word for "rediscovery," is a peer-support program that is led by couples who have successfully resolved their serious marital problems using the Retrouvaille program. The program consists of a retreat weekend that teaches couples how to open the door to healthy and safe communication and marital healing and continues with six follow-up sessions addressing various topics throughout the year. Retrouvaille does not take the place of counseling but provides excellent complementary support and training for struggling couples. I strongly encourage all couples who are going through difficulties to take advantage of this wonderful resource. For more information, visit www.HelpOurMarriage.com or contact your diocesan family life office for information on local weekends.

- *Third Option* is an ongoing program that focuses on skill-building workshops and peer support. It takes its name from the fact that it presents a healthy alternative to the two options most couples vacillate between when dealing with problems—namely, stuffing their anger and lashing out at each other. Couples meet regularly for training and encouragement both in groups and with sponsor couples. There are fourteen two-hour meetings, each covering the development of a particular marital skill. In addition, trained sponsor couples are available to help participating couples through crises at any time. Like Retrouvaille, Third Option is not meant to take the place of counseling, but it can be an invaluable source of marriage-friendly support and training for struggling couples. You can learn more by visiting their website at www.TheThirdOption.com or by contacting your diocesan marriage and family life office.

• *PREP* is a marital skill-building course led by a trained leader (who could be a pastor, a couple, a mental-health professional, or any other person). PREP groups have been established internationally at more than a thousand sites, and their program is backed by thirty years of research. PREP's well-designed program covers a variety of topics in a group format, involves up to fourteen hours of training on various marital skills, and has a strong track record of helping couples transform struggling relationships into happy marriages. For more information, visit www.PREPinc.com.

Whether or not you choose to utilize these resources (and I highly recommend that you do) when you seek advice, whether from friends, pastors, or professionals, make sure you talk to someone who—by experience or training, or both—knows what a truly healthy marriage looks like and who is prepared to challenge both you and your mate to develop habits that will heal your marriage. Anyone who is too quick to agree with you or suggest an easy path to relief from your troubles should be avoided. There are many excellent resources available to assist you. Cultivate healthy help seeking by using these resources instead of those sources of pseudo-support that make you feel better in the moment while actually undermining your chances of healing your marriage.

They seek marriage-friendly advice.

We all want to be told that we're right. When we're angry with our spouse, we all want to find someone who will support all the negative things we are saying in our heads about what an awful person we married; how he or she is beyond repair; that we would be better off without him or her. This kind of "advice," however, does nothing but feed our pride, and, as Scripture notes, pride goes before destruction (Prov. 16:18) of both life and marriage.

When we have lost rapport with our spouse and lost hope in our marriage, we are afraid to seek "marriage-friendly" advice because we're concerned it will be preachy and insensitive. It will tell us that we have to hang in there no matter how awful it is and just settle for being miserable for the rest of our lives. After all, God never promised you a happy marriage. Life is hard. Suck it up. *This is not marriage-friendly advice.* This is awful advice, even if there is some arguable truth to it. It isn't pastoral, and it certainly isn't useful. It only makes the speaker feel full of himself without doing any real good for anyone. So, if this was your fear, fear not.

Rather, marriage-friendly advice comes from people who are familiar — either through lived experience or professional training, or both — with what a healthy marriage looks like. Keeping this awareness in mind, the advice giver shares thoughts he or she thinks will challenge *both you and your spouse* to make changes that are more consistent with this vision of marriage. It helps if the person knows and likes both you and your mate. Don't ever take advice from a friend who doesn't know — or worse, dislikes — your spouse. By contrast, it is possible to work successfully with a marriage-friendly therapist who does not know your spouse as long as that therapist has actually been trained in marriage-friendly approaches to solo-spouse marital counseling (see the point about choosing a competent professional). But, as a general rule, marriage-friendly advice is rooted in a clear sense of what a healthy marriage looks like and is directed at the things both the husband and the wife will have to do to adjust their behavior and attitudes in order to be capable of a healthy marriage with anyone.

This last point is important. Most couples who have marital problems think they were just unfortunate and married the wrong person. They think that if they just had another chance to pull the arm on the marriage slot machine, they'd come up a winner next time. It is because of exactly this type of thinking that there is more than a 67 percent divorce rate for second marriages. With rare exceptions, if you don't have the skills to make your present marriage work, then you don't have the skills to make any marriage work. You will need to learn those skills before you will be able to be happy in any relationship, so you might as well learn them now to see if you can get this relationship to work.

If a marriage-friendly therapist tells you that, based on actual research, you are doing everything a healthy spouse should be doing and the relationship still isn't working, it might be prudent to discuss with your pastor whether your spouse was capable of entering into marriage as the Church defines it. But my recommendation to my clients and to you is to use the marriage you have to become the healthiest spouse you can be. That is what professional marriage-friendly advice does. It helps the husband or wife become the healthiest spouse he or she can be using the present circumstances. As a result, the marriage as a whole is either strengthened or the (now) stronger and healthier spouse can make the decision to end the marriage from a position of strength and relative certainty regarding his or her ability to have a healthier relationship in the future (although, in most cases, when a spouse does this work, the marriage does actually improve significantly).

Spouses who do not seek advice that will help them be the healthiest people in their own right doom themselves to the illusion that getting out fast to seek greener fields elsewhere is a viable option. Most people who do this end up even lonelier the second time around.

They know who is good at what.

Knowing what kind of help you can get from various sources is incredibly important when you are seeking marital help. Friends and family, psychoeducational groups, pastors, and marriage counselors all do different things and can help you in different ways. Unfortunately, since all of these different groups "talk about marriage," it can be difficult to tell which kinds of support you can and can't get from these various sources.

 • *Family and friends.* In general, family and friends can offer *moral support*, encouraging you to keep trying and gently nudging you toward marriage-friendly resources they may be aware of. That said, for reasons I discussed with you above, friends and family are terrible sources of practical advice. We are living in the third generation of the culture of divorce. Many people have parents and grandparents, and in some cases, great-grandparents who are all divorced. That means most people intuitively know much more about what it takes to end a marriage than how to save it. In fact, our culture has largely forgotten what it takes to make a marriage work. Even couples who seem happy may not really know what they are doing, why their marriage is working, or whether what they are doing will work for you. That doesn't mean they won't be happy to give you advice. It just means it may not work. I don't mean to imply that you should never under any circumstances seek practical help from friends and family. I just mean that they are usually the weakest and most flawed source for advice, despite the fact that these are the people toward whom most struggling couples turn first. *Caveat emptor!*

• *Psychoeducational groups.* These involve programs such as Retrouvaille, Third Option, PREP, and others. Although these programs teach psychological concepts and provide some support, they are more like classes than counseling. Couples can learn a great deal by participating in these programs, and I highly encourage your involvement in all of them. That said, many couples struggle to apply the lessons these programs teach when they get back home. These same couples can become discouraged and feel that nothing will work for them. This is not true. The reason the lessons from these programs don't stick is often because of certain personality or thinking quirks that particular husbands or wives have that stop them from actually applying these skills consistently. Counseling can help couples work through this faulty programming so that they can take better advantage of the things they have learned in whichever marriage-education groups they participate in. If you need new skills, and most struggling couples do, these programs can be tremendously helpful. Just don't make the mistake of thinking that this is all there is.

• *Pastors.* Pastors are a wonderful, frontline source of spiritual and moral support. You should know up front, however, that talking to your pastor about your marriage problems has as much to do with marriage counseling as talking to your pastor about your broken leg has to do with going to the doctor. Both can be helpful, but in radically different ways. For instance, your pastor can give you Anointing of the Sick for your broken leg, giving you the grace you need to heal more quickly and face your suffering with peace and patience, among other things. And while miracles are certainly possible, you will most likely still need to go to a doctor, who will use the latest technical skills available to walk you through the physical process of healing your leg.

In the same way, talking to your pastor about your marriage problems can be tremendously helpful for acquiring the grace you need to speed your marital healing and bear your sufferings well in the meantime. And while miracles are always possible, you will still, most likely, need to seek the help of a professional marital therapist, who will use the latest technical skills available to walk you through the practical process of healing your marriage. Both speaking with your pastor and speaking with a counselor involve talking, but for the most part, that's where the similarities end. Unless your pastor is a trained marital therapist, he will most likely not be qualified to provide counseling.

Your pastor can, however, do three very important things. First, as I already noted, he can bless your efforts and your struggle (through confession or other means that are available to him) so that you can receive the grace you need to participate more effectively in the process of healing your marriage and be able to stand strong in the face of the challenges you may meet along the way. Second, your pastor can help you clarify the Church's vision of marriage so that you will have a sense of the type of relationship you are working to create and what having a marriage—as the Church defines it—requires of you. Third, through spiritual direction, your pastor can give you advice on how to use both the strengths and challenges of your marriage as opportunities for spiritual growth. This can include how to use the sufferings of your marriage to great spiritual benefit. This last point bears some additional clarification, however.

Sometimes clients will tell me in the course of counseling that they no longer need to work on their marriage because

"Father said" that their marital sufferings will bear great fruit all on their own and they just need to trust God's grace to heal their marriage in God's good time. I can tell you that I have spoken to enough pastors over the years to know that, most likely, "Father said" nothing of the sort. It would be the rare priest, indeed, who would ever counsel someone to stop counseling and trust God to work things out in time. That may be what Scientologists or what Christian Scientists believe, but it is not what Catholics believe.

The problem often comes down to a simple misunderstanding of the difference between counseling and spiritual direction. Spiritual direction is not, generally speaking, about making life changes (Barrette, 2002). It is primarily about learning to use whatever one is going through — good or ill — for spiritual gain. Learning, in spiritual direction, how useful your marital suffering is to your spiritual growth is not the same as saying you should not still try to end that suffering as quickly as possible! If your pastor tells you that you are blessed to be able to join your marital sufferings to the cross of Christ for the benefit of your soul and the salvation of the world by bearing your sufferings well, that is a very powerful and valuable message indeed. It does not, however, mean that God would not necessarily like to bless you in an even more powerful way by also healing your marriage.

I want to be clear that I am not diminishing the importance of spiritual direction. In fact, I teach pastoral and spiritual direction in a graduate theology program, and I integrate spiritual direction into the counseling work that I do. I am a great supporter of the value of spiritual direction, and I strongly encourage all serious Christians to find a good spiritual director to assist them on their journey. Spiritual direction can be a tremendously important source of support in marital healing, but be careful not to confuse it with marriage counseling. Spiritual direction teaches you to use the circumstances of your life to grow closer to God. It takes counseling, however, to teach you how to change the circumstances of your life so that God may bless you in new ways.

They know how to choose a competent professional.

Couples with good help-seeking skills know that there are many different kinds of mental-health professionals, and while they may be quite competent in other areas, not all of them are competent marital therapists.

When you decide to seek professional marital counseling, it is important to choose well. Chances are it has taken you a while to get to that point. Most couples wait four to six years from the onset of problems to initiate therapy, which means it is especially important to work with a professional who genuinely knows what he or she is doing. Your choice matters a great deal. Research shows that marital therapists who have professional training and supervised experience in marriage and family therapy have over a 90 percent success rate with marital therapy clients, while general practice therapists can have as low as a 30 percent success rate (Gottman, 2011).

The problem is that despite ethical rules stating that no therapist may work outside his or her area of competency, it is left to the individual therapist to judge his own competency, and therapists often think they are more competent at more specialties than they actually are. Many therapists who do marital counseling—even ones who have been doing it for more than twenty years—have no training in marital counseling and have simply been making the same mistakes with clients throughout their professional practice. When it is time to choose a therapist, you want someone who is marriage-friendly (as defined earlier in this chapter) and who can describe, in detail, his or her actual training (both classroom and post-graduate seminar training) and supervised experience in marital therapy. If you ask a therapist to describe his training in marital therapy and he answers, "I've been counseling couples for years," you have the wrong counselor. The answer you want is something like, "I did graduate coursework in marriage and family therapy and had supervised internship experience in a marriage and family counseling center. Additionally, I have done X, Y, and Z training in such-and-such type of marriage therapy."

The actual words the therapist uses to fill in the blanks above matter less than that he *can* fill in the blanks. You wouldn't understand the difference, for instance, between systems theory or Gottman therapy or solution-focused marital therapy. You shouldn't have to. It doesn't matter. The point is therapists with the best marital-counseling success rates have specific graduate or post-graduate training and supervision in marital counseling. If your therapist can't describe that training to you, find another marital therapist.

Finally, if possible, it is helpful to find a therapist who is both familiar with and supportive of your faith tradition. For instance, research shows that faithful Catholics prefer eleven different counselor competencies — including training in moral theology, and both Catholic and current secular approaches to marital problems — than Protestant Christians seek from their counselors. Every faith tradition has a somewhat different vision of what marriage should look like. Working with a therapist who is unfamiliar with, or worse, unsupportive of, your Church's understanding of marriage can make counseling a challenge. This becomes an even more relevant consideration with a faith like Catholicism, which has a particularly deep and involved theology of marriage.

For local resources, the best place to turn for qualified, marriage-friendly therapists is the National Registry of Marriage-Friendly Therapists at www.MarriageFriendlyTherapists.com or, for Catholic-integrated marriage-friendly counseling, contact the Pastoral Solutions Institute at www.CatholicCounselors.com or by calling 740-266-6461.

Wrapping Up

Throughout this chapter, we've discussed healthy and unhealthy approaches to help seeking. Everyone needs assistance from time to time. Every single couple hits a point in their relationship when they will need to learn new skills and get outside support. This is particularly true in our current marriage-hostile culture. It is my hope that, having reviewed the information in this chapter, you will have a clearer idea of the kind of help you may need to move forward in your marital journey and where you might best turn to receive that assistance.

The most important thing to keep in mind at the conclusion of this chapter is that you don't have to go it alone. In fact, you shouldn't try. The popular legal saying "The man who serves as his own attorney has a fool for a client" applies to marital therapy as well. While this is a self-help book filled with ideas to give you hope and start you down the road toward marital healing, the vast majority of readers would definitely benefit from more intensive training and support. I hope that you will be among those readers who will seek help early and often and from many sources throughout your journey toward marital healing.

Pray

Lord Jesus Christ, in Genesis, we are told that it is not good for us to be alone. Help us to remember this as we work

*toward healing our marriage. Help us to overcome the
pride that might stop us from reaching out for assistance.
Give us the wisdom we need to seek good counsel and the
humility we need to accept and use the help we receive.
Walk with us on our journey, and grant us the ability
to cooperate fully with your abundant grace. We place
our marriage at the foot of your Cross. As we join our
struggle to your Cross, we ask that you would allow us to
also rise with you so that the love you would rekindle in our
hearts would be a sign to us and the world of the wonders
your grace can do. We ask this through Christ our Lord.
Amen.*

Our Lady of Good Counsel, pray for us!

Discuss

• Think of the people you have been asking for support
through your marital difficulties. Do they fit the criteria
discussed in this chapter? Do they know and like both
you and your spouse? Does their advice challenge both
you and your mate to change? Are their marriages models
you would like to follow? Do any of your friends or family
meet this criteria?

• Have you taken advantage of the informed peer support
offered by Retrouvaille, Third Option, or PREP? Do you
know when the next offering of these programs is in your
area?

• What are three things that distinguish "marriage-friendly
advice" that you would like to remember in your own
help-seeking efforts?

• Have the help-seeking recommendations in this chapter differed from your own approach to help seeking so far?

• If you have been to counseling, do you know if you have seen a therapist who is marriage-friendly and has the kind of training and supervision experience in marital therapy recommended in this book? If you decide to enter into counseling (either again or for the first time), how will you make sure to choose a therapist who meets the criteria listed in this chapter?

Chapter 12

Is It Worth It?

While reading this book, chances are you have, at some points, wondered if all the effort is really worth it. Why *should* you work on your marriage? If you don't really feel it anymore, if it looks as if your spouse wants out, if you haven't enjoyed being married for a long time, isn't it better just to call it quits? Why beat your head against a wall? Why put up with the exasperated looks from your friends and family, and maybe even a less-than-marriage-friendly therapist? Maybe they're right. Maybe it really would be easier and better to throw in the towel.

I toyed with not including this chapter at all. I thought that the last thing you'd need was someone to preach at you about why you should do the work anyway, even if all of the above is true. After all, it isn't really my job or desire to talk you into anything. I am a marriage-friendly therapist, and I would very much like you to follow through with all the suggestions in this book — suggestions I genuinely think will heal your relationship. But I can't make you do anything, and I don't intend to try. All I can do is extend an invitation and show you ways that it could be possible to heal your marriage. The rest is up to you.

And yet, because there may very well be any number of people lining up to tell you how crazy you are for trying to make this mess of a relationship work, I thought I would at least offer a few reasons why it might be worth keeping up your efforts because there are some very good reasons. It is not my intention to preach at you or make you feel guilty. It is only my hope that on those days when you need a little extra encouragement or need some other reasons to keep trying, you might draw some strength from these thoughts. The list here is hardly exhaustive, but I've tried at least to hit the high points.

Why You Might Want to Stick It Out

The rest of this chapter will look at the following practical and important reasons why working on a troubled marriage — even one as troubled and unsatisfying as yours may be — is worth it.

1. Your Faith asks you to try.

2. Divorce isn't the end of anything.

3. You value your mental health.

4. Divorce impacts physical health to a surprising degree.

5. Your kids want you to stay together.

6. It is easier to mediate negative effects of your spouse's behavior on your kids if they aren't alone with him or her for long periods.

7. Divorce threatens your financial health.

8. Second-marriage divorce rates are even higher.

9. Being alone stinks, and dating (especially when you have kids) is horrible.

10. Divorce is hard on the environment. (Hey, every reason counts, right?)

Let's take a look at each one. You might be surprised what you discover, and having the right reasons to go on at the right moment just might save your marriage.

Your Faith asks you to try.

Despite what you may have heard, the Church does permit divorce. Catholics consider divorce a serious matter, but paragraph 2383 of the *Catechism of the Catholic Church* states, "If civil divorce remains the only possible way of ensuring certain legal rights, the care of the children, or the protection of inheritance, it can be tolerated and does not constitute a moral offense." That said, divorce is a very serious and even grave offense against the moral order. Entering into it for anything less than the most serious reasons is considered a sin (although this is not the case if divorce is either necessary for the above reasons or if one is the unwilling spouse in a divorce brought about by one's mate).

One might liken divorce to an amputation. Amputations are morally permissible under certain circumstances, but they are always bad things. They should never be entered into lightly, and they must be done only for the most serious and life-threatening reasons. The same is true for divorce. Marriage constitutes a visible sign to the world of Christ's commitment to the Church. Christ will never divorce the Church, but saying this can become meaningless in a culture in which divorce is seen as the cheap and easy answer. Your struggle to keep even your difficult marriage together has deep spiritual significance for both yourself and the world. Remaining faithful to even a troubled marriage gives the world an image of how God can be faithful to us even when we are difficult, ugly, nasty, broken, sinful, and undeserving of love. Staying in your marriage is a powerful witness to the fidelity God has to each of us. Even though it is hard—in fact, especially because it is hard—God will generously bless your decision to remain in your marriage despite all the reasons piling up that seem to justify your leaving.

Divorce doesn't end anything.

First off, even if you get divorced, you need to remember that, as far as the Church is concerned, you are still married. Unless you receive a declaration of nullity (an annulment) stating that you and your spouse either did not enter into marriage as the Church defines it or were, for some reason, incapable of doing so, you are still married to your spouse even after a civil divorce is contracted.

This might seem stupid on the face of it, but this isn't just a Catholic thing. It is a psychological reality. Divorce actually sets you free from very little. Imagine all the arguments you have now—all the fights about kids, money, respect, religion, and so forth. Now imagine having them with someone who will still be in your life for the rest of your life, except now you have even less ability to influence him or her. That's divorce.

Especially if you have kids, your spouse will be a thorn in your side for the rest of your life. People imagine having an "amicable divorce," but if these people were really capable of being amicable in conflict, they'd still be married. Divorce gets you some physical distance from your spouse, but it doesn't get you emotional or psychological distance. You will still argue about money. You will still argue about kids and rules. You will still argue about schedules and priorities and lifestyles. Only now, you will have even less influence over what your spouse does and will have to suffer the consequences of a spouse who may make more and more decisions just to spite you.

Is It Worth It?

It is not just the Catholic Church that says that divorce is little more than a tax document that ends nothing. The lived experience of millions of divorced couples shows that divorce ends nothing. It just freezes arguments in time and stretches them out over decades with no hope of ever resolving them without lawyers and money being spent every time you need something. Is this pessimistic? Yes. It also happens to be true more often than not.

Sometimes this can't be helped. Sometimes things are so dangerous and awful that getting physical distance is the only way to live a reasonably healthy life. If this isn't your situation, however, divorce makes no sense for you from either a spiritual or practical perspective. Better to work things out in an environment where you can still effect some change over time.

You value your mental health.

I could easily write an entire book on this point alone. If you wanted to do something to yourself and your children that would exponentially increase your (and your kids') risk of depression and suicidality, anxiety, drug and alcohol abuse, school and work problems, and behavioral problems, then you would be hard pressed to find something more effective than divorce. It's just bad news. Here are just a few examples.

One major study found that the use of psychotropic medications (antidepressants and anti-anxiety meds) significantly increased in the time leading up to and immediately following divorce and continued at higher levels than the general population for up to four years after divorce (Metsa-Simolen, Martikainen, 2013). The same study found that people heading into divorce were twice as likely to need medications as people in unhappy marriages who were not divorcing. Adult male children from divorced families have a 300 percent higher incidence of suicidal thoughts, and adult female children from divorced families have an 83 percent greater incidence of suicidal thoughts than adult children from intact families (Fuller-Thompson and Dalton, 2011). A recent Gallup-Healthways Well-Being Survey found that divorced and separated people scored more poorly than any other group of people across six measures of well-being: general life satisfaction, emotional health, work satisfaction, physical health, healthy behaviors, and access to basic necessities (2012).

You get the idea. Sometimes, for very serious reasons, divorce may be advisable, but most of the reasons people divorce simply do not justify the tremendous drain on mental health and well-being for themselves and their children that divorce entails. Again, there are very good reasons for working it out.

Divorce impacts physical health to a surprising degree.

Many people are surprised to discover that divorce impacts physical health, but to be honest, the degree to which it impacts physical health over the course of a lifetime surprised even me. A study in the *Journal of Health and Social Behavior* found that divorced persons were 20 percent more likely than married persons to develop chronic health problems such as heart disease, diabetes, and cancer (Hughes and Waite, 2009). They were also 23 percent more likely than married people to develop disabilities that impair physical mobility. Even more shocking, researchers found that remarriage does not heal the damage to physical health done by divorce. Divorced people remained at higher risk of these chronic health problems even if they remarried. In essence, your body wants you to make your marriage work.

Is It Worth It?

Your kids want you to stay together.

Research shows what a lie it is that children are happier after divorce. The best study of the matter to date, presented in the book *Between Two Worlds: The Inner Lives of Children of Divorce*, looked at over 1,700 adult children of divorce (Marquardt, 2006). The participants were young adults from so-called "good divorces" who all graduated college and had good relationships with both parents. Marquardt found that even children of divorce raised in these ideal post-divorce circumstances were less happy with their lives, more doubtful of their own abilities to form healthy attachments, less likely to attend church or believe in God, and more likely to struggle with mental-health issues. Almost all participants agreed that they would have been better off if their unhappily married parents had found a way to stay together.

The only group Marquardt found had benefited from divorce were those who were raised in households where marital conflict reached sustained, abusive levels. With that one exception, all participants expressed the desire that their parents had been able to either find a way to work things out or stay together despite their unhappiness.

Marital stability is essential to a child's sense of well-being, at every stage of that child's development—including adulthood. This is important. Marquardt makes the point that parents who wait until their children are older to divorce do as much, if not more, damage to their children's sense of well-being. Children of late-divorcing parents tend to feel that everything they learned about relationships and what it takes to lead a stable, secure life is a lie. The point is that your efforts to work it out, even against challenging odds, are absolutely worth it.

**It is easier to mediate negative effects of
your spouse's behavior on your kids if they
aren't alone with him or her for long periods.**

I have had many clients who thought seriously about divorcing their spouse because of that spouse's negative influence on their children's behavior. People who feel this way need to take a page from a very astute client of mine who shared that she chose not to divorce her husband because if she did, he would have the kids all to himself for days and even weeks on end, and she simply couldn't trust him not to undermine her values and perhaps even jeopardize their safety in the time that he was in charge of overseeing them. Obviously, this was a terrible marriage, but my client had a point. If you are already doing battle with your spouse over parenting issues, imagine what it will be like when you no longer have any say whatsoever regarding what happens when your spouse has visitation. All the co-parenting classes in the world can't make your spouse follow good post-divorce parenting rules. Everyone does what he thinks is best, regardless of what his ex says.

And here is one more consideration for my readers who are people of faith. My experience shows that spouses who have higher standards for their children's behavior are always the losers after divorce. You will either need to relax your standards or work ten times harder to maintain both your standards and your rapport with your children if they can just go to your ex's house and do what they want.

Divorce threatens your financial health.

Divorce is one of the worst financial decisions you can ever make, especially as a woman. A University of Connecticut study that followed six hundred women over forty years found that divorced women continued to suffer the financial effects of divorce well into their retirement years (Weiss, 2011). Men are negatively affected by divorce too, as they continue to bear the burden of dividing their assets and retirement savings and paying child support and possibly alimony for years after the divorce.

People often complain about the cost of marriage counseling, but the cost of counseling is nothing compared with even the short-term expenses of lawyer fees and court costs, which, as of 2014, average between fifteen and twenty thousand dollars for an uncomplicated divorce. To put this in perspective, assuming an average rate of a hundred dollars per session, you could do almost four full years of weekly sessions (which is almost unheard of) with a marital counselor before you would approach the high-end cost of an inexpensive divorce. On average, marital counseling is able to make significant improvements in a relationship over the course of fifteen to twenty weekly sessions. What is more, many insurance plans will cover a significant percentage of the costs of your marital therapy.

Keep in mind that these numbers comparing the cost of self-pay counseling with the cost of divorce do not even begin to calculate the costs of the division of marital assets and retirement, as well as years of child support and alimony payments. Working things out is much better for your present and future financial outlook.

Second-marriage divorce rates are even higher.

Many people believe that they just married the wrong person. If they could just get divorced and get a second chance, things would be better. I have addressed this issue elsewhere in the book, but it bears a second look.

In the first place, remember that, if you are Catholic especially, divorce does not end your marriage. A civil divorce is just a tax document. It has no bearing on your marriage in the sight of God and the Church. Attempting to date or marry again after a civil divorce is, in fact, the sin of adultery. Before you may consider looking for another spouse, you must be willing to seek an annulment, which does not undo the marriage. Rather, it determines that, for a particular reason, you or your spouse did not—or were not able to—enter into marriage as the Church defines it. It is extraordinarily important to remember that just because you have a civil divorce, you are not free to marry someone else.

But let's say that you do receive an annulment and you do find someone to marry. The divorce rate for second marriage is over 67 percent, and the divorce rate for third marriages is 75 percent. As I argued earlier in this book, it simply makes more sense to use your present marriage to learn to become the healthiest person you can be. Chances are, if you do this work, you will be able to bring greater health to your whole relationship, but if you do not do this work, you will most likely bring the same problems into your next marriage.

You may say, "But I would never get married again!" Almost every divorced person says this, but 75 percent of divorced people do, in fact, remarry. Don't kid yourself. Leaving no stone unturned to save your marriage now is the best chance of living a healthy and happy life.

Being alone stinks, and dating (especially when you have kids) is horrible.

Sometimes we need to be by ourselves, but this is very different from being alone. Human beings are social beings. We were made to love and be loved, and it is not good for a person to be alone (Gen. 2:18). This is why, despite all the protestations to the contrary, 75 percent of divorced people do remarry, and a higher percentage either date or cohabit.

But for most people, dating wasn't much fun the first time around. Who wants to go through all that again? Why would you want to complicate your life that way? Worse, children simply do not react well to having people come in and out of their lives. When you date after divorce, many children will work hard to distance themselves not only from your boyfriend or girlfriend but from you as well. Children want their parents to be models of stability. Their sense of well-being and security is not supported by watching Mom and Dad go through all the stupidity and awkwardness they themselves are experiencing.

Divorce is hard on the environment.

We all aspire to be green these days, but someone should have told Al and Tipper Gore (the environmentalist couple who divorced after forty years of marriage) the inconvenient truth that divorce is horrible for the environment. A study in the *Proceedings of the National Academy of Sciences* found that the carbon footprint of divorced families was twice that of intact families because you need twice the number of rooms, power, and energy to shelter the same number of people. For instance, the study found that if divorced couples had stayed married, divorced households in the United States alone could have saved more than 38 million rooms, 73 billion kilowatt-hours of electricity, and 627 billion gallons of water in a single year (Liu and Yu, 2007)! You can't make up for this environmental impact with any recycling program.

The bottom line is that divorce is bad. It's bad for you, your health, your mental health, your social life, your kids, your finances, your community, your Church, and your environment. In fact, except in cases where a household is characterized by sustained violence, there is not a single instance where divorce has a positive impact on any aspect of life or functioning. *Not one.* As common as it is, it would be hard to invent a worse thing to do to a person, much less a child.

Again, my point is not to guilt you into staying married. My point is to strengthen you, to give you other reasons to hang in there and work harder on those days when it just doesn't seem to make sense to keep trying. Even when your heart isn't in it. Even when your spouse is against it. Even when other people tell you that you are crazy. It makes sense to work on your marriage.

Epilogue

Marriage and the Cross:
"It Is Consummated!"

As this book draws to a close, I want to take a moment to thank you. I want to thank you for being among those strong, brave few who believe that marriage is worth fighting for even through the difficulties, trials, and struggles and sometimes even when it makes no emotional sense to keep trying.

Your fight is an inspiring witness, and God wants to use your struggle to change the world. In our disposable society, it is simply too easy to throw people and relationships away as if they were broken tools that no longer served us well. You are among those people who realize that people and relationships are not objects that can be thrown away just because they become inconvenient, difficult, or even problematic.

We are all broken, but to face that brokenness head on and work with all your heart, mind, soul, and strength to cooperate with God's grace to heal those wounds is a truly inspiring witness to what God can do when we let him reign in our lives.

I know that this journey has not been easy, and I know that it may not get easy again for some time. But you should never doubt that God is walking along with you and understands your pain more than you could know.

It is perhaps not by accident that I am writing this epilogue on Good Friday. I am caught up in the significance of this coincidence of events. You may not know that on Good Friday we celebrate a marriage. *The* marriage between Christ, the Bridegroom, and his Church, the bride. The great Archbishop Fulton Sheen once pointed to the Cross and said to his congregation, "Do you know what is going on there? Nuptials! I tell you, nuptials!" This comment has a long theological pedigree. If you do an Internet image search for "Christ the Bridegroom," you will see a famous icon whose origin goes back to the earliest days of Christianity. An icon of the suffering Christ with a crown of thorns fixed upon his head.

Earlier today, I participated in the reading of the Passion narrative at my parish's Good Friday service. Most modern translations of Jesus' last words have our Savior saying, "It is finished." The Douay-Rheims translation of John 19:13 is: "It is consummated!" The Cross is the wedding of heaven and earth, but as the scene suggests, it is a not an easy marriage.

The truth is that we the Church are not a particularly faithful, easy bride to love. We have many other lovers. We are very bad at standing by our Bridegroom's side. We wander off. We become selfish, whiny, argumentative, cruel. We are the very picture of a terrible spouse. And yet God does not let any of that stand in his way.

Pope Benedict XVI, in his 2007 Lenten Love Letter, wrote that the Cross is a sign that nothing can separate God, our lover, from us, his beloved.

On the Cross, God's eros for us is made manifest. *Eros* is indeed—as Pseudo-Dionysius expresses it—that force "that does not allow the lover to remain in himself but moves him to become one with the beloved" (*De divinis nominibus*, IV, 13: PG 3, 712). Is there more "mad *eros*" (N. Cabasilas, "Vita in Cristo," 648) than that which led the Son of God to make himself one with us even to the point of suffering as his own the consequences of our offences? Dear brothers and sisters, let us look at Christ pierced on the Cross! He is the unsurpassing revelation of God's love, a love in which *eros* and *agape*, far from being opposed, enlighten each other.

In her book, *Strange Gods*, Elizabeth Scalia picks up this theme when she writes,

> Look at the profundity of God's love for his people, Israel, and for those of us grafted onto that branch.... God takes pity on human limitations and tries another way of teaching and reaching, a better way to know the transcendence. He says, in essence:
> My love and my law are not enough? You need a corporeal king? All right then, I will come down and be your corporeal king. I will teach you what I know—that love serves, and that a king is a servant—and I will teach you how to be a servant in order to share in my kingship. In this way, we shall be one—as a husband and wife are one—as nearly as this may be possible between what is whole and holy and what is broken. For your sake, I will become broken, too, but in a way meant to render you more whole and holy, so that our love may be mutual, complete, constantly renewed, and alive. I love you so much that I will incarnate and surrender myself to you. I will enter into you (stubborn, faulty, incomplete you, adored you, the you that can never fully know me or

love me back), and I will give you my whole body. I will give you all of myself unto my very blood, and then it will finally be consummated between us, and you will understand that I have been not just your God but also your lover, your espoused, your bridegroom. Come to me, and let me love you. Be my bride; accept your bridegroom and let the scent and sense of our love course over and through the whole world through the church I beget to you. I am your God; you are my people. I am your bride-groom; you are my bride. This is the great love story, the great intercourse, the great espousal, and you cannot imagine where I mean to take you, if you will only be faithful ... as I am always faithful, because I am unchanging truth and constant love.

This is the love your broken marriage bears witness to — the painful, passionate, transformative love of the Cross. And I believe that God has great plans for you and plans to take you to places that you have never even dreamed of, if you let him and if you can remain faithful to his plan in your life.

I know that what I am inviting you to do is hard. I know there are many days it will not make sense, but I know that what I am asking you to do will also make you whole, because embracing the challenge to love your spouse as God loves you leads not only to a kind of crucifixion, but to the resurrection that comes after your cross.

This is my prayer for you. That on this Good Friday, and every day in your marriage that feels like Good Friday, God might remind you of how much he loves you and that he would fill you to overflowing with that love so that maybe a little bit of that love can spill over into your spouse as well through your generous service, your patience, your forgiveness, your thought-fulness, and your caretaking. I pray that through this generous gift of yourself to your spouse, your marriage will be transformed into something amazing; a witness to the love of the Cross and to the Resurrection that can come only from such a love rooted in the "mad *eros* and *agape*" of the Bridegroom himself.

A Note from Dr. Gregory Popcak

Dear Reader,

Thank you for allowing me to walk with you during this part of your marital journey. In the epilogue, I asked you to take as your model the image of Christ the Bridegroom, who exchanged vows with his bride, the Church, on the Cross when heaven was wedded to earth. While this can be a powerful and inspiring image, it is important to remember that not even Jesus was asked to carry his Cross alone. If, at some point on your journey toward marital healing, your cross becomes too difficult to bear, I hope that you will allow either me or one of my associates at the Pastoral Solutions Institute to be your Simon of Cyrene and help you carry your burden.

Each year, the Pastoral Solutions Institute provides thousands of hours of Catholic-integrated, marriage-friendly counseling services by telephone to couples just like you and your spouse. We use empirically validated methods combined with inspiring insights from our Catholic Faith. If you would like to learn more about how the Pastoral Solutions Institute can help speed you along your path to a joyful, loving marriage, family, and personal life, I would invite you to contact us through our website at www.

CatholicCounselors.com or by calling us at 740-266-6461 to make an appointment.

I promise we will do all that we can to help you experience the love and wholeness God has planned in his heart for you. In the meantime, please be assured of my prayers for you and all those who read this book, that you would be blessed abundantly and be filled with his passion and transforming love.

Yours in Christ the Bridegroom,
Dr. Gregory Popcak

Exercises

Taking Charge of Your Marriage Exercise

(Chapter 1: The Secret of Saving Your Marriage)

To begin to take charge of your marriage, consider the following questions. Write your answers in the spaces provided:

1. Does your marriage dynamic reflect more of the Happys' marriage pattern, the Dramatics', or the Flatliners'? Why do you think so?

_____

_____

_____

2. Think about times when your marriage is just naturally better. What do you do differently? Be specific. (For instance, don't just say, "We go on vacation." How do you interact with each other on vacation that makes a difference? E.g., "We spend more time together." "We take time to play together." "We are more friendly to each other." "We snap less at each other.")

_____

_____

_____

3. Couples with a stable marital dynamic are aware of the kinds of behaviors that make their marriage work better and take personal responsibility for making those things happen in their marriage (even when their spouse forgets or is distracted). To bring more stability to your marital dynamic, what would you, personally, need to do to increase the presence of the kinds of behaviors you identified in question 2 in your everyday life with your spouse?

_____

_____

_____

4. No doubt you have the best of intentions, but without some way to remind yourself to follow through, you will probably forget to do the things you listed in question 3 or get distracted by your daily life. To prevent this from happening, review your answers to questions 2 and 3 each morning. Answer the following:

    a. What might make it challenging for you to follow through with these things today?

_____

_____

_____

    b. What will you need to do today to overcome those challenges and distractions and make sure you do the things that make your marriage naturally better?"

_____

_____

_____

5. Celebrate successes; learn from mistakes. Each evening, review your progress. How well did you overcome the challenges and distractions that tried to get in the way of doing the things you identified in your answer to question 3? What do you need to do tomorrow to be more effective at overcoming these challenges and distractions? Be specific and concrete.

_____

_____

_____

6. Pray.

> *Lord, Jesus Christ, I give you my marriage. Help me to be an effective instrument of grace in my home. Help me to stop blaming my marriage, my spouse, or my circumstances for my unhappiness. Give me the wisdom I need to see that I can change my marriage for the better. Give me the fortitude I need to make a consistent effort and avoid either dramatic swings or flatlining in my marriage. Help me become the change I seek in my marriage. Amen.*

Mindset Exercise

(Chapter 2: What "I've Tried Everything" Really Means)

The following exercise will help you begin to look out for the times when you give in to the Misery-Making Mindset and its three powerless personas. No one wakes up in the morning saying, "I think I'll behave childishly today." Most people are simply not aware that they are slipping into one of the powerless personas until it is too late to do something about it, if at all. Awareness is the key to change, however. In chapter 6, on self-regulation, we'll discuss how to leave behind the powerless personas of the Misery-Making Mindset for good. For now, use the following steps to become more aware of how you act when you are in the Solution-Focused Brain versus how you act when you allow yourself to fall into the Misery-Making Mindset.

1. Divide a piece of paper into two columns. Label the column on the left "Misery-Making Mindset" and the column on the right "Solution-Focused Brain."

2. Imagine a handful of situations in which a problem makes you feel stressed, powerless, and unproductive. Ask yourself, "When I allow myself to fall into the powerless personas of the

Misery-Making Mindset, how do I think, feel, and behave? What sorts of things do I say to myself about my life, the people I am working with, or the situation in which I find myself? How does the stress affect me? List these thoughts, feeling, and behaviors in the "Misery-Making Mindset" column.

3. Now imagine a handful of situations in which you are handling a problem, but you feel confident, competent, and capable. You may or may not be upset, but you are definitely in control of yourself and your responses, and you are dealing well with the situation at hand. How do you think, feel, and behave in these situations? What sorts of things go through your head about yourself, the people around you, and your situation when you are in this mindset? How do you manage the stress and focus on solutions? List these thoughts, feelings, and behaviors in the "Solution-Focused Brain" column.

4. Orient yourself. Go through your day with these two columns in mind. At various points throughout your day, ask yourself whether you are leaning more toward your Misery-Making Mindset or your Solution-Focused Brain. Often this awareness alone will help you shift out of a less productive mindset and find a healthier perspective. Chapter 6 will build on this first step, but the better you become at identifying the shift from one mindset to the other, the easier it will be for you to learn to stay in the Solution-Focused Brain, no matter what your marriage (and life in general) throws at you.

5. Pray.

Lord God, I praise you for the grace you are giving me to learn to take control of myself and my marriage. I give these painful times to you and the painful feelings and reactions that go with them. Help me respond to these difficulties with grace, wisdom, and patience. Give me the self-control, assertiveness, patience, understanding, and courage I need to do better, both for my sake and the sake of my marriage. Be glorified in all my actions, especially my actions in times of struggle and stress. Make me an instrument of your grace and healing in my marriage. Lord, change me. Amen.

Love List Exercise

(Chapter 5: Emotional Report and Benevolence)

In my book *For Better . . . FOREVER!*, I use the Love List Exercise to help couples negotiate between differing *Lovestyles* (what Gary Chapman [2009] refers to as "Love Languages"). But this exercise can be used to help couples take the guesswork out of learning the steps of Emotional Rapport and Benevolence. There are four steps, and you can do them whether or not your partner is doing it with you.

1. *Identify your likes.* First, you and your spouse should each — independently — write down *at least* twenty-five simple things that make you feel cherished. (If you are doing this exercise alone, you will focus on developing a list for your mate and worry about your own list at some future point, when your spouse is more on board with the process. To begin, write down about twenty-five simple things that you and others have done for your spouse over the years that seemed to please him or her.)

In developing this list, be *positive*, *concrete*, and *specific*. Being *positive* means that you must resist the temptation to make this a complaint list. *Do not*, under any circumstances, write things like, "I'd feel cherished if you ever picked up your socks!" Items like this defeat the entire purpose of the list. It is a Love List Exercise, not a Complain List Exercise.

Second, being *concrete* means avoiding vague, passive, "I didn't want to think about this exercise too hard" items like, "I feel cherished when you take care of the kids"; or, "I feel cherished when you go to work." I'm sure you do genuinely appreciate these things that your spouse does, but they are not ways you cherish each other. They are ways you take care of your life together, and that is important, but these activities do not build Emotional Rapport and Benevolence because both of you know that you would have to do them whether you were married or not. To cherish one another means, "I am doing this thing specifically with you in mind to demonstrate that you are special to me."

Finally, keeping it *simple* means two things. First, it means don't overthink it. Little things count a lot. For instance, "I feel cherished when you smile at me"; or, "I feel cherished when you hold the door for me"; or, "I feel cherished when you text me to say, 'I'm praying for your meeting'"; or, "I feel cherished when you help me in the yard." Second, keeping it simple means breaking down big categories into lots of smaller things. For instance, "I feel cherished when you're affectionate" could easily be broken down into at least ten different things like, "I love when you hold my hand when we walk"; or, "I feel cherished when you give me a real kiss on the lips (instead of just a peck on the cheek)"; or, "I really like when you sit next to me on the couch with your arm around me."

People often struggle to write twenty-five things because they aren't dividing their big items into simple activities. Be simple, specific, and concrete, and you'll have a great list in no time.

Alexis said, "It was really hard for me to come up with twenty-five things Carl could do for me. It had been so long since we had really tried to be thoughtful to one another. I could think of plenty of things to complain about and loads of things I wanted him to stop doing, but it was tougher to make a list of how he could take care of me, cherish me. I didn't like making myself that vulnerable.

Carl agreed. "I'm not good at telling people what I want to begin with. It feels wrong, or selfish, or something. I understand that Alexis can't know what I need if I don't tell her, but boy, coming up with stuff was no picnic."

"I'm glad we did it, though," said Alexis. "It gave us some ways to try to take better care of each other, and it helped us know when we were getting it right. It's only been a couple of weeks, but I can see it making a difference already."

Again, if you are doing this exercise without your spouse, try to identify the types of things he or she has visibly appreciated when you or others have done them for him or her. Then brainstorm other, similar activities to round out the list.

2. *Trade lists.* Once you have your own list of twenty-five things that make you feel loved and cherished, trade your lists with each other and review them. There may be many things you are familiar with and a few things that surprise or even upset you. Try your absolute best not to react. The self-donation that lies at the heart of a healthy marriage really requires husbands and wives to be as generous as possible about the items on each other's list. Unless your spouse is asking for you to do something that is against the Commandments or Church teaching, or is

objectively degrading, I'm going to ask you to work hard to do it. This is your chance to love your spouse more than you love your comfort zone—which is the definition of benevolence.

What's in it for you? Think of it this way. Let's imagine that it really is true that God brought the two of you together. Chances are he did it because he knew that by responding to each other's unique needs, you would be challenged to grow in ways you never would have if you were left on your own. Why would God do that? Presumably because he wants to heal your broken parts. Or because he wants to love you through channels that are currently blocked to him. Or perhaps because he wants to develop those aspects of your personality so that he can use you to share his love with the world in even more powerful ways. The bottom line is that he is challenging you to do these things for your mate more for your sake than for your mate's. If you refuse this invitation, I believe you would be refusing an invitation, not from your spouse to be more loving toward him or her, but rather from God to become the person he needs you to be instead of the person you're comfortable being. Dying to ourselves is hard work. It's the hard work people talk about when they say, "Marriage is hard work." But if you're Christian, there's really no getting around it or wishing we could. The sooner you realize this and stop fighting the call to love your mate more than your comfort zone, the sooner you'll find the happiness and grace you crave.

If you are doing this on your own, you can, of course, skip this step until your spouse is on board with the process.

3. *Just do it!* Assuming that you can make it past any initial negative reaction to your mate's list, your daily goal is as follows: Each day, choose two relatively easy things on your mate's list

and one challenging thing ... and do them. Don't keep track of whether your spouse did anything. Just focus on your own efforts to become the truly loving person God wants you to be. Likewise, try to do something different every day. If you repeat something you did the day before, good, but don't count it. Choose two relatively simple and one more challenging *new item* every day in addition to any other loving things you have done.

> Caren is working on the relationship by herself. Ben is disengaged and refuses to do counseling. "It was tough coming up with things that I thought he might like at first, and then it was tough making myself do them. There's this little voice inside my head that keeps screaming, 'But what about me? When do I get *my* turn?' Honestly, I don't know the answer to that question, but I've been trying to be more intentional about being present to Ben, and things seem to be a little more pleasant the last few weeks. We haven't even watched TV together in weeks, but last night we hung out and talked about our days. It probably sounds pathetic to admit this, but that was a really big deal for us. I'm feeling hopeful for the first time in a while. Before I started doing the Love List Exercise, I was always trying to talk about the things we needed to do to fix the marriage, but he would tune me out. It never dawned on me that I could just start doing things to make it better on my own, but doing has definitely been working better for us than talking. I hope we get to the point where we can talk through things together, but I'll take this as a first step!

4. *Review daily.* Sometime before bed, take ten minutes to discuss what you did for each other. (This would be a great, positive talk

ritual if you're looking for one.) Don't critique the other. Simply talk about yourself. Consider:

1. What did you do for your spouse today?

2. Why did you pick this? (I.e., *not* because "It was the easy thing to do," but presumably you thought your spouse really needed X; explain why this might be.)

3. Ask each other if there is anything specific you could do for the other tomorrow. This is your chance to practice building intimacy by asking for your needs. Your natural tendency will be to respond to the question, "What can I do for you tomorrow?" by answering, "Nothing" or "I don't know." Resist this. Look at your list. Think about your day, and ask for something that might make your day a little easier or more pleasant. Keep in mind that this request is not a command. It is not an order. It may or may not happen, based on how the day turns out. This is just an opportunity for both of you to be more honest about your likes or dislikes. You might say something like, "I don't know. I guess if you came and gave me a hug before I left for work, it would mean a lot to me"; or, "It would really make me feel good if you called me to see how I was doing with the kids after lunch." Or something similar.

Some spouses say, "Well, what if I ask for something and it doesn't happen?" I can guarantee that this will definitely happen more often than not at first. You aren't used to taking care of each other. It may be hard to remember. Never mind. Challenge yourself to take care of your mate anyway. Let your loving actions, not your judgments, criticisms, and scorekeeping, remind your spouse to remember to do something for you. It is very hard, but this is what it takes to have a grown-up kind of love.

Healthy marriages value equity as opposed to equality (Schwartz, 1995). In other words, where equality looks at balancing the ledger every day and making sure you don't do more than your spouse every time you do something, equity assumes that some days and maybe even some weeks, one of you is going to work harder than the other on the marriage. That's okay, because in the long run, you will both take your turns taking care or being taken care of. This can be hard to trust at first, but commit yourself to focusing on your own efforts for at least a month before mentioning any perceived imbalance to your spouse. This way, you will have the credibility to say, "I don't know if you've noticed, but I've really been trying hard to take better care of you and show you that I care about you. I plan on continuing to do that, but some days it's harder than others, and I could use some encouragement. It would mean a lot to me if you would look at my Love List and try to do the exercise with me."

If you follow these suggestions, you will have the credibility to ask for more effort from your spouse because you will have been working for several weeks without looking for an immediate cookie for your effort. Incidentally, this approach is the best one to take if you are doing this exercise on your own. Build credibility by doing the exercise whether your spouse is responding or not; then invite your mate to participate more directly.

If your spouse remains resistant to this exercise or is willing—for weeks on end, not hours or days—to enjoy the benefits of your service without responding in kind, it is most likely time for counseling. Pope St. John Paul the Great reminded us that the secret to a happy marriage is *mutual self-donation*, which means *both* the husband and wife must, over the long run, be committed to serving each other in order for this to work. It's okay to give some credit to each other at first for any instances of accidental or benign neglect. But if you have been making an honest effort over the course of several weeks to make the Love List Exercise work on your own and your spouse is unresponsive, then there is probably a deeper problem that would benefit from some professional attention.

Clarification Exercise

(Chapter 7: A Positive Intention Frame)

This Clarification Exercise will help you to develop your ability to use charitable interpretation. The steps are pretty straightforward; it's the practice that's hard.

1. *Don't respond. Take a breath.* When you encounter an offense, the first thing to do is *shut your mouth*. Stop. Take a breath. It doesn't have to be a deep, cleansing breath. Any old breath will do. Just press "pause" before you say something defensive. Research shows that intentionally delaying a response by even a split second significantly improves your ability to choose well (Teicher, Ferrara, Grinband, 2014). Your emotional brain gets information before your problem-solving brain becomes aware something is going on (thereby allowing your emotional brain to activate your fight, flight, or freeze response in light of a threat). Pausing even for a split second allows the rest of your brain to catch up, shut down any undue threat reaction that has already started, and respond rather than react. Whenever possible, practice this "pause button" technique when you are having a conversation with anyone—especially when it is not a difficult conversation. Let the other person stop talking. Pause (for about

as long as it took you to read the word *pause*). Let what the person said settle in. Then speak. If the person asks why you aren't jumping in right away, just tell him that you're practicing being a better listener and you're trying to let what he said settle in before you respond. It happens to be true, and the other person will actually appreciate the effort you're putting into the conversation.

The more you practice this "pause button" technique in your general conversations (even though it will feel a bit unnatural at first), the more you will improve your ability to pause under pressure. Fair warning, though: if you wait until you feel attacked to try this, you will fail. This is one case where practice definitely means progress.

2. *Restate what you heard.* You need not do this for "normal" conversations, but only when you feel attacked or feel the rising need to defend yourself. Stop, as in step 1, and then, instead of defending yourself, check to make sure you understood what the other person said. Start with a simple, polite gesture of deference (e.g., "I'm sorry," or "Just a second"); then say, "It sounds as if you're saying ..." and tell the person what you heard him say. Then ask, "Did I get that right?" (Note, the "I'm sorry" doesn't constitute an actual apology for anything. It's just a social convention that says, "I'm taking this seriously, but let's not fight." It has the effect of disarming the offender, who expects you to be defensive, not sensitive.)

3. *Listen and decide.* At this point, the other person may tell you that you got it right or wrong. If he tells you that you got it wrong, ask him to restate what he was trying to tell you. He'll probably use different words this time. Repeat steps 2 and 3.

When the other person tells you that you got it right (whether the first or fifth time he has clarified his original comments) and understood what he was trying to communicate, then and only then should you respond. If both you and your spouse are doing this exercise, your spouse should now follow the same steps in response to your comments. If you are working on your own, just use this exercise to improve your responses.

This Clarification Exercise will feel artificial at first, but your delivery will become more natural with time. Feel free to play with the wording. The actual words you use to invite the clarification from your husband or wife are less important than the fact that you are both pausing to let your brain catch up, and you are slowing down the whole conversation, which will also help decrease the stress temperature discussed earlier.

Let's try this technique with two brief scenarios. The first responds to a direct attack. The other responds to content that, while not representative of an attack, could certainly precipitate a very angry discussion.

Spouse: You are such a jerk!

You: I'm sorry, it sounds like you're upset about something I did. Am I right?

Spouse: Yes! I can't believe you forgot to let the dog out before you left, as I asked.

You: (*Pause, breath.*) Oh, actually, I did let the dog out before I left. Jennifer brought her back inside when she got home from school.

Or:

Spouse: I don't think I ever want to have another baby!

You: (*Pause, breath.*) Just a second. Are you saying you want to stop using Natural Family Planning?

Spouse: No! Not at all.

You: (*Pause, breath.*) I'm sorry, I don't understand. Can you try again?

Spouse: We never get any time together. We're always running after the kids. I'm sick of never getting any time with you.

You: (*Pause, breath.*) Wow, it sounds like you're really wanting a date.

Spouse: Of course I do! Don't you?

It is fairly obvious from both examples that these conversations could have gone very differently if not for the Clarification Exercise. Taking a pause, restating what you heard, asking for clarification, and getting confirmation before you respond is a simple but powerful way to take control of both your reactions and the flow of the conversation. By making sure you know what you are responding to before you speak, you are practicing the art of charitable interpretation and allowing the discussion to proceed on a more positive and productive course.

Reframing Exercise

(Chapter 9: Mutual Respect, Accountability, and Boundaries)

This exercise will help you see the value of activities your spouse enjoys, even if you don't enjoy them.

1. Consider some of your mate's most important interests. Write those here. Start with the biggest interests or values. The things your spouse spends the most time and energy doing. The same process can apply to other things once you've gotten the exercise down.

_____

_____

_____

2. Next, imagine that you are your spouse. From this position, ask yourself what you enjoy or how you benefit from these activities. State your answer in the positive manner your spouse might. Avoid the tendency to use false or snarky positives (which actually represents your critical view of the activity). Here are a few examples of the difference.

• Example 1. Going to church

"Snarky positive" benefit: It allows my wife not to have to think for herself and gives her a reason to feel better than me.

Actual benefit as spouse sees it: A place she feels safe and loved; where she gets encouragement to face the week.

• Example 2. Watching sports

"Snarky positive" benefit: He can relive his glory days and have a socially appropriate way to vent his aggression and competitive nature.

Actual benefit as spouse sees it: It's exciting and inspiring to watch people who are really good at an activity he has been actively involved with in the past. It gets him in touch with good times he had as a kid and gives him a way to feel connected to friends in the present.

• Example 3. Shopping

"Snarky positive" benefit: She gets to indulge her materialistic nature.

Actual benefit as spouse sees it: She enjoys looking as much as buying. It gives her ideas about how to make the house more of a home.

Notice that the correct way to do this exercise is to kindly check your armchair psychoanalysis and value judgments and simply describe the benefits your spouse gets from this activity as your spouse actually would.

Now you try.

Reframing Exercise

Activity 1:

_____

_____

_____

Benefit as my spouse would describe it:

_____

_____

_____

Activity 2:

_____

_____

_____

Benefit as my spouse would describe it:

_____

_____

_____

Activity 3:

_____

_____

_____

Benefit as my spouse would describe it:

_____

_____

_____

3. Next, identify how (or if) you pursue the same or similar benefit in your own life and in your own way. For instance, maybe you don't like to shop, but chances are you do something to get more ideas on how to take better care or improve upon the things you treasure (e.g., the imagined benefit identified above). Or again, maybe you don't like to go to church, but there must be someplace you go or something you turn to that makes you feel safe and loved and gives you the strength to face the week ahead (e.g., the actual benefit identified above). What is that thing you do to accomplish this benefit in your life?

Activity 1:

_____

_____

Benefit to spouse:

_____

_____

How do I get that similar benefit in my life?

_____

_____

_____

Reframing Exercise

Activity 2:

_____

_____

Benefit to spouse:

_____

_____

How do I get that similar benefit in my life?

_____

_____

_____

Activity 3:

_____

_____

Benefit to spouse:

_____

_____

How do I get that similar benefit in my life?

_____

_____

_____

4. For this last step, you have a choice. If you were able to identify a way that you pursue that similar benefit in your life, you will need to remind yourself that when your spouse does X (e.g., shops), it's the emotional equivalent of your doing Y (e.g., subscribing to car magazines) for you. You might object. For instance, many faithful readers will no doubt have a hard time comparing their religious involvement to their spouses' hunting or golfing. After all, religion isn't just a habit or a hobby. It's a way of life. As a sincere Catholic myself, I agree. But we aren't looking at the objective value of these activities. All we're considering are the emotional and psychological benefits you gain from doing that thing you do, so that you can develop some basic appreciation for those things you couldn't previously relate to at all or perhaps related to in a negative way.

For instance, my wife never really understood why I "need" to go buy fireworks and set them off on the Fourth of July. She's always afraid I'm going to burn down the house, and she thinks the city displays are nicer and safer—and on that count, she's probably right. But one summer day, she said to me, "I think I get the fireworks thing now. If I want to add a little sparkle in my life, I might buy a piece of costume jewelry, but you don't have anything like that. Fireworks are kind of like 'guy bling.' My complaining about it would be like you complaining that I spent a few dollars on a new inexpensive necklace or something. I'm going to try to see it that way and stop complaining about your fireworks." Frankly, the comparison doesn't really resonate for me, but it made her more sympathetic to my pyromania, so I'm happy she was willing to be generous enough to reframe this activity and appreciate it a little more with me.

On the other hand, maybe you weren't able to find a way that you pursue that particular benefit in your life. Maybe you don't have a way to think about how you might do a better job making your house a home, or feeling God's love, or gathering strength to face the week, or whatever it is your spouse gets out of doing what he or she does. Since you don't have a way to achieve that benefit, why not join your spouse in doing what he or she does? You just might start to wonder how you ever managed without this thing in your life. Or at least, you might wonder what you were dreading so much.

Increasing Accountability Exercise

(Chapter 9: Mutual Respect, Accountability, and Boundaries)

This exercise will help you to be open to your spouse's feedback without subjecting yourself to abuse or control.

1. *Identify the criticisms.* Write down three criticisms your spouse makes about you. It does not matter if you think these complaints are fair or legitimate. In fact, this exercise will work better if you think the criticisms are absurd, unreasonable, even offensive. Here are some examples:

> "My wife says that I am thoughtless and unfeeling."
> "My husband says that I am a stick in the mud."
> "My wife accuses me of not ever listening to her."
> "My husband is always telling me that I'm hysterical."

Write down three criticisms your spouse makes about you.

_____

_____

_____

Increasing Accountability Exercise

Again, at this point, we're not concerned with whether you agree with your spouse's assessment or if what your spouse said was particularly charitable, kind, or remotely true. Even in all of these instances, it is still an important marital skill to learn to listen to the message behind the criticism and respect your spouse enough to be accountable to his or her opinion of you.

2. *Identify the problem behavior and desired response.* Next we try to provide a practical context for these criticisms. To this end, you must do your best to identify both the problem behavior your spouse is trying to address and the response your spouse is trying to inspire with these criticisms. If you aren't sure, you can ask your spouse to clarify. If your spouse can't or won't tell you, ask yourself what you are usually doing that provokes the criticism. That will at least give you a general starting point. I will use the previous examples to illustrate my point.

Criticism: "My wife says that I am thoughtless and unfeeling." *Problem behavior:* "I lose track of time when I'm working or talking with people." *Desired response:* "She wants me to call or text her if I'm going to be late."

Criticism: "My husband says that I am a stick in the mud." *Problem behavior:* "He tries to be affectionate by grabbing at me, and I push him away." *Desired response:* "He wants me to treat his advances as playful affection and not as a violation."

Criticism: "My wife accuses me of not ever listening to her." *Problem behavior:* "I don't know what she wants me to say when she asks me for feedback." *Desired response:* "She wants me to be able to answer her questions or ask her questions about what she's told me."

Criticism: "My husband is always telling me that I'm hysterical." *Problem behavior*: "When I get upset, I yell or sometimes cry." *Desired response*: "He wants me to stop yelling or crying when I get upset about things and just talk to him."

Now, it's your turn. Write the behaviors that you believe are most closely associated with the criticism your spouse lobs at you.

Criticism 1. Problem Behavior:

_____

_____

Desired Response:

_____

_____

Criticism 2. Problem Behavior

_____

_____

Desired Response:

_____

_____

Criticism 3. Problem Behavior:

_____

_____

Increasing Accountability Exercise

Desired Response:

_____

_____

3. *Generous effort/personal motivation:* In this step, the most challenging one, it is your job to talk yourself through what you would need to do to generate this desired response. Don't worry. I am not asking you to commit to anything at this point. I'm just asking you to entertain what you would have to do (not what your spouse would have to do) to grant the desired response. While this can be challenging, I would ask you to recall what we discussed with the Love List Exercise. Specifically, that unless we are convinced that what we are being asked to do doesn't just make us uncomfortable, but is objectively immoral, then we ought to at least consider granting the request. The generosity that lies at the heart of a healthy marriage requires nothing less.

Plus, by responding generously to requests to step outside my comfort zone, I respond to God's invitation to me to grow in ways I never would if I were left on my own. Presumably God gave your spouse to you and you to your spouse. That means God knew the kinds of requests your spouse would be making of you when you married him or her and anticipated that you would be challenged by these requests. Therefore, it's not unreasonable to think that God would like you to rise to the challenge. You do not have to be 100 percent certain why God might be inviting you to do what your spouse is asking. You just have to be able to say that what you are being asked is not objectively immoral or degrading. Assuming that's the case, ask yourself what you would have to do to grant the request.

Secondly, ask yourself how you might grow as a person if you were to grant this request. At first, you will want to be negative about it and say that you will somehow be worse off. Work through this and get to the place where you can see how you might possibly actually be better off in at least some small way if you were to learn to be more generous regarding your spouse's request. Here are some examples of both the generous effort and the personal motivator.

> *Criticism*: "My wife says that I am thoughtless and unfeeling." *Problem behavior*: "I lose track of time when I'm working or talking with people." *Desired response*: "She wants me to call or text her if I'm going to be late." *Generous effort*: "I would need to set my cell-phone alarm to tell me when I need to start wrapping up at work or at least call and let her know what's going on." *Personal motivator*: "I would become a more thoughtful, trustworthy, and reliable person."

> *Criticism*: "My husband says that I am a stick in the mud." *Problem behavior*: "He tries to be affectionate by grabbing at me, and I push him away." *Desired response*: "He wants me to treat his advances as playful affection and not as a violation." *Generous effort*: "I would have to remind myself that he is not trying to use me, that he does love me and cares for me. And I would need to flirt back in some way." *Personal motivator*: "I would become a more playful, affectionate, and affirming wife."

> *Criticism*: "My wife accuses me of not ever listening to her." *Problem behavior*: "I don't know what she wants me to say when she asks me for feedback." *Desired response*:

"She wants me to be able to answer her questions or ask her questions about what she's told me." *Generous effort*: "I would need to interrupt her periodically either to summarize what she said (so I don't get lost) or ask a question to clarify her meaning." *Personal motivator*: "I would become a better listener and more of the caring husband I'd like to be."

Criticism: "My husband is always telling me that I'm hysterical." *Problem behavior*: "When I get upset, I yell or sometimes cry." *Desired response*: "He wants me to stop yelling or crying when I get upset about things and just talk to him." *Generous effort*: "I would need to use some of the techniques in the self-regulation chapter to take down my emotional temperature first and then try to talk about things once I was in a better place emotionally." *Personal motivator*: "I could become more emotionally mature and make others less responsible for helping me manage my emotional reactions."

Couples who are in happy marriages—whether or not they have a faith life—try very hard to see how they might grow personally by granting even their spouse's difficult requests. They understand intuitively that their growth as persons is dependent upon listening generously and attentively to even the difficult things others—and especially close others, like a spouse—have to say. Even when they are not sure they are willing to commit to a change, they at least begin to imagine how a change might be possible and whether and how they could benefit by making such a change, not just for their spouse, but for themselves. This imaginative process may not result in a final decision to commit to the change or not or how to pursue the change, but it allows respectful conversation to move forward. Having seen a few examples, list the generous effort you would need to make to grant your spouse's request and the personal motivation you would need to focus on.

Criticism 1:

_____

_____

Generous effort:

_____

_____

Personal motivator:

_____

_____

Criticism 2:

_____

_____

Generous effort:

_____

_____

Personal motivator:

_____

_____

Increasing Accountability Exercise

Criticism 3:

_____

_____

Generous effort:

_____

_____

Personal motivator:

_____

_____

4. *Discuss.* As I promised at the beginning, you have not committed to anything. You may still have reservations or concerns. It is perfectly acceptable to discuss those issues and to reserve any decision pending the resolution of those concerns. The purpose of this exercise is not so much to ask you to change anything (although that would be the ideal). Rather, the intention is to make you more open-minded about the possibility of change and to give you a more productive way to discuss these hot-button topics with your spouse. For the final step, this is exactly what you will do. Here is how the spouses in two of the four examples I've walked you through would approach the discussion with their mate, having completed this exercise.

Example conversation 1: Husband who loses track of time.

This husband approaches his wife at a time when they are not arguing about this or any other issue and things are relatively calm. "Honey, I've been thinking. I know that you feel like

I'm sometimes thoughtless and unfeeling because I lose track of time when I'm working or talking with people. I know I haven't always been willing to hear that, but I've been thinking about it. I'm not completely sure how to guarantee changing this once and for all, but I have an idea. I'm going to set my phone alarm when I'm at work to remind me to either wrap up or give you a call to let you know what's happening. I'm going to do the same thing before I meet a friend or go out. I think that would help at least some—maybe even most—of the time. I hope that could at least make you feel like I'm trying to take your concern seriously. I really want to be a better husband to you. What do you think about my idea?"

Example conversation 2: Wife who pushes husband away.

This wife approaches her husband at a time when things are calm and they are not already arguing about this or any other issue. "Honey, I've been thinking. I know you feel like I'm not very playful and flirtatious with you, especially because I get really uncomfortable when you try to be affectionate with me. Sometimes I've even told you I feel grabbed at. I know I'm not always very receptive when you've tried to explain that you really do care about me and you're just trying to show me I'm desirable. I'm not totally sure how to resolve this once and for all, but I have an idea. I'm going to focus my attention on the things you do to show me that you love me and want to take care of me to remind myself that you're not trying to use me in some way, and I'm even going to try to flirt back. I think I could probably do that at least some—maybe even most—of the time. I hope that would make you feel like I'm at least trying to hear what you're telling me. I really want to make you happy. What do you think about what I'm saying?"

Obviously, you will use your own words, but try to follow the flow of the above examples. 1) Approach when both of you are calm. 2) *Briefly* state the problem. 3) Acknowledge you haven't always been receptive. This will take tension out of the discussion. 4) Propose your idea, explaining that it might not work perfectly but that you wanted to find some way to show a sincere effort. 5) Finally, ask for input.

Chances are your spouse will either be grateful or offer some helpful input. If so, mission accomplished. Sometimes, though, there is so much anger and resentment built up around an issue, a spouse will take the opportunity to lash out in response to this generous effort. If that happens, it is almost always necessary to seek some professional assistance to work through the depth of pain your mate feels about the problem.

Either way, however, you will have demonstrated a generosity of spirit that has the greatest chance of convincing your spouse that you are sincere in your efforts to take the marriage to a better place. You will have demonstrated a sincere willingness to be accountable for even the difficult things your spouse suggests and even when he or she fails to state these requests perfectly.

One last note: Some of you may be concerned that this process rewards criticism. That might be true if you committed to changing regardless of how your spouse responded to this effort. This is not what you are doing. Rather, you are being generous and opening up a conversation that, as far as your mate knew, was either closed or futile. In response, you are expecting a respectful, productive, even grateful response. If you do not get such a response, the offer goes off the table for the time being, and you seek professional assistance. Insisting on a change in your spouse's behavior as a good-faith response to your initial efforts, coupled with the consequence of counseling if you don't experience that generosity in return, prevents you from being taken advantage of. It is admirable to make the first effort at reconciliation, but you are not obliged to suffer every humiliation or cruelty in your efforts to make things work. Make the effort. Assume the best about the both of you. If that doesn't work, seek help. Regardless, you will be responding to these issues in a more charitable and effective way than ever before.

Boundary Clarification Exercise

(Chapter 9: Mutual Respect, Accountability, and Boundaries)

This exercise will help you to respect your spouse's boundaries.

1. *List the boundaries.* Think of your past few arguments. What things have you done or said that made your spouse claim you had crossed a line? You don't have to agree with your spouse's assessment. Just write down the things your spouse has indicated he or she wishes you would stop doing or saying when you are arguing.

Examples:

"My wife hates when I swear during arguments."

"I drive my husband crazy when I correct his account of what happened."

What things do you say or do in your arguments that your spouse says cross the line?

_____

_____

_____

2. *Identify the alternative.* Consider how you would change your behavior if you accepted your spouse's limit. What would you do differently? Keep in mind that "I wouldn't get upset" isn't an acceptable answer. Your initial reactions will change with time and practice, but you can't control your initial reactions at first. Instead, focus on what you would actually do or say instead of doing or saying the offensive thing.

> *Example 1:* "My wife hates when I swear during arguments." *Alternative behavior:* "I would have to take breaks and maybe even end the argument a lot sooner than I usually do."

> *Example 2:* "I drive my husband crazy when I correct his account of what happened." *Alternative behavior:* "I need to stop getting hung up on details and really listen for his larger point."

Write your alternative behavior for each of the boundary issues you identified in step 1.

_____

_____

_____

3. *Make a plan and gather resources.* Next reflect on what you would need to do to use this alternative response successfully.

> *Example 1:* "My wife hates when I swear during arguments." *Alternative behavior:* "I would have to take breaks and maybe even end the argument a lot sooner than I usually do." *Make a plan:* "I'm going to work on becoming more aware of the Stress Temperature Scale (see chapter

6) and be sure to take a break at 7 instead of waiting until 8 or 9, as I currently do."

Example 2: "I drive my husband crazy when I correct his account of what happened." *Alternative behavior*: "I need to stop getting hung up on details and really listen for his larger point." *Make a plan*: "I will ask regular questions about his larger point so that I can stay focused and avoid falling into the Contemptuous Expert Persona."

Write your example of what you will do to employ your alternative response successfully.

_____

_____

_____

4. *Commit*. Finally, tell your spouse that even though you haven't been willing to listen in the past, you are going to respect this boundary in the future. Explain what you are going to do differently and how you plan to follow through. Ask your spouse to be patient if you forget or mess up, but also to remind you gently of your commitment if you do forget. Promise to do your best to respect these boundaries even if you don't always understand them because you want your partner to feel safe and loved even in his or her arguments with you.

References

Arriaga, X. B. (2001). "The Ups and Downs of Dating: Fluctuations in Satisfaction in Newly Formed Romantic Relationships." *Journal of Personality and Social Psychology* 80: 754-765.

Barrette, G. "Spiritual Direction in the Roman Catholic Tradition." *Journal of Psychology and Theology* 30, no. 4, 290-302.

Benedict XVI (2007). Lenten Love Letter. Retrieved April 18, 2014 at http://chiesa.espresso.repubblica.it/articolo/121716?eng=y.

Burns, D. (2008). *Feeling Good. The New Mood Therapy.* Harper.

Chapman, G. (2009). *The 5 Love Languages: The Secret to Love That Lasts.* Northfield Publishing.

Cozolino, L. (2014). *The Neuroscience of Human Relationships.* W. W. Norton.

Dorsett, K. (2011). "Signs You May Have a 'Work Spouse.'" CNN, February 16. Retrieved March 3, 2014 at http://www.cnn.com/2011/LIVING/02/16/workspouse.relationship.at.work/.

Fiese, B., T. Tomcho, and M. Douglas (2003). "A Review of 50 Years of Research on Naturally Occurring Family Routines and Rituals: Cause for Celebration?" *Journal of Family Psychology* 16, no. 4.

Fiese, B. (2006). *Family Routines and Rituals*. Yale University Press.

Fredrickson, B., K. Grewen, and K. Coffey (2013). "A Functional Genomic Perspective on Human Well-Being." *Proceedings of the National Academy of Sciences*. Retrieved March 3, 2014, at http://www.pnas.org/content/early/2013/07/25/1305419110. short.

Fuller-Thomson, E., and A. D. Dalton (2011). "Suicidal Ideation among Individuals Whose Parents Have Divorced: Findings from a Representative Canadian Community Survey." *Psychiatry Research* 187:150-155.

Gallup (2012). "Separation, Divorce Linked to Sharply Lower Well-Being." Retrieved April 19, 2014, at http://www.gallup.com/poll/154001/Separation-Divorce-Linked-Sharply-Lower-Wellbeing.aspx?ref=image.

Gottman, J. (2011). *Bridging the Couple Chasm. Workshop for Clinicians*. Gottman Institute.

Gottman, J. (1995). *Why Marriages Succeed or Fail and How to Make Yours Last*.

Gottman, J. (1993). "A Theory of Marital Dissolution and Stability." *Journal of Family Psychology* 7, no. 1 (June 1993): 57-75.

Gröpel, P., H. M. Kehr (2013). "Motivation and Self-Control: Implicit Motives Moderate the Exertion of Self-Control in Motive-Related Tasks." *Journal of Personality*.

References

Hawkins, M., S. Carrere, and J. Gottman (2002). "Marital Sentiment Override: Does It Influence Couple's Perceptions?" *Journal of Marriage and Family* 64, no. 1.

Hughes, M. E., and L. Waite (2009). "Marital Biography and Health at Mid-Life." *Journal of Health and Social Behavior* 50, no. 3.

Kelly, M. (2007). *The 7 Levels of Intimacy: The Art of Loving and the Joy of Being Loved.* Fireside Press.

Larson, P., and D. Olsen (2004). "Spiritual Beliefs and Marriage: A National Survey Based on ENRICH." *The Family Psychologist* 20, no. 2: 4-8.

Lewandowski, G. W., Jr., and R. A. Ackerman (2006). "Something's Missing: Need Fulfillment and Self-Expansion as Predictors of Susceptibility to Infidelity." *The Journal of Social Psychology* 146: 389-403.

Manes, S. (2013). "Making Sure Emotional Flooding Doesn't Capsize Your Relationship." Gottman Institute Relationship Blog. Retrieved February 14, 2014 at http://www.gottmanblog.com/2013/08/making-sure-emotional-flooding-doesnt.html.

Marquardt, E. (2006). *Between Two Worlds: The Inner Lives of Children of Divorce.* Harmony.

McKnight, D. H., and N. Chervany (2001). "Trust and Distrust Definitions: One Bite at a Time." *Trust in Cyber Societies Lecture Notes in Computer Science* 2246: 24-37.

Metsa-Simolen, N., and P. Martikainen (2013). "Divorce and Changes in the Prevalence of Psychotropic Medication Use: A Register-Based Longitudinal Study among Middle-Aged Finns." *Social Science and Medicine* (October 1994): 71-80.

Northwestern University (2013). "Twenty-One Minutes to Marital Satisfaction: Minimal Intervention Can Preserve Marital Quality over Time." *Science Daily*. February 5, 2013. Retrieved March 4, 2014, at http://www.sciencedaily.com/releases/2013/02/130205123702.htm.

Pargament, K. (2011). *Spiritually Integrated Psychotherapy: Understanding and Addressing the Sacred*. The Guilford Press.

Popcak, G. (1999). *For Better . . . FOREVER!: A Catholic Guide to Lifelong Marriage*. Our Sunday Visitor.

Popcak, G. (2000). *The Exceptional Seven Percent: Nine Secrets of the World's Happiest Couples*. Kensington Press.

Rushnell and DuArt (2011). *Couples Who Pray*.

Scalia, E. (2013). *Strange Gods*. Ave Maria Press.

Schwartz, P. (1995). *Love Between Equals: How Peer Marriage Really Works*. Touchstone.

Seigel, D. (2013). *Pocket Guide to Interpersonal Neurobiology*. W. W. Norton.

Stanley, S. (2005). *The Power of Commitment*. Jossey-Bass.

Teichert, T., V. Ferrera, and J. Grinband. "Humans Optimize Decision-Making by Delaying Decision Onset." *PLoS ONE* 9, no. 3.

Thigpen, P. (2001). *The Saint's Guide to Making Peace with God, Yourself, and Others*. Charis.

Toglia, M., D. Reed, and D. Ross (2006). *The Handbook of Eyewitness Psychology: Vols. 1 and 2*. Psychology Press.

Weiner-Davis, M. (1993). *Divorce Busting*. Fireside.

References

Weiss, C. (2011). "Divorce Is Costly to Women." *UConn Today.* September 28, 2011. Retrieved April 19, 2014, at http://today.uconn.edu/blog/2011/09/divorce-is-costly-for-women/.

Yu, E., Liu, J. (2007). "Environmental Impacts of Divorce." *Proceedings of the National Academy of Sciences* 104, no. 51.

About the Author

Dr. Gregory Popcak (POP-chak) is the Founder and Executive Director of the Pastoral Solutions Institute, an organization dedicated to helping Catholics find faith-filled solutions to tough marriage, family, and personal problems. The author of almost twenty popular books and programs integrating solid Catholic theology and counseling psychology, Dr. Popcak is an expert on the practical applications of Pope John Paul the Great's Theology of the Body.

Through the Pastoral Solutions Institute, he directs a group pastoral tele-counseling practice that provides over ten thousand hours per year of ongoing pastoral psychotherapy services to Catholic couples, individuals, and families around the world. He and his wife, Lisa Popcak, have hosted several nationally syndicated, call-in radio advice programs, including *Heart, Mind and Strength* (Ave Maria Radio), *Fully Alive!* (Sirius/XM-The Catholic Channel), and most recently, *More2Life* (Ave Maria Radio—airing Monday through Friday, noon to 1 p.m. Eastern time). They have also hosted two television series for EWTN (*For Better . . . FOREVER!* and *God Help Me!*). In addition to hosting *Faith on the Couch*, a popular faith and psychology blog on Patheos.com, Dr. Popcak writes articles that appear regularly in periodicals such as *Catholic Digest*, *Family Foundations*, *Tender Tidings*, *Columbia*, and others, and his work has been featured on FoxNews, NPR's *Here and Now* and in the *Los Angeles Times*, the *Washington Post*, *Ladies' Home Journal*, and the *National Enquirer*. A sought-after public speaker, Dr. Greg Popcak has been honored to address audiences across North America, as well as in Australia and Hong Kong.

In addition to his ministry work, Dr. Popcak serves on the adjunct faculty of both the undergraduate psychology and graduate theology departments at Franciscan University of Steubenville, where he teaches Spirituality and the Helping Professions and Pastoral and Spiritual Direction, respectively. He also serves on the doctoral faculty of the Harold Abel School of Behavioral Health.

Other Books and Programs by Greogry K. Popcak

Marriage and Sexuality

Just Married
The Catholic Guide to Surviving and
Thriving in the First Five Years of Marriage

Holy Sex!
The Catholic Guide to Toe-Curling,
Mind-Blowing, Infallible Loving

For Better . . . FOREVER!
A Catholic Guide to Lifelong Marriage

The Exceptional Seven Percent
Nine Secrets of the World's Happiest Couples

Parenting and Family

Then Comes Baby
The Catholic Guide to Surviving and Thriving
in the First Three Years of Parenthood

Beyond the Birds and the Bees
Raising Sexually Whole and Holy Kids

Parenting with Grace
The Catholic Parents' Guide to
Raising (Almost) Perfect Kids

Faith and Life

God Help Me, These People Are Driving Me Nuts!
Making Peace with Difficult People

God Help Me, This Stress Is Driving Me Crazy!
Finding Balance Through God's Grace

The Life God Wants You to Have
Discovering the Divine Plan When Human Plans Fail

Programs

Living a Joy-Filled Marriage
Marriage Preparation Starter Pack (with Leader's Guide,
Couple's Workbook, and Marriage Action Plan)

A Marriage Made for Heaven
Twelve-Session Marriage Enrichment Program
(with DVD, Leader's Guide, and Workbook)

An Invitation

Reader, the book that you hold in your hands was published by Sophia Institute Press. Sophia Institute seeks to nurture the spiritual, moral, and cultural life of souls and to spread the Gospel of Christ in conformity with the authentic teachings of the Roman Catholic Church.

Our press fulfills this mission by offering translations, reprints, and new publications that afford readers a rich source of the enduring wisdom of mankind.

We also operate two popular online Catholic resources: CrisisMagazine.com and CatholicExchange.com.

Crisis Magazine provides insightful cultural analysis that arms readers with the arguments necessary for navigating the ideological and theological minefields of the day. *Catholic Exchange* provides world news from a Catholic perspective as well as daily devotionals and articles that will help you to grow in holiness and live a life consistent with the teachings of the Church.

Sophia Institute Press also serves as the publisher for the Thomas More College of Liberal Arts and Holy Spirit College. Both colleges provide university-level education under the guiding light of Catholic teaching. If you know a young person seeking a college that takes seriously the adventure of learning and the quest for truth, please bring these institutions to his attention.

www.SophiaInstitute.com
www.CatholicExchange.com
www.CrisisMagazine.com

Sophia Institute Press® is a registered trademark of Sophia Institute.
Sophia Institute is a tax-exempt institution as defined by the
Internal Revenue Code, Section 501(c)(3). Tax I.D. 22-2548708.